73 642A

18"

9au

Personal styles in neurosis

The International Library of Group Psychotherapy
and Group Process

General Editors

Dr Malcolm Pines
Institute of Group Analysis (London) and the Tavistock Clinic, London

Dr Earl Hopper
Institute of Group Analysis (London) and the London School
of Economics and Political Science

The International Library of Group Psychotherapy and Group Process
is published in association with the Institute of Group Analysis (London)
and is devoted to the systematic study and exploration of group
psychotherapy

Personal styles in neurosis

Implications for small group psychotherapy and behaviour therapy

T.M. Caine
O.B.A. Wijesinghe
D.A. Winter

Routledge & Kegan Paul
London, Boston and Henley

First published in 1981
by Routledge & Kegan Paul Ltd
39 Store Street, London WC1E 7DD,
9 Park Street, Boston Mass. 02108, USA,
Broadway House, Newtown Road,
Henley-on-Thames, Oxon RG9 1EN
Set in Press Roman 10/12 by
Hope Services, Abingdon, Oxon.
and printed in the USA by
Fairfield Graphics
The Arcata Book Group

British Library Cataloguing in Publication Data

Caine, Thomas Mackenzie

Personal styles in neurosis. − (The international
library of group psychotherapy and group
process).
1. Neurosis   2. Behavior therapy
I. Title   II. Wijesinghe, O.B.A.
III. Winter, D.A.   IV. Series
616.8'5   RC489.B4   80-41393
ISBN 0-7100-0617-9

Contents

Foreword

Too many books are published in the field of psychology at the present time. Every week brings another fistful of publishers' catalogues and leaflets describing books which add nothing to what is already known, stimulate no new thought, but simply add impetus to a current bandwagon, fuel a fleeting but lucrative controversy, or, less likely, expound some ephemeral idea scarcely worth its conception.

This is not one of those books. As a report of research work in the field of psychological treatment, it displays a range of virtues encountered only too rarely in the present-day social science publications. The work reported is relevant to important problems confronting those who work in the psychological therapies, and indeed indicates ways in which those problems may fruitfully be tackled. Despite its use of the methods and techniques of traditional scientific psychology, it is not difficult for the non-technical to understand, and is written in an historical and cultural perspective which (in contrast to the impression given by so many 'psychological scientists') suggests that the authors do not inhabit a world which sprang into being, complete and entire, *circa* 1970.

At some points in the text the authors almost apologize for the fact that their research work has been constrained by their involvement in the practical conduct of psychological therapy. And yet this, to me, seems to be one of the book's main strengths – the work reported has been carried out in response to a long-standing concern with problems posed by the actual *experience* of psychotherapy, and is, thus, no mere academic exercise (aimed, for example, as so many academic exercises are, at the advancement through 'publication' of a university career). There is an encouraging feeling of continuity about this work: an elaboration of concerns which have preoccupied the authors, to a greater or lesser extent, over a period of many years.

Most practising psychotherapists who have not become closed off to their own experience have for some time been dissatisfied with orthodox theoretical accounts of the therapeutic process, and there has been an increasing recognition that 'non-specific' factors in therapy seem to be as important as any of the technical phenomena which are invoked to explain its efficacy (or, indeed, lack of efficacy). It is perhaps not surprising that the conventional schools tend to fight shy of coming to grips with such factors, which include the personality, expectations, attitudes and prejudices of the therapists as much as of their patients, since to do so threatens psychological treatment in its guise of professional, technical discipline. The very expression 'non-specific' signifies a relegation of such considerations to a sphere which cannot be encompassed in the 'scientific' enterprise so beloved of traditional psychology. Yet, if we are to be true to the experience of psychotherapy (and being true to experience must be what science is all about), then our task must surely lie in rendering specific, i.e. central to our enquiry, precisely these non-specific factors.

It is in this area which the present work makes its main contribution: it underlines the recognition that psychological therapies are activities which involve people who bring to the undertaking their own styles, expectations and values, and that the therapeutic process cannot be satisfactorily understood unless these are properly scrutinized and elaborated. In this direction there is much to be learned in these pages.

Also to be appreciated is the way in which the authors have shunned the kinds of theoretical dogmatism and methodological obscurantism which bedevil so much of psychology. They have remained true to their experience, using only those techniques of enquiry which promise to elucidate their concerns. For example, they neither espouse nor reject 'trait psychology', but rather make flexible use of the undeniable fact that people do conduct themselves in consistent ways over long periods of time. On the one hand, the authors do not fall into the trap of suggesting that these consistencies are fundamentally definitive of 'personality' nor, on the other, of eschewing them as doctrinally incompatible with freedom and change.

However much one may regard psychological therapy as a fundamentally personal undertaking, as I do, this does not mean that each therapeutic encounter is totally unique, mysterious and ineffable; although it can be argued that regularities and common strands cannot hope to give a complete and finished account of the therapeutic process it is still a worthwhile undertaking, at least as carried out in the manner reported in this book. Patients do not come to their therapists at random, nor should they. The basis on which treatment selection and allocation takes place, however, is often haphazard, if not irrational. While the importance of matching therapist to patient has been recognized by some writers, it is only with the publication of this book that the question receives the kind of systematic attention which is of real value to practising psychotherapists.

D. J. Smail
Nottingham

Acknowledgments

We would like to express our gratitude to all those staff and patients who have so willingly completed our questionnaires and without whose cooperation this book could not have been published. Thanks are also due to our colleagues at Claybury Hospital, Chase Farm Hospital and University College Hospital for their support, to Dr Patrick Slater's M.R.C. Service for help in analysing our repertory grid data and to Mrs Janet Ziff for her excellent preparation of the manuscript. A special debt is owed to Dr Malcolm Pines of the Group Analytic Society and the Institute of Group Analysis, for his constant encouragement and support.

Introduction

The present work has developed, to a large extent, as a response to some of the problems and issues that have confronted us as clinical psychologists closely involved in psychotherapy, behaviour therapy and research. The limitations of 'the medical model' for the understanding and the psychological treatment of neuroses is now widely recognized. It has been variously argued, for example, that for such conditions the term 'mentally ill' should be replaced and that the patient's conflicts can be conceptualized more appropriately as problems in living (Szasz, 1967), a function of interpersonal conflicts (Laing, 1967), a reflection of a socio-political organization (Levine, 1972), or a natural and even adaptive reaction to stress (Albee, 1969). In response to these ideas an assortment of treatment methods, largely of the psycho-social variety, has arisen. From a practical point of view, however, no consistent evidence has been forthcoming demonstrating the superiority of any one method. Nevertheless, their respective protagonists have been much concerned to impress upon us the scientific basis (and hence, presumably, the respectability) of their particular approach. Unfortunately such claims have been subjected to severe criticism for a number of reasons, not least of which is the restricted view of science taken by the various therapeutic schools (Smail, 1978). In addition, we have been warned by writers such as Rollo May (1958), Barbara Wootton (1960), and Jerome Frank (1973) that psychological disorder and its treatment cannot be defined in scientific terms which are completely free from subjective moral judgments and the prevailing values of a society or class within a society.

In considering this situation and the sparse and contradictory nature of the literature on treatment selection, Professor Yalom of Stanford University School of Medicine has stressed the pressing need for a system of classification to be developed for patients which is capable

1

of providing predictive information about interpersonal behaviour within a given treatment situation. This lack of a systematic framework for selection for treatment ventures is particularly evident in the area of small group psychotherapy where it is commonly reported that one third of group members drop out within the first few months of starting treatment.

Thus the present-day clinician is faced with the problem of deciding what treatment to recommend to what patient, with no indicators firmly based in practice or theory to guide him. Our task, therefore, has been to develop a framework for the allocation of neurotic patients to the psychological methods of treatment. We have selected small group psychotherapy for special study, with behaviour therapy as a contrasting treatment model, because of their widespread practice within the National Health Service and because of our own particular involvement.

A basic assumption in our work has been that the individual patient is an active agent in his transactions, in health as well as in illness. Thus we maintain that a person seeking help for his psychological distress presents with a characteristic integration of adjustment strategies, attitudes, and expectancies which we have called his 'personal style' and we have found in our researches that these various elements have considerable predictive power with regard to the allocation and response to the two treatment methods we have investigated. Although it can be argued that this 'personal style' is a unique integration as far as the individual is concerned, the various elements, we suggest, are shared with others to a greater or lesser extent. Thus we may expect to find groups of individuals who employ similar adjustment strategies, and who share somewhat similar beliefs concerning many issues, including psychiatric treatment. The systematic investigation of adjustment strategies, beliefs and expectancies in relation to the neuroses and their treatment is the main focus of this book.

With regard to the adjustment strategies which we have found to be relevant to our problem, we have brought together a number of different, although related, dichotomies which have an acknowledged place in social psychology and the psychology of personality. The first of these is based on Jung's (1933) adjustive concept of introversion-extraversion, which we have designated as 'inward' or 'outward' directions of interest, and which we have discussed in detail in Chapter 1. In Chapter 2 we have described a second strategy much investigated by Wilson (1973) and traditionally designated in the literature as 'conservatism-radicalism'. The third strategy (in Chapter 5) is one popularized by Hudson (1966) and referred to as 'convergent-divergent thinking'. The fourth and fifth strategies involve the 'openness' and 'control' attitudes identified by Coan (1974) which we have discussed in Chapter 6. Although there are undoubtedly considerable differences in the genealogies of these variously named strategies, we have argued that different writers have simply stressed and measured rather different aspects of two profound polarities or principles operating in both the inorganic and organic worlds and which have been recognized by mystics, philosophers and scientists through the history of human thought.

With regard to our own research, we have related the elements of the 'personal style' to the neuroses in a number of ways. In the various chapters describing the adjustment strategies, clinical group differences have been reported. In Chapters 3 and 4 we describe the development and validation of our measures of treatment expectancies and attitudes to patient care. We have identified two broad approaches, namely a 'psychological' and an 'organic', and we have found that they are represented institutionally by the therapeutic community on the one hand and the traditional psychiatric hospital on the other. Their relationship to the adjustment strategies has been found to be consistent over a large number of different samples. Initial studies of the complaints of psychological distress have suggested links between particular patterns of presentation, the adjustment strategies and treatment expectancies (Chapter 7).

As we have indicated, we have regarded the patient as an active agent in his own treatment and, as such, we have been concerned with the meaning of his conflicts to him. Although his expectancies concerning his treatment may be seen to be an aspect of such meaning, by the use of repertory grids, in Chapter 8, we have been able to extend our investigations to other areas including the relationship of general construing to adjustment strategies.

In Chapter 9 we argue that the assumptions underlying small group psychotherapy and behaviour therapy, far from being based on hard facts and dispassionate observation, stem in part from the theorists' more general orientations to life. These theoretical assumptions reflect the same 'personal style' elements that have been identified in the patients. Like Goldstein and Stein (1976), we believe that for treatment ventures to be successful, such critical, operative variables for patient, therapist, and treatment must be matched.

In Chapter 10 we report our preliminary attempts to develop and evaluate a selection framework for small group psychotherapy and behaviour therapy. The research findings suggest particular predictive power for a composite measure in relation to a stringent outcome criterion involving psychological test score changes and progress ratings by both patient and therapist. However, our research was carried out under National Health Service conditions and thus the staff involved varied considerably in terms of training, experience, and therapeutic commitment. Patient allocation to treatment, too, was simply in terms of psychiatric symptom pattern derived from clinical observation. Nevertheless, Chapters 1, 2, 3, and 4 describe significant institutional, professional and patient sample differences in adjustment strategies and treatment attitudes, suggesting that considerable self-selection in our terms was proceeding gratuitously within the Health Service. Thus we would argue that sufficient matching has indeed given rise to findings of positive therapeutic outcome in all the studies of treatment response we have carried out. However, we suggest that a more systematic selection procedure, along the lines discussed, would reduce the general frustration associated with high drop-out rates and unresolved 'resistance', 'transference' and 'counter-transference' problems. Our task in the future is to refine the selection framework presented here and to this end, a number of specific research proposals have been suggested in Chapter 11.

In drawing together this somewhat amorphous and wide-ranging research material involving adjustment strategies, personal constructs, general attitudes and interests, specific attitudes to psychiatric treatment, neurotic symptom clusters, small group psychotherapy, and behaviour therapy we have been faced with the dilemma of presentation alternatives. We have found it impossible to devise a completely logical order of presentation since, inevitably, some relationships have had to be presented before all the relevant variables have been fully discussed. In Chapter 1, for example, the significance of direction of interest for attitudes to patient care has been indicated before the full discussion of the latter in Chapter 4. Rightly or wrongly the best solution to this problem, we have decided, is to present our data in a roughly historical sequence, as one research programme has led to another. We are aware of the deficiencies in terms of a perfectly consistent sequence in this arrangement and we apologize for any irritation our presentation may arouse in this respect.

Chapter 1
The structure of personality and direction of interest

The present authors' concern with certain general areas of personality functioning has arisen as a result of their preoccupations with a number of specific practical problems, such as why some people make good psychotherapists and why some patients accept and respond to some forms of psychological treatment and not to others. In our search for answers we have been influenced primarily by our personal clinical involvement in psychotherapy and behaviour therapy. Tenaciously held opinions about the nature and treatment of 'mental illness' on the part of both staff and patients, without supporting evidence, suggested to us that these were simply the reflection of more basic personality attributes. Some staff, for example, strongly resisted the attempt to transform a humanitarian, traditional mental hospital into a therapeutic community. Indeed, after more than a decade of exposure to the new ideas, resistance was still so strong that the attempt was virtually abandoned. What seemed to be involved was a threat to a very much more general life style or value system of great importance to resistant staff members. We noticed too that other staff, presumably for similar reasons, found the therapeutic community way of treatment immediately compatible with their values without training or indoctrination. Similar attitudes were encountered among the patients admitted to the hospital.

One clue to a possible personality variable underlying treatment preferences was the finding by one of the authors (Caine, 1964) that committed therapeutic community nursing staff indicated a preference for working with ideas whereas their general hospital colleagues preferred to work with things. This clearly had some affiliation with Jung's theory of direction of psychical 'libidinal' flow or the inward or outward orientation of the individual. Further study of staff and patient attitudes (Caine and Smail, 1969) suggested that some staff and some patients preferred a conventional, traditional approach to patient care

5

whereas others preferred the more revolutionary, therapeutic community orientation. This led us to a consideration of social attitudes and the use of Wilson's Conservatism Scale (Wilson, 1973) in our studies.

We believe, with Lecky (1951), that there is a self-consistency in the value system a person adopts, in the meaning that he places upon life's experiences, and in the methods he uses in coping with the basic problems of living. In this we find ourselves in sympathy with such apparently divergent personality theorists as Allport (1937), Eysenck (1953), Jung (1920), Lecky (1951), Foulds (1965) and Coan (1974). If in little else, these writers all agree that personality is a matter of structure and organization and they reject the alternative doctrine of the specificity of behaviour. Exponents of the latter doctrine hold that there are no broad, general traits making for consistency of behaviour and stability of personality. Rather, there are only independent, specific, stimulus–response bonds or habits. Eysenck traces this theory back to its roots in the experimental tradition. Thus the Thorndikian type of learning theory conceived of the learning process in terms of S-R (stimulus-response) bonds similar to those of the reflex or the conditioned reflex. These bonds are regarded as being entirely specific to the particular situation which evokes them. It follows that if the organization of personality is largely dependent on the learning process, then the adult personality should reflect the basic specificity of the learning process itself. Learning is specific to the task learned. Finally, the much quoted studies of deceit by Hartshorne and May (1928) purported to show that children might cheat in one situation but not in another, thus indicating the specificity of deceitful behaviour.

This approach has come under heavy fire from Allport (1937) and from Eysenck (1953) amongst others. Eysenck, for example, has questioned the wisdom of directly applying the theoretical implications derived from the study of learning processes to personality theory. He maintains that the principles of the organization of personality should be derived from the study of personality rather than from the study of learning. The Hartshorne and May studies are more to the point and Eysenck has marshalled some impressive arguments invalidating their interpretations of their results. In a re-examiniation of the test data themselves he writes:

> Hartshorne and May advance the view that the very low intercorrelations between the different tests for each one of the various personality qualities measured — honesty, persistence, self-control, and

so on — make the assumption of the existence of such qualities very unlikely. Yet on the specificity theory these correlations should be zero; in fact they are almost in every case positive. Thus it is reported that the twenty-three tests used in securing our total character score, for example, intercorrelate .30 on average. Such intercorrelations are admittedly lower than those found between intelligence tests, but we must be careful not to compare an intelligence test, composed of fifty to a hundred items, with a single test of honesty, or persistence, which in truth would correspond rather to an item in a much larger test battery for the measurement of honesty, or persistence, made up of fifty to a hundred such items. We shall see, in our discussion of the detailed results of this experiment, that reliabilities and validities approaching and sometimes even exceeding values of .85 and .90 are found in Hartshorne and May's own work for such batteries of 'honesty' or 'persistence' tests. Such results are inconceivable on any strict specifistic hypothesis, and must therefore be held to controvert that position.

On the basis of his analysis of his personality inventory data Lecky (1951) maintains that confidence in social situations, cooperation, optimism, a friendly attitude towards other members of the family, companionship with the opposite sex, efficient work dispositions, freedom from nervous symptoms, and a feeling of physical well-being are closely interrelated and tend to increase or decrease together. He writes 'The data support this conclusion with such convincing uniformity that the presence of a dynamic organisation of some kind can scarcely be open to serious question.' He goes on to say that behaviour is characteristic of a person not because his separate acts are related to one another, but because all his acts have the goal of maintaining the same structure of values. In support of this contention, Bromley (1966), in his study of the ageing process, has concluded that the elements of adjustment are much the same throughout life, the individual and his circumstances being modified as a consequence of goal-directed mental and behavioural activities. Although in the process one desire may replace another, measurable age-changes in actual personality structure and dynamics are slight. A similar finding has been reported by Reichard, Livson and Peterson (1962). Perhaps enough has been said to indicate that the present authors are not alone in their bias towards an organizational, structural, and self-consistency approach to the theory and study of personality.

Granted that many leading personality theorists are in agreement on the organizational aspect of personality, there is little general agreement on what is, in fact, being organized. For Adler it is the 'life style'; for Allport it is the forming of patterns or hierarchies of ideas and habits and the principle of functional autonomy by which the proliferation of unique dynamic traits within an individual can be explained; for Foulds it is the degree of success in establishing and maintaining mutual personal relationships, since for him a person is a person only in relation to others; for Coan it is the flexible attainment of balance and integration between an 'openness' towards experience on the one hand and its successful ordering and controlling on the other. Coan sees his system as basically the same as Jung's differentiating and integrating components of the process of individuation.

With regard to our studies of staff/patient orientations to psychiatric treatment, doctors' interests and adjustive strategies have been found to parallel our results regarding those of therapeutic community and general hospital nurses. The consistent finding is that doctors who are psychologically orientated in their approach to treatment tend to score higher on tests of 'introverted thinking' than do their more physically orientated colleagues (Kreitman (1962), Walton (1966, 1969), Walton and Hope (1967), Walton and Last (1969) and Mowbray and Davies (1971)). The term 'introverted thinking' seems to have been coined to denote a general orientation towards, or interest in, the realm of ideas, imagination and theory rather than that of facts, practical problems and issues. Although this may seem straightforward enough, a closer examination of the term 'introverted thinking', particularly with regard to its ancestry, leads one into a conceptual jungle which indicates only too obviously the subjective nature of the study of human personality. At the very root the difficulties encountered in distinguishing conceptually between interests, attitudes, and personality traits are obvious from any scrutiny of introductory text books of psychology. The conceptual confusion about the nature of extraversion and introversion, for example, is reflected in this respect by its varied classification by different authors. For Jung (1920, 1933), the originator of the terms, and for Drever (1952) they are the attitudes and interests; for Thouless (1958), Munn (1966) and Katz and Schank (1938) they are personality traits. Further, some authors seem to regard them as units along with such other attributes as dominance, perseverance, altruism, etc. Others give long lists of traits which in combination go to make up the extravert or the introvert. In addition to these problems there is no doubt that the terms over the years have been so distorted that they no longer have their original meaning — a point that we will return to later.

Since our measure of interest, the Direction of Interest Questionnaire, is directly based upon a test designed to measure Jung's personality typologies, it may be worthwhile to present a brief summary of his ideas. The following condensation of Jung's theory and description of psychological types is put forward with some trepidation. The scope of his work is enormous and any attempt to reduce his arguments for the more limited purpose of this book is bound simultaneously to detract from the acuteness of his observations.

For Jung (1933) introversion and extraversion are the basic essentials which underlie the whole psychic process. They establish the habitual reactions and determine not only the style of behaviour but also the nature of subjective experience and 'the kind of compensatory activity of the unconscious which we may expect to find'. In defining introversion and extraversion Jung writes:

When the orientation to the object and to objective facts is so predominant that the most frequent and essential decisions and actions are determined not by subjective values but by objective relations, one speaks of an extraverted attitude. When this is habitual, one speaks of an extraverted type. If a man so thinks, feels and acts, in a word, so lives, as to correspond directly with objective conditions and their claims, whether in a good sense or ill, he is extraverted.

His entire consciousness looks outwards to the world, because the important decisive determination always comes to him from without. But it comes to him from without only because that is where he expects it . . . . The extravert's libido or psychical energy is directed to the external world so that all interests, values and attitudes are directed towards the physical and social environment.

With the introvert the contrary is the case. He selects the subjective determinants as the decisive ones. This type is guided, therefore, by the factor of perception and cognition which represents the receiving subjective disposition to the sense stimulus . . . . whereas the extraverted type refers pre-eminently to that which reaches him from the object, the introvert principally relies upon that which the outer impression constellates on the subject.

The introvert is thus fundamentally involved with his inner world. With each of these two types, at the unconscious level, the opposite tendencies hold sway. The extravert has repressed his introversion and vice versa.

Jung derived some of these ideas from his observation of psychiatric patients. Hysteria, he contended, is characterized by a centrifugal tendency of the libido, whilst *dementia praecox* (schizophrenia) is characterized by a centripetal tendency. These tendencies vary with the state of the 'illness' and are reversed 'where the illness has fully established its compensatory effects'. The hysteric takes to his bed, the *dementia praecox* patient draws attention to himself and becomes directly aggressive.

In carrying out these observations beyond the psychopathological, Jung argued that a study of literature reveals numerous examples of this dichotomy. In his opinion the best observations on the subject were made by William James, who maintained that in his philosophy the professional philosopher is simply expressing his own temperament. James divided philosophers into two classes, namely, the 'tenderminded', who are only interested in the inner life and spiritual things, and the 'tough-minded', who lay stress on material things and objective reality. The tender-minded person is intellectual, idealistic, optimistic, religious, a partisan of free-will, a monist and a dogmatist. The tough-minded person is positivistic and an empiricist. He is concerned only with matters of fact. It is only empirical phenomena demonstrable in the outside world which count. Thought is merely a reaction to external experience and principles are never of such value as facts. Values as such are reduced to elements lower than themselves. He explains the higher by the lower, arguing that it is nothing but such another thing and therefore of no value in itself. Jung quotes further examples drawn from the descriptions of scholars and artists. In psychology Freud's system is centrifugal or extraverted. It is a theory which is essentially reductive, pluralist, causal and sensualist. The theory limits itself rigidly to empirical facts and traces back complexes to their antecedents and their elemental factors. It regards the psychological life as only a reaction to the environment and accords the greatest role and the largest place to sensation. Adler's, on the other hand, represents a centripetal or introverted theory. Phenomena are not reducible to earlier and very primitive factors but are conceived as 'arrangements' — the outcome of intentions and of ends of an extremely complex nature. The history of the patient and the concrete influences of the environment are of much less importance than the dominating principles of the individual. He is not dependent upon an object for subjective enjoyment. Rather, he protects his own individuality and dominating ideas from the hostile influences of the environment.

Jung came later to recognize the inadequacy of these two very global descriptive types and elaborated his theory to include ways of judging and ways of perceiving. If in judging ideas one concentrates on whether they are true or not before one accepts them, one is using thinking predominantly. If one is conscious first of like or dislike, of whether concepts are sympathetic or antagonistic to other prized ideas, one is using feeling. In perception one can depend upon one's senses or one's intuitions. Extraversion and introversion determine the direction that these other psychological 'functions' will take.

It is clear from Jung's writings that he regarded extraversion and introversion as very basic attitudes or orientations towards the outer world of objects on the one hand and the inner subjective world on the other. Together with the psychological functions, they represent dynamic adjustment strategies. Jung also associated certain personality traits with each of his eight possible types. In his system, then, he seems to be utilizing three 'levels' of psychological functioning. Extraversion and introversion are the basic universal psychological phenomena having, in some way, their biological precursor.

Over the years Jung's system has suffered considerable mutilation. Extraversion and introversion as basic interest/attitude orientations have been redefined by the search for measurements of the possible related personality traits by which to define the underlying orientation. These modifications stem primarily from the work of Guilford and his colleagues. In an influential review of studies in this field up to the 1930s, Guilford and Braly (1930) point out that in bringing Jung's 'poetic terminology within the reach of experimental methods', extraversion and introversion had acquired a number of distinctions. Emphasis by various writers had been placed on the subject's direction of interest; others emphasized sociability, while others selected degree of expressive inhibition. These authors conclude that 'there is a considerable agreement among psychologists upon the existence of a bipartite distinction known as introversion-extraversion and there is some agreement upon its definition, although the intellectual, emotional and social aspects are variously emphasized.' In their view factor analysis is to solve the riddle of the nature of extraversion and introversion and, indeed, of personality in general.

With hindsight and the increasing recognition of the essentially subjective nature of factor analysis in terms of data selection, choice of statistical methodology, and the interpretation of factors, we can see now that their belief was unjustified.

The three main factor analytically orientated protagonists in this area since the 1930s are Guilford, Cattell, and Eysenck. The amount of published work of each of these authors is prodigious and full reviews evaluating the relative statistical merits of their personality descriptions are to be found in Carrigan (1960) and Eysenck and Eysenck (1969).

In her review of over thirty multivariate analyses of the nature of extraversion/introversion, Carrigan found that each analysis produced one or more factors having some resemblance to Jung's type descriptions. In spite of this core of agreement there was much disagreement in the number and nature of the factors found, due, no doubt, to differences in the original set of variables being measured and to differences in the statistical procedures used, the choice of which may simply reflect the researcher's bias towards one particular theory of extraversion/introversion.

In Marshall's (1967) view Cattell's work in this area escapes some of these criticisms but he considers that Cattell's primary factor M (autia-praxernia) is a better measure of extraversion/introversion than is his second order factor. Cattell himself speculated on the relationship between this empirically discovered factor as measured by his personality test and Jung's clinically derived concepts. He considered that the extravert type corresponded not to factor M alone but to a correlated group of six or eight of his factors which included M. Marshall argues that this broader description of Cattell's may fit Jung's subsequent descriptions of the secondary personality traits associated with the extravert or the introvert. In his view factor M remains the purer measure of the latter.

Marshall, too, criticizes the popular equation of sociability with extraversion, particularly with regard to the construction of personality tests of extraversion/introversion. For example, in constructing a test of extraversion, it is not sufficient to ask 'Would you rather spend an evening reading or seeing friends?' It would be more accurate to ask 'Did you, as a child, prefer stories of battle or conquests or imaginary fairy tales?' Or similarly, 'Would you rather marry someone who is socially admired or someone who is gifted in art and literature?' Such questions ask the person to choose between inner and outer interests within the activity of story-telling or within the activity of relating with others. In any event, it is clear that there has been a considerable shift by some writers from the original Jungian dichotomy of a basic orientation towards the internal world of ideas versus the external world of objects to the behavioural level of personality traits. Be that as it may, for the clinician, perhaps, the crucial test of a personality measure is its usefulness in clinical practice. We would argue, from this point of view, that nomothetic attempts to provide one complete and final map of personality should be abandoned. Rather, research might more profitably be directed towards determining which aspects of personality are enduring and which are transient; which aspects are experienced as distressing and alien and which as ego-syntonic; which are constitutionally determined and which environmentally; which aspects have general application and which are idiosyncratic. A step in this direction has been made by Foulds (1959, 1965). In his system psychiatric symptoms, attitudes and personality traits are distinguished conceptually and tests have been specifically devised to measure these different aspects of personality functioning. Reports showing different stabilities, following psychiatric treatment, in the measures directed towards these varying aspects of personality have been published by, for example, Mayo (1966) and Caine and Smail (1969). As Griffiths (1970) has argued, from the applied psychology point of view clinical experience and research could determine what aspect of personality functioning will be of importance for any one particular problem. The hysteroid-obsessoid personality trait constellations might be more important for vocational guidance than for the evaluation of treatment results. In the latter area psychiatric symptoms, attitudes of hostility and guilt, personal constructs, expectancies, openness and control may be of greater relevance. In this connection, Walton (1969) has found that the extraversion scale of the Maudsley Personality Inventory was not related to psychiatric career preference whereas such a preference was related to 'thinking introversion' and 'complexity of thinking'.

The development of the Direction of Interest Questionnaire

In the particular set of problems being investigated in this book 'direction of interest' seemed to be a fundamental issue. From the individual test item point of view and from general description a number of test constructors have developed scales measuring this dimension. These include the C Scale of the Kuder Preference Record Personal Form A (Kuder, 1952), the M Scale of the Sixteen Personality Factor Questionnaire (Cattell and Eber, 1957) and the S/N Scale of the Myers-Briggs Type Indicator Form F (Myers, 1962). All these scales emphasize an interest in ideas and imagination on the one hand and facts and practicality on the other. Again, the naming of this orientation or interest pattern varies from author to author. Kuder calls it simply a preference for working with ideas. Cattell describes it as 'bohemian, introverted, absent minded versus practical, concerned with facts'. Myers considers that his S/N Scale is measuring the sensing versus intuiting dimension postulated by Jung. Although his inventory is based directly on Jungian typology, Myers seems to have fallen into the same trap as other test constructors and has built up his extraversion-introversion scale with items having to do with sociability or so-called social extraversion. This is borne out experimentally in that the scales going to make up Cattell's extraversion factor, the extraversion-introversion scale of the Myers-Briggs Type Indicator and the Hysteroid-Obsessoid Questionnaire (a personality questionnaire which has been found to correlate highly with Eysenck's Extraversion Scale (Caine and Hope, 1964)) loaded on one factor whilst the M Scale and the Sensing-Intuiting Scale loaded on another when a battery of tests was factorized (Caine and Smail,1969). The distinction being made between the personality traits of sociability and of the hysteroid-obsessoid kind versus the direction of interest in terms of orientation towards the world of ideas or the world of objects is thus supported. This is confirmation also of the Mowbray and Davies (1971) finding of no correlation between the two aspects.

The Direction of Interest Questionnaire (compiled with the help of Dr D. J. Smail) is a short, fourteen-item composite of the C Scale, the M Scale and the S/N Scale described above. It distinguishes between an interest in ideas, imagination, theory, religion, philosophy, unconventionality and emotional problems on the one hand and facts, practical problems, biochemistry, common sense, engineering, domestic science, power and action on the other.

The validation of the Direction of Interest Questionnaire was carried out in two ways, namely by determining its correlation with a criterion measure and by the use of criterion groups.

The correlation with the criterion measure

Since the Myers-Briggs Type Indicator is the personality inventory directly based upon Jung's typology, the S/N Scale was selected as the criterion measure. Both scales were administered to three groups of subjects, namely fifty-three occupational therapy students, thirty-five members of the general population and twenty-six neurotic patients attending a psychotherapy clinic. The mean age for the group as a whole was 24.54 (sd 7.70). The means and standard deviations for the Direction of Interest Questionnaire for the groups separately are shown in Table 1.1. No significant difference was found between these groups.

Table 1.1 Means and standard deviations of various samples for the Direction of Interest Questionnaire

	n	Mean	sd
Occupational therapy students	53	15.00	6.96
General population	35	16.06	7.66
Neurotic patients	26	14.08	5.96
Total sample	114	15.11	7.00

When the total sample was compared for sex differences no significant difference emerged (men: mean 14.94, sd 6.75; women: mean 15.22, sd 7.28). 104 of the subjects also completed the Hysteriod-Obsessoid Questionnaire. The correlations of the Direction of Interest Questionnaire with the Myers-Briggs S/N Scale, the Hysteroid-Obsessoid Questionnaire and with age are shown in Table 1.2.

Reliability

Forty-two of the occupational therapist students were retested on the Direction of Interest Questionnaire after three months' practical experience in a progressive mental hospital where therapeutic community techniques are applied in varying degrees depending on the type of ward. The retest correlation was 0.84. It is of considerable interest, however, that there was a significant shift to a more inward direction of interest on the part of a sub-sample of twenty-seven students responding to a follow-up, suggesting that their experience, however limited in many instances in the therapeutic community ethos, had modified their orientation to some degree. This shift was found to be maintained in more than half the group followed up a year after taking up their first job. In contrast, there was no siginificant change at any point in the students' hysteroid-obsessoid personality trait score, supporting the distinctions drawn by Foulds (1965) and Caine and Smail (1969) between symptoms, attitudes and traits.

Validation by the use of criterion groups

Both Cattell and Myers link their scales to certain occupation groups. According to the *Handbook of the Sixteen Personality Factor Questionnaire* a high M score occurs in artists, researchers, planning executives and editors. A low M is associated with occupations requiring mechanical

Table 1.2 Correlations of the Direction of Interest Questionnaire and the Criterion Measure, the Hysteroid-Obsessoid Questionnaire and age

	r	p <
Myers-Briggs S/N Scale (Criterion Measure)	0.81	0.01
Hysteroid-Obsessoid Questionnaire	0.37	0.01
Age	−0.06	−

sense, realism, and alertness. Research is quoted demonstrating that a high M score distinguishes the more creative researchers and artists from administrators and teachers of the same eminence. In the same way top-level advertising planners can be distinguished from routine salesmen. Automobile accident rates are lower for the low M individuals. The S/N Scale has a high positive correlation with the Strong Vocational Interest Blank occupational scales of artist, psychologist, architect, physician, minister, social worker, author-journalist and advertising man. It is negatively correlated with accountant, office man, purchasing agent, banker, mortician and sales manager.

A large number of patients and normal subjects have completed the Direction of Interest Questionnaire and one would expect the means of the various occupations represented to follow roughly the same order as that indicated by the Cattell and Myers studies. Since a high score on the questionnaire indicates an inward direction of interest and a low score an outwardly directed interest one would expect the means of the occupations involving these orientations to arrange themselves in this way. Table 1.3 shows the means of the Direction of Interest Questionnaire scores of the various occupations available in descending order of value.

It is indeed the case that the occupational groups have arranged themselves along a dimension from those concerned primarily with relationships, psychology, imagination and theory to those more concerned with concrete, practical tasks. However, in order to rule out the operation of a possible intelligence factor further studies were carried out comparing the psychologically orientated and the physically orientated members of the same profession or training groups. Table 1.4 shows a comparison between (1) general hospital doctors and psychotherapeutically orientated psychiatrists and (2) psychology, human biology, and engineering university students.

The large number of nurses who have completed the questionnaire enable us to make yet another comparison along these lines. Three types of nursing were represented in our samples, namely general

Table 1.3 Mean Direction of Interest Questionnaire scores of various occupational groups

	Mean	sd
Psychiatric social workers (9 trained, 10 trainees)	23.26	3.93
Undergraduate psychology students on a clinical option course (20)	22.65	4.23
Psychotherapists (19 trained psychiatrists)	21.21	5.37
Clinical psychologists (7 trained, 4 trainees)	19.83	4.52
Mature students on a group psychotherapy introductory course (116)	19.8	5.5
Trained artists (29)	19.66	6.45
Secretaries (11)	17.27	4.56
Research biochemists (13)	16.00	6.38
Theology students (23)	15.87	6.67
Pre-clinical medical students (98)	14.62	6.14
Clerks (25)	13.40	6.05
Metallurgists (28)	11.36	5.50
Salesmen (14)	10.92	6.23
Engineers (craftsmen) (40)	9.92	5.82

nurses, psychiatric nurses and psychiatric therapeutic community nurses. The latter are nurses who would be expected to form psychotherapeutic relationships with the patients, to attend ward meetings, small group meetings and generally participate in the psychotherapeutic ethos of their units. They should therefore be expected to have the highest Direction of Interest Questionnaire Scores (show more inwardly directed interest), the general nurses should have the lowest score (show more outwardly directed interest) and the psychiatric nurses should fall in between. The psychiatric nurse in most mental hospitals is less

Table 1.4 Comparison of Direction of Interest Questionnaire scores of groups of comparable intellectual ability and educational attainment

	n	Mean	sd	t	p <
1 Psychiatrists	19	21.21	5.37	4.309	0.001
General hospital doctors	30	14.10	5.77		

	n	Mean	sd	t	p <
2 Psychology students	54	18.44	5.68		
Engineering students	19	15.00	4.37 ⎫ n.s. ⎫	3.667	0.001
Human biology students	90	14.48	6.23 ⎭ ⎭		

involved in a formal psychotherapeutic way with the patients than are the therapeutic community psychiatric nurses and he may well be more concerned with the physical treatment aspects of the job. For the purposes of this comparison the three groups were matched for nursing grade so that each group consisted of fifteen sisters or charge nurses, nine assistant matrons and two tutors. The means, which are all significantly different from each other, are shown in Table 1.5.

Table 1.5 Comparison of Direction of Interest Questionnaire scores of various groups of nurses

	n	*Mean*	*sd*
Therapeutic community nurses	26	18.38	6.42
Psychiatric nurses	26	12.35	5.92
General nurses	26	9.50	5.48

Cattell has suggested that his high M scorers are characterized by a vigorous individualism and subjectivity which may tend to lead to poor relations with society. It is of considerable interest in this connection that young persons referred to one of the writers for occupational guidance tended to obtain high Direction of Interest scores (mean 19.25, sd = 5.48, n = 31). They presented, mainly, as an intelligent, socially alienated group, unable to fit into society educationally and occupationally. One presented his problem in the following terms:

My basic problem is not knowing what I want out of life, therefore I don't know what life style to adopt. Being a romantic, I would ideally like to become a beachcomber on an island or a boatbuilder or fisherman in a Cornish village but I am realistic enough to know that I must earn a living. Recently I tried the 'simple life' by returning to the sea and working as a seaman. I found the life boring, hard, limiting and dangerous (end of dream of being a sailor)! I am now looking for a job that will bring me into contact with creative and stimulating people. I thought art teaching would provide this, but it turned out to be humdrum and I found myself not dedicated to the profession. I want to be able to make decisions and act on my own initiative.

This client achieved a maximum inward Direction of Interest Questionnaire score.

From these data it may be concluded that the Direction of Interest

Questionnaire has a high coefficient of correlation with the criterion validation measure. Occupations thought to be related to direction of interest have been found to arrange themselves in the expected order in terms of mean score. Within single occupations and amongst university students differences in mean score in the expected direction have been found. The questionnaire has a high level of reliability on retest. The questionnaire may be said to be measuring an interest in the subjective in terms of imagination, ideas, theories and psychological events as opposed to an interest in the objective in terms of concrete, practical situations and events. In our validation sample a medium-sized significant correlation emerged with the Hysteroid-Obsessoid Questionnaire. The latter has been found to correlate highly with the Extraversion Scale of the Maudsley Personality Inventory (Caine, 1965a). Thus in our terms it can be observed that an inwardly directed interest is associated with hysteroid personality traits (Eysenckian 'extraverts'). This underlines rather forcibly the difficulties of conceptualization in this area.

Over the years it has been possible for us to collect data concerning the Direction of Interest Questionnaire in relation to other tests from various non-patient groups as opportunity presented itself at lectures, conferences and in the course of other research work. These relationships are shown in Tables 1.6, 1.7, 1.8, 1.9 and 1.10. From these tables it can be seen that in non-psychiatric patient samples the Direction of Interest Questionnaire is consistently related to the general factor of conservatism, is positively related to the musical/literary/artistic triad of the Kuder Preference Inventory and negatively to the scientific and computational scales and is unrelated to any of the Eysenck scales. There are consistent significant correlations between the Direction of Interest Questionnaire and attitudes to treatment as represented by the Attitude to Treatment Questionnaire and the Treatment Expectancies Questionnaire over a large number of samples of nursing staff and a more varied group composed of health care professionals of

Table 1.6 Correlations between the Direction of Interest Questionnaire and the Conservatism Scale[*] in various samples

Sample	n	r	p <
Medical students, sundry volunteers, and neurotic patients	81	0.39	0.001
Pre-clinical medical students	98	0.24	0.05

[*]See chapter 2.

different kinds, medical students and hospital voluntary workers. The evidence is thus very strong that in non-patient samples the Direction of Interest Questionnaire is measuring a musical/literary/artistic interest as opposed to a scientific/computational one and that this interest pre-disposes a 'psychotherapeutic' as against an 'organic' set towards psychiatric treatment, both on the part of those with experience and those without (pre-clinical medical students, for example).

Table 1.7 The correlations between the Direction of Interest Question-naire and the Kuder Preference Inventory (Vocational) sub-scales in a sample of males attending for occupational guidance ($n = 31$; mean age 19.25, sd = 5.48)

Musical	*Literary*	*Artistic*	*Scientific*	*Computational*
0.57[*]	0.50[*]	0.47[*]	−0.46[*]	−0.42[*]

Persuasive	*Mechanical*	*Social service*	*Clerical*
−0.33	−0.26	−0.15	−0.13

[*]$p < 0.01$.

Table 1.8 Correlations between the Direction of Interest Questionnaire and the Attitude to Treatment Questionnaire[*] in various samples

Sample	*n*	*r*	*p* <
General, psychiatric and mental handicap nurses of various grades (attending a conference)	94	−0.32	0.05
Trained general, psychiatric and mental handicap nurses (attending a conference)	36	−0.33	0.05
Nurses attending a psychiatric nurses' conference:			
students	63	−0.33	0.01
trained	52	−0.52	0.01
General hospital student nurses	64	−0.26	−
General hospital trained nurses	29	−0.20	−
Pre-clinical medical students	98	−0.24	0.05
Sundry health care professionals, medical students and hospital volunteers	219	−0.40	0.01

[*]See Chapter 4

The relationships of the Direction of Interest Questionnaire and other data in neurotic patient samples are derived from our pre-treatment assessments of patients referred to out-patient clinics at Claybury and Chase Farm Hospitals. These relationships are shown in Tables 1.11, 1.12, and 1.13.

Table 1.9 The correlations of the Direction of Interest Questionnaire with the sub-scales of the Eysenck Personality Inventory in a group of general hospital student nurses (n = 27; mean age 19.92; sd = 1.70)

Neuroticism	Extraversion	Lie
0.04	−0.11	−0.20

Table 1.10 Correlation between the Direction of Interest Questionnaire and the Treatment Expectancies Questionnaire[*]

Sample	n	r	$p <$
Sundry health care professionals and medical students	212	−0.33	0.001

[*]See Chapter 3

Table 1.11 shows that patients allocated to group therapy are more inwardly directed than are patients allocated to behaviour therapy. This allocation was carried out by the consultant psychiatrists in charge of the clinics in consultation with the therapist likely to carry out the treatment. Allocation was in terms of psychiatric symptom pattern only, without knowledge of the patient's psychological test results. This consistent link across three large independent samples of patients between direction of interest and symptom pattern is explored further in Chapter 7.

Table 1.12 shows the relationships between direction of interest, conservatism and treatment expectancies in the three samples of patients, confirming the pattern found previously in our normal samples. Table 1.13 shows the relationship between the Direction of Interest Questionnaire and age and other tests used in clinical work. Only one sample shows a significant correlation with age although the other shows a non-significant correlation in the same direction. The most consistent finding is a correlation with total hostility at a significant level in both samples. Thus the inwardly directed patient admits to more interpersonal and personal difficulties in terms of hostile and guilty feelings than does the more outwardly directed patient, who seems to confine himself to his symptoms. This, no doubt, is reflected in the initial treatment allocation.

Table 1.11 The Direction of Interest Questionnaire scores of three samples of neurotic patients entering a psychotherapy clinic

Sample	n	Mean	sd
1* Behaviour therapy (males)	38	10.76	5.00 ⎱ n.s.
Behaviour therapy (females)	44	11.36	5.70 ⎰
Small group therapy (males)	50	15.12	7.88 ⎱ n.s.
Small group therapy (females)	50	13.90	6.87 ⎰
2 Behaviour therapy (mixed)	25	11.36	6.60
Small group therapy (mixed)	30	15.27	6.95
3 Behaviour therapy (mixed)	100	11.14	—
Small group therapy (mixed)	153	13.92	—

For sample 1: $f = 11.97$, $p < 0.001$.
For sample 2: $f = 2.12$, $p < 0.02$ (1-tail).
For sample 3: $f = 4.74$, $p < 0.001$.

*See Caine and Wijesinghe (1976).

Table 1.12 The correlations of the Direction of Interest Questionnaire with the Conservatism Scale (C) and the Treatment Expectancies Questionnaire (TEQ) in three samples of neurotic patients (age partialled out as appropriate)

Sample	n	C	TEQ
1*	182	−0.42***	−0.36***
2	181	−0.28**	−0.30***
3	64	−0.21	−0.34**

*   See Caine and Wijesinghe (1976).
** $p < 0.01$.
*** $p < 0.001$.

In addition to these data Smail (1972) and Wood (1977) have reported statistically significant correlations between the Direction of Interest Questionnaire and repertory grid measures of empathy, despite the very small number of patients involved in the studies ($r = 0.83$ and 0.73 respectively).

Summary

The Direction of Interest Questionnaire is a short, fourteen-item test

Table 1.13 The correlation of the Direction of Interest Questionnaire with age and other psychological tests in two samples of neurotic patients (age partialled out as appropriate)

Sample	N	Age	Mooney Problem Check List Total	Personal Disturbance Scale	Hostility and Direction of Hostility Questionnaire		Hysteroid-Obsessoid Questionnaire
					Total Hostility	Direction of Hostility	
1	66	−0.35**	0.22	0.12 (n=62)	0.24*	−0.29*	0.26* (n=64)
2	64	−0.24	0.40**	0.08	0.29*	−0.08	0.01

* p < 0.05.
** p < 0.01.

based on scales held in common by three well-established personality and interest inventories, namely the Cattell 16PF (M Scale), the Myers-Briggs Type Indicator (S/N Scale) and the Kuder Personal Preference Record (C Scale). Conceptually, these three scales are concerned with an 'inner' direction of interest in terms of an interest in ideas, imagination, theory, religion, philosophy, unconventionality, and emotional problems on the one hand and an 'outer' direction of interest in terms of facts, practical problems, science, engineering, power, action and common sense on the other. Experimental evidence has been presented in support of this dichotomy involving a factor analytic study and a correlational study using the Kuder Preference Inventory (Vocational).

The questionnaire has high reliability and an acceptably high validity with respect to a criterion measure and the ordering of occupational groups in terms of the interest patterns likely to be involved. Direction of interest has been found to be consistently related to the general factor of 'conservatism', with the more inwardly directed subjects adopting more radical attitudes with regard to a wide variety of social issues. The more inwardly directed psychiatric patients tend to express a larger number of critical attitudes towards the self and others. There is some evidence to suggest that an inner direction of interest is associated with a greater degree of empathic skill.

The questionnaire has been found to be consistently related to attitudes to psychiatric treatment in general population, medical, nursing, and psychiatric patient samples. An inner direction of interest has been found to correlate with a more psychological approach to patient care and treatment. An outer direction of interest has been found to correlate with a more organic, physical, scientific approach. Direction of interest has been found to relate to treatment allocation (psychotherapy or behaviour therapy) in a number of studies and it would appear to have implications for vocational guidance.

Chapter 2
Conservatism

Our experience in various hospital settings has impressed upon us the wide range of patterns of authority within the general therapeutic milieu. These patterns may range from the semi-military ethos of some traditional, organically orientated psychiatric units to the relatively democratic, psychologically orientated therapeutic community (see also Chapter 4 in this connection). As we have indicated in the previous chapter we have encountered considerable differences between staff and between patients in their reactions to these varying authoritarian structures and concomitant therapeutic approaches. Our research suggests that direction of interest is one adjustment strategy underlying attitudes to treatment in both staff and patients and that conservatism may well be a second. The present chapter examines this possibility. In our studies we have employed a recently developed test tapping a wide range of social attitudes and beliefs (Wilson's (1973) Conservatism Scale) which, in factor analytic studies, has been found to measure a general factor of conservatism-radicalism. However, before presenting our research findings with regard to the Conservatism Scale in relation to psychiatric treatment, a brief discussion of the nature of social beliefs and attitudes, together with a description of the history and construction of the Scale will be presented.

According to George and Handley (1957) beliefs may be regarded as relatively permanent states of the central nervous system. They are those stored memories whose contents specify for the organism what may be expected to happen. At any given moment relatively few of the totality of stored beliefs will be in action. Those beliefs which are actually influencing behaviour at any given instance of time may be called expectancies. For Eysenck (1954) attitudes are very similar to habits. Both are learned modifications of the central nervous system. Both are dispositions to act which cannot be observed directly. Both are hypothetical constructs which require linking up with antecedent conditions and consequent behaviour for their measurement, and both denote a persisting state of the organism. In his view attitudes so defined show a considerable degree of organization or structure. This emphasis on organization and persistence with regard to attitudes, beliefs and expectancies is common in the literature, as is the emphasis on their importance for actual behaviour. Although inevitably linked to other aspects of personality functioning such as personality traits, for the purpose of conceptualization and measurement some sort of delineation must be made. The distinction made by Eysenck (1954) is that attitudes have reference to an object, problem or social issue whereas personality traits refer to general dispositions to behave — largely regardless of object, problem or issue. In terms of the devising of measuring instruments such as attitude or personality tests of questionnaire type, Ray (1973) considers that an attitude item asks a subject to state his opinion about something in the world outside himself. A personality item, on the other hand, asks the subject to rate, describe or assess himself or his own behaviour.

With these distinctions in mind we may regard the Conservatism Scale — the C scale — as the latest of a series of attitude measures concerning a wide range of social issues such as pacificism, divorce, capital punishment, racialism, socialism, religion and institutional authority. The study of the underlying relationships between attitudes to these apparently relatively specific issues has provided a rich research harvest for social psychologists and sociologists.

Wilson and Nias (1973) have justified the construction of yet another attitude scale by pointing to the weaknesses involved in previous social attitude questionnaires. They point to the ambiguity of many of the questions going to make up the scales. Logically distinct aspects of an issue may be included in one question. Multi-negative grammar, leading questions and evaluative wording are common and two of the most frequently used tests (the California F-Scale and the Dogmatism Scale, to be discussed later) may well be open to 'response bias'. Thus both scales in scoring 'key' all of their items in one direction. Agreement with any statement is thought by the constructors to indicate authoritarianism or dogmatism respectively. Unfortunately there is experimental evidence to show that some subjects tend to agree with any statement made to them regardless of its meaning or content. Without correcting for this bias (technically known as 'acquiescence') by reversing some of the questions systematically, one's resultant scores are not a true reflection of what one is trying to measure. However, a somewhat embarrassingly high correlation between the new C scale and the F Scale of 0.68 reported by Wilson (1973) detracts from the force of these arguments.

In spite of the fact that some of its items are already dated and some appear to be sex biased, the C Scale does seem in its format to escape some of the pitfalls of traditional questionnaires. In place of questions the constructors of the scale have used single words, catch-phrases or labels representing various controversial social issues. For example, an item from Eysenck's Social Attitudes Inventory 'Unrestricted freedom of discussion on every topic in the press, in literature, on the stage, etc.' was replaced by Censorship' (Yes? No?). The authors view this new format as differing from the old in that evaluation occurs only in the response and not in the question. The old formula 'X' is a good/ bad thing (agree? disagree?) is replaced by 'X' (good? bad?). In addition, because the item is reduced to attitude content or referent alone, we might expect contamination due to grammatical confusion, ambiguity, task conflict, acquiescence, etc., to be minimized.

In the main the research evidence is consistent in demonstrating a small number of very general orientations or sets which underlie the more specific attitudes to a wide range of social issues, regardless of the methodological and statistical approach adopted. Research workers have differed, however, in their definitions of these emergent underlying orientations in accordance with the particular theory of personality they have wished to promote. A further subjective element arises in that the designation of a name to any resultant emergent statistical factor is a subjective procedure which can frequently carry value laden implications. In reading the literature concerning conservatism it becomes quite clear, for example, that in the eyes of the researchers the conservative is the baddie whereas the liberal/radical is the goodie. Aetiological explanations carrying psychopathological connotations have been advanced to explain the former but not the latter. No doubt this bias has its roots in the early studies of authoritarianism which were concerned with the rise of Fascism in the 1930s and the subsequent atrocities perpetrated by the Nazis.

It seems to the present writers that what is involved in the Conservatism Scale is, in part, an underlying generalized attitude to authority and control. If this is a dimension, at one extreme will be individuals who favour strong external authority and at the other will be those who reject all external authority in favour of their own personal sovereignty. The latter merit the label 'anarchistic' rather more than 'liberal', and since man is not an island and develops only within a human society, such an extreme position may be seen to warrant as much criticism as the former. Furthermore, such an anarchistic attitude to all external authority lends itself to psychodynamic analysis in terms of parental relationships as readily as does extreme conservatism.

Examples of the anarchistic type of person, namely one who rejects all external control, social responsibility and the like, can easily be cited. The biographies of many artists and political activists of this orientation are well known. Certainly many had chaotic personal lives fraught with anxiety, depression and despair, and ending in alcoholism, drug addiction and suicide. Their rejection of dependence on society ended in a dependence on alcohol, drugs or death. The psychoanalytic literature provides a number of studies of just such people. Presumably these orientations arise as a means of coping with life, on the one hand by the imposition of organization and control, and on the other by their abandonment. As in most things some sort of balance between the two extremes is achieved by most of us. Those at risk may well be the inflexible extremists at both ends.

There would seem to be an overlap here with the concept of internal versus external control expectancies (Rotter, 1966). A number of writers have developed the theory that belief in one's own power or powerlessness in the world has the status of a fundamental attitude or expectancy. Adler, of course, is the classical personality theorist to have argued along these lines. According to this theory situations will be evaluated in terms of the extent to which one feels capable of influencing them. Behavioural response may well be determined by the nature of the expectation of power or powerlessness as, for example, whether the person sees himself as unable to determine outcomes because the world is unpredictable (luck) or predetermined (fate) or controlled by others (appreciation of secular power). The crucial (and frightening) influence of the latter has been demonstrated by Milgram (1974) in a series of experiments demonstrating his subjects' willingness to inflict excruciating pain on helpless victims in obedience to authority.

The link between experienced power and conservatism was originally made by Adorno, Frenkel-Brunswick, Levinson and Sanford (1950) in their studies of conservatism and superstition as a power belief. Later experimental work by Boshier (1973) has only partially supported their hypothesis that superstition is a central component of the extreme conservative. In Boshier's subjects older conservatives demonstrated more superstitious behaviour than did his older liberals but the difference did not hold in his younger age group.

One of the most extensive writers in this field and one firmly entrenched in the factorial approach is Eysenck (1953, 1954). In his books *The Structure of Human Personality* and *The Psychology of Politics* he has given a full account of the early research of the 1920s and 1930s on social attitudes which culminated in the establishment of the Conservatism Scale with which we are concerned.

For the clinician it is something of a relief to move from the wrangles of the static personality profile map-makers to the dynamic, clinically orientated advocates of the conceptual approach, the chief proponents of which are Adorno, Frenkel-Brunswick, Levinson and Sanford (1950) and Rokeach (1960). Although for these authors personality is still regarded as a more or less enduring organization of forces within the individual which gives consistency to verbal and physical behaviour, they are concerned also with the analysis of the external and internal dynamics of the situation and the person. Adorno *et al.* are psychoanalytically orientated and Rokeach is concerned with the structure rather than the content of attitudes. For him, conservatism is not a constellation of attitudes which place an individual somewhere in three-dimensional space, but is rather the individual's inability to shift or modify his attitudes. It is the dogmatism with which these attitudes are held.

Rokeach has taken up the ideas of Frenkel-Brunswick experimentally. He accepts the view that every emotion will have its cognitive counterpart and that a study of the latter may well throw light on the complexities of emotional life. This general approach is much in line with a modern theory of emotion. Strongman (1974) has pointed out that the drawing of a sharp distinction between emotion and reason (or, more generally, cognition) is an out-dated procedure, since these elements can now be seen to be fused. Emotions may be seen as alerting us to various aspects concerning the situations which confront us and therefore help us to analyse them, make choices and carry out actions. Thus emotions help in the organization of our perceptions and our behaviour. Strongman too quotes experimental evidence suggesting a possible link between the personality trait of general emotional sensitivity and the ability to identify emotional experience in others, intelligence, and general verbal ability. The extensive experimental work on perception, both liminal and sub-liminal, in relation to personality, is underpinned by such a belief.

To return to Rokeach, during the course of his investigations he has come to view personality as an organization of expectancies involving an individual's particular belief-disbelief system. Man's cognitive processes take place within this already formed system of belief-disbelief which can be described and measured. The two basic systems of belief-disbelief which have primarily concerned him he has labelled the open and closed mind. He sees the open system as being set to receive, evaluate and act on information from outside on the basis of its own intrinsic merits, relatively uncontaminated by irrelevant pressures arising from within the perceiver such as anxiety based on power needs, fear of external authority, and intolerance of ambiguity.

On the other hand, the closed system is characterized by a greater difficulty in distinguishing between the intrinsic information derived from the outside and personal needs and fears. Thus, for example, what an external source says is true about the world may become mixed up with what the perceiver believes or imagines the external world wants him to think and do. Perceptions and interpretations of what is going on will be more influenced by his anxiety aroused by power needs, fear of external authority and intolerance of ambiguity.

Rokeach argues that all belief-disbelief systems serve these two powerful and conflicting motivational systems at the same time, i.e. the need for a cognitive framework to know and to understand on the one hand and the need to ward off threatening aspects of reality on the other. Although these two systems are inevitably interwoven, the former system will predominate in the open mind whereas the latter will predominate in the closed. The more closed the mind the more psychoanalytic defence mechanisms of repression, denial and projection will be enlisted.

With regard to these concepts of the open and closed mind and internal-external control Coan (1974), on the basis of an extensive body of research data, has achieved a remarkable and important integration, which restores some balance to the situation. As we have discussed in Chapters 5 and 6 it is the flexible integration of the two concepts that is important for individual growth and creativity.

Our own researches have been concerned with the relation between conservatism and attitudes to 'psychiatric illness' on the part of hospital staff and patients. In addition it has been possible to relate this dimension to various treatment programmes and to personality and diagnostic measures (Caine, 1970; Caine and Smail, 1969; Caine and Leigh, 1972; Caine, Wijesinghe and Wood, 1973; Caine and Wijesinghe, 1976).

We have argued that much of psychiatry, in contrast to physical medicine, is a pretty subjective affair which has little in the way of hard-core 'scientific' evidence on which to base itself. Due to the nature and complexity of the problem this is likely to remain the case. Our contact with both staff and patients convinces us that most people are really well aware of this but few are willing to face the position openly. Such a situation provides great scope for the operation of personal assumptions and biases which may, if expectancies are met, provide a basis for successful treatment. Indeed, practically all treatments report some successes. Our research has been concerned with the elucidation of these expectancies and with relating them to personality structure. In this respect it is to be anticipated that the general factor of conservatism will play a not inconsiderable part in the adoption of certain beliefs and practices concerning the nature of so-called mental illness and its treatment. This factor should be an operative one in both staff and patients.

Lillie (1973), in his review of work in this field, points to the paucity of research on staff and patients' attitudes in psychiatry. He suggests that the restrictive applications of the 'medical model', and the assumptions that go with it, may well have hindered the development of such studies. The same charge might well be levelled at the practice of physical medicine when its activities are confined to the treatment of organisms and diagnoses rather than people in a social and cultural environment.

1 Conservatism and the patient

The data to be reported were obtained from samples of neurotic patients referred to a psychotherapy clinic at Claybury Hospital. The conservatism scores of patients allocated to the different treatment settings are shown in Table 2.1. Table 2.1 indicates that the Conservatism Scale is a less efficient predictor of treatment allocation than either the Treatment Expectancies Questionnaire or the Direction of Interest Questionnaire (see Chapters 1 and 3). In Sample 1 only the group therapy males indicated a lower conservatism score than the behaviour therapy patients. In Sample 3, however, in comparison with patients allocated to behaviour therapy, a significantly lower conservatism score was obtained for the group therapy patients as a whole.

The correlations with the other two measures in three large samples of patients are shown in Table 2.2.

Thus in these three samples high conservatism tends to be associated with an outer direction of interest and a more traditional, symptom- and doctor-centered orientation to psychiatric treatment as opposed to a more psychological, relationship approach.

Table 2.1 Mean conservatism scale scores of three samples of neurotic patients entering a psychotherapy clinic

Sample	n	Mean	sd		
1[*] Behaviour therapy (males)	38	42.56	9.51	n.s.	F=6.19
Behaviour therapy (females)	44	43.38	11.24		
Small group therapy (females)	50	41.10	11.50		p<0.05
Small group therapy (males)	50	35.92	13.26		
2 Behaviour therapy (mixed)	25	42.88	10.90	t=1.14	
Small group therapy (mixed)	29	39.17	12.79	n.s.	
3 Behaviour therapy (47 males, 53 females)	100	44.55		F=2.91	
Small group therapy (24 males, 79 females)	153	39.53		p<0.02	

[*]See Caine and Wijesinghe (1976).

In addition, a number of the group therapy patients had completed other psychological tests used in clinical work. The correlations of the Conservatism Scale with these latter in two large samples of patients (n = 66 and 64 respectively) are shown in Table 2.3. In Sample 1, four of the patients failed to complete the Personal Disturbance Scale, and two failed to complete the Hysteroid-Obsessoid Questionnaire.

From Table 2.3 it can be seen that conservatism is unrelated to the tests typically associated with patient groups, namely the Personal Disturbance Scale, total hostility, and the total Mooney Problem Check List score. On the other hand the usual association with age is found, with older patients tending to be more conservative. The scale is significantly correlated with the Hysteroid-Obsessoid Questionnaire in one sample only, with patients of obsessoid personality being the more conservative.

To explore further the relation of conservatism to neurosis, a group of 34 student general hospital nurses was equated for age with a group of 27 female neurotic patients and the comparison of their conservatism scores is shown in Table 2.4. As with the psychological test data, Table 2.4 does not support a connection between conservatism and neurosis. The student nurses also completed the Eysenck Personality

Table 2.2 The correlation of the Conservatism Scale with the Direction of Interest Questionnaire (DIQ) and the Treatment Expectancies Questionnaire (TEQ) in three samples of neurotic patients (age partialled out)

Sample	n	DIQ	TEQ
1[*]	182	−0.42[**]	0.30[**]
2	181	−0.28[**]	0.20[**]
3	64	−0.21	0.34[**]

[*] See Caine and Wijesinghe (1976).

[**] $p < 0.01$.

Inventory but none of the three scales Neuroticism, Extraversion and Lie were found to be significantly related. In terms of psychological defensiveness, no significant correlation was found between conservatism and the K Scale of the Minnesota Multiphasic Personality Inventory in a sample of 83 neurotic patients.

The earlier writers on conservatism have suggested a link between extreme conservatism and maladjustment. Two more recent reports (Robertson and Kapur, 1972 and Coan, 1974) have linked psychological distress with extreme liberalism. Our data does not support either of these positions.

2 *Conservatism and the staff*

A number of studies have related conservatism scores to various nursing and medical groups and these comparisons are shown in Table 2.5. With regard to the nursing staff, the general and psychiatric nurses were balanced in terms of age and staff grade. Statistical analysis showed that the difference between the general and psychiatric nurses was significant as was the difference between the psychiatrists untrained in psychotherapy and those who were trained. The difference between the eclectic psychiatrists and the committed psychotherapists is in the right direction, since our hypothesis was that the physically and medically orientated staff should be more conservative than the psychotherapeutically orientated.

A number of studies relating social attitudes to attitudes to patient care as measured by the Attitude to Treatment Questionnaire (ATQ) have been reported (see Chapter 4). For example, Caine and Leigh (1972) have reported correlations of 0.50 and 0.22 in large samples

Table 2.3 The correlation of the Conservatism Scale with age and other psychological tests in two samples of neurotic patients (age partialled out as appropriate)

Sample	Age	Mooney Problem Check List Total	Personal Disturbance Scale	Hostility and Direction of Hostility Questionnaire		Hysteroid-Obsessoid-Questionnaire
				Total Hostility	Direction of Hostility	
1	0.31**	−0.14	0.04	−0.06	−0.04	−0.27*
2	0.36**	−0.18	−0.01	−0.13	0.03	−0.01

* p < 0.05.
** p < 0.01.

Table 2.4 Conservatism scores of female student general hospital nurses compared with the conservatism scores of neurotic patients of the same mean age

	n	Mean	sd	t	p
Student nurses	34	37.41	9.79		
Patients	27	37.70	9.68	—	—

of nursing groups with nursing fields and grades approximately balanced. In a further sample of seventy-two psychiatric nurses the correlation was 0.44. For doctor samples Pallis and Stoffelmayr (1973) found a correlation of a similar order: 0.44 between the C Scale and the ATQ in a sample of forty-two psychiatrists. Thus in both nursing and medical staff social attitudes are related to their attitudes to patient care and treatment preferences, with the conservative staff favouring a traditional medical approach and an organic orientation and the liberal staff adopting a more psychological orientation.

The vexed problem arises, of course, as to whether staff learn their attitudes to patient care in the course of their training and experience or whether they are drawn to work in areas compatible with their already formed social attitudes and personality structure. In the studies of nurses no correlation was found between the ATQ and age in any of the groups, and trained staff were not significantly different from the

Table 2.5 C Scale means of staff samples in various treatment situations

	n	Mean	sd	t	p
General nurses	42	51.98	12.00		
Psychiatric nurses	40	41.15	11.75	4.10	<0.001
Psychiatrists untrained in psychotherapy[*]	20	37.7	—		
Psychiatrists trained in psychotherapy	20	28.4	—		
Eclectic psychiatrists[**]	21	33.0			
Psychotherapeutically orientated psychiatrists	13	29.4			

[*] Panayotopoulos and Stoffelmayr (1972); sds not reported but a statistically significant difference claimed (p < 0.05, one-tail test).

[**] Pallis and Stoffelmayr (1973): sds not reported; no significant difference.

students. This does suggest that length of experience and training in nursing is unrelated to attitudes to patient care. A similar result for the C Scale in two of the nursing samples was also found, but in the third a significant moderate correlation was found with age.

In their doctor samples Panayotopoulos and Stoffelmayr found the C Scale and the ATQ to be unrelated to age or length of psychiatric experience in one of their studies (Panayotopoulos and Stoffelmayr, 1972), but in a later study (Pallis and Stoffelmayr, 1973), they found that the less conservative doctor chose his psychiatric career earlier than the more conservative. This supports an earlier study by Sharaf, Schneider and Kantor (1968) showing that social attitudes are related to certainty of choice of psychiatric speciality.

Summary

The research evidence is consistent in demonstrating a link between the general factor of conservatism and attitudes towards 'psychiatric illness' and treatment in both staff and patients. The more conservative staff and patients tend to support a traditional, organic, medical approach whereas the more radical tend to support a psychological, therapeutic community orientation. Conservatives were not found to be more maladjusted than radicals. Indeed there is some evidence pointing to the psychological difficulties of extreme radicals. Conservatives were found to be more obsessoid in personality in one study and to be more outwardly directed in their interests.

Chapter 3
Patients' expectancies in psychiatric treatment

Traditionally the selection of patients for psychotherapy has frequently been made on the basis of such classifications as psychiatric diagnosis, ego-defence system, social class, age, intelligence level and the like. In contrast to this approach based on the observations of a clinically trained observer, the present chapter is concerned with selection in terms of the meaning of the treatment situation to the patient himself. It can be argued that in psychological treatments the patient must become actively involved in the treatment process if change is to occur and this is unlikely to happen if the situation has no meaning for him and carries no positive expectation. For Dent (1978), 'the patient's expectations about treatment, and how they are met, are critical variables in the outcome. We will never understand the psycho-social therapies so long as we ignore these expectations.'

In their discussion of the nature of meaning Osgood, Suci, and Tannenbaum (1957) state the apparent truism that how a person behaves in a situation depends upon what the situation means to him or, in other words, his expectancies about it. In examining the experimental evidence in support of this belief, however, Griffiths (1970) finds a number of studies in which measures of such expectancies, including measures of interests and attitudes, do not, in fact, correlate with actual behaviour. Nevertheless, the considerable evidence in favour of the link between conception and behaviour suggests to him that further research may well show that these sorts of measures can provide important aids in prediction. This is certainly the position adopted by Gestalt psychologists and is the assumption of Kelly (1955), Bannister (1962) and Smail (1978). For these authors meaning and change of meaning would seem to be the most important factors in social activity regardless of whether they are expressed in terms of attitudes, values, constructs, expectancies or other such terms (see Chapter 8).

The influence of personality factors, including expectancies, on perception and memory has been the subject of intensive study by experimental psychologists for many years. Historically, Kulpe (1904) and Jaensch (1930) were among the first to suggest that individual typologies may be related to characteristic forms of perception and imagery. Bartlett's (1932) work on schemata and memory has become a classic. Zangwill (1937) pioneered experimental work on expectancies and showed how different anticipations produce different perceptions of the same contoured surfaces, and that later inability to recognize these stimuli is traceable to differences in the earlier perceptual context.

With the advent of highly sophisticated experimental and statistical techniques in recent years the research output in this area has become a flood. The evidence is consistent in demonstrating that what one sees in a perceptual experiment (or recalls in a memory experiment) is the result of a complex process involving the meaning of the experiment to the subject, the set he is given, his attitudes, and his reactions to what may be to him value laden or emotionally charged material. The selective reporting of socially 'undesirable' material even in the compulsive world of the psychotic has been demonstrated by one of the authors (Caine, 1966). Similarly, some recent studies suggest that hospitalized psychiatric patients can give a favourable or unfavourable impression of themselves on tests or in interviews according to the goals they wish to achieve. For example, if they wish to remain in hospital they present a less favourable picture of themselves psychiatrically than if they wish to be discharged (Braginsky, Grosse and Ring, 1966; Braginsky and Braginsky, 1967; Braginsky, Braginsky and Ring, 1969; Kelly, Farina, and Mosher, 1971). Although unable to support these researches unequivocally, Ryan and Neale (1973) found that schizophrenics may indeed respond differently to the same questionnaire when given an illness or neutral orientation in the instructions. Thus even with deeply disturbed patients the response to test material is not primarily determined by the material presented but rather by the meaning of the total situation to the subjects. At a more 'unconscious' level Allen, Weins, Weitman and Saslow (1965) have demonstrated that an experimentally induced expectancy in an interviewee that he would talk to either a 'cold' or 'warm' interviewer markedly influenced the interviewee's 'latency' (defined as the period of time between two speech units) before answering the interviewer in an otherwise free employment interview. Kiesler (1973) has reviewed the research findings in this area demonstrating the importance of underlying attitudes, moods and motivational states in relation to client and therapist interview patterns in terms of speech/silence/latency variables.

In line with this approach Lennard and Bernstein (1969) have adapted the concepts and methods developed in the social sciences to the study of psychotherapy. In their view psychotherapeutic intervention has traditionally located pathology within the individual and has concentrated on the management of intrapsychic variables. In their researches, however, they have focused on the 'interactional environment' within which the patient's behaviour is inevitably embedded. The shift in research emphasis is matched precisely in the psychotherapeutic developments of recent years of group therapy, therapeutic communities and family therapy. What is important for the viewpoint being presented here is the emphasis placed by these authors on the importance of expectancies in the therapeutic situation:

> In therapy the patient not only 'learns' a set of expectations appropriate to the therapeutic relationship, and how to behave in accordance with such expectations; but in learning this . . . he acquires insight into the principles underlying the learning of role expectation in general. These principles are then available for use in learning or relearning other patterns of expectations governing relationships in which he participates.

The relative neglect, in clinical and medical psychology, of the influence of such conscious aspects of experience on behaviour has been pointed out by Smail (1968, 1978). Something of a corrective, in his view, has come from the existentialist and phenomenological school of psychologists and psychiatrists which includes such writers as Rogers (1961), Jourard (1964) and Laing (1960). The emphasis in this approach is upon the person himself as the 'fountain of power', to use Maddi's (1967) phrase (borrowed from Emerson), in that his beliefs about himself and the nature of the world are basic motivational factors. In line with this position we would argue against imposing a rigid theoretical framework or treatment programme on a patient and his conflicts. Instead we will be concerned with trying to understand some of the possible ways that psychiatric patients may interpret their emotional problems and the meaning to them of the treatment procedures applied to resolve them. We would regard these interpretations on the part of the patient as fundamental in the treatment process. For example, it seems to us that in psychiatry the active involvement of the patient in his treatment increases as one moves from the physical to the psychological methods. Such active participation, requiring an element of commitment, is unlikely to eventuate in a treatment situation which has no meaning for the patient, which seems to him to be irrelevant as far as his problems are concerned, and which is alien to his typical adjustment strategies.

Credit must be given to Goldstein (1962) for his pioneering cross-fertilization of experimental and clinical psychology in the area of patient and therapist expectancies in psychotherapy. In reviewing the results of perceptual experiments in general psychology he lists five central principles regarding expectancy strength and frequency:

1   The greater the strength of the expectancy the greater its likelihood of arousal in a given situation, the less the amount of appropriate information required to confirm it and the more the amount of contradictory information necessary for its abandonment.

2   The smaller the number of alternative hypotheses held by the person at a given moment concerning the event, the greater their strength will be.

3   The more frequently an expectancy has been confirmed in the past, the greater will be its strength.

4   The larger the number of supporting hypotheses or the more integrated the supporting system of hypotheses, the stronger the hypotheses become.

5   The more basic the confirmation of a hypothesis is to the carrying out of goal-striving activity, the greater its strength will be.

In Goldstein's view these considerations regarding expectancy strength and frequency hold considerable relevance for understanding the complexities of participant expectancies in the pschotherapeutic setting. He then goes on to draw supporting experimental evidence of the influence of set and expectancy in such diverse fields as learning theory, personality theory, levels of aspiration experiments, group organization, stress reaction, stuttering, reactions to physical disability, experimenter bias and psychological testing procedures.

As we have indicated, one of the foremost exponents of the 'expectancy approach' is Kelly (1955). In his view:

The client's conceptualization of psychotherapy represents a body
of constructs whose permeability determines how extensively
he can envision therapeutic change in himself. If the client sees
only certain minor adjustments and certain interview room exercises as constituting psychotherapy, he will not be prepared to assay

sweeping changes in his style of life. If he is to move, he needs
to have a framework within which that movement may take place.

Kelly has listed seven specific types of patient expectations regarding
psychotherapy, namely:

1   An end in itself rather than a means to an end.
2   A way to produce a 'healthy state of mind'.
3   A virtuous act which will be rewarded by relief of difficulties.
4   A means of altering circumstances.
5   A confirmation of one's illness.
6   Proof of the objective difficulty of one's life circumstances.
7   An environment in which already imminent changes may take place.

To broaden the argument, Goldstein quotes a paper by Rosenthal and
Frank (1956) in which it is maintained that since placebos can significantly modify a patient's physiological functioning, the relief of any
particular complaint by a given medication is not sufficient evidence of
the specific effect of the medicine unless it can be shown that the relief
is not obtained as a placebo effect. Hence the need for 'double blind'
trials in the assessment of drug effectiveness in which neither the doctor
nor the patient is aware of whether a placebo or a drug is in fact being
administered. Similarly patients entering psychotherapy will have varying degrees of belief in its efficacy, and this belief or set of expectancies
may be an important determinant of the results of therapy. Any progress that might result from a particular form of psychotherapeutic
treatment might have been achieved equally well by any other form in
which the patient had confidence. In addition to expectations about
treatment, the patient's confidence in the therapist and his suggesti-
bility will also be determinants.

Cartwright and Cartwright (1958) have suggested that a patient's
expectations concerning psychotherapy can be broken down into at
least four different types of belief, namely:

1   A belief that certain effects will result.
2   Beliefs about the therapist as the major source of help.
3   Beliefs concerning the techniques or procedures as the major source of help.
4   A belief in himself as the major source of help.

In their view, not all beliefs are therapeutically effective. The first three types will not necessarily be positively related to subsequent improvement. For example, a strong belief that certain effects will result may well be unrelated since there is often little resemblance between what the patient believes is wrong with him in the initial interviews and what is eventually cleared up. In this connection, just what a patient presents as his problem in an initial psychiatric interview, and the reasons for doing so, are presumably also a matter of expectancies and this is an area which needs to be better understood. A patient entering psychotherapy with a strongly held expectation that the therapist will be the major source of help may well be the type of patient who shuns the responsibilities associated with successful psychotherapy and who sits back and waits to be helped. This may be paticularly true of group psychotherapy and therapeutic community treatment, in which the therapists are shared among a number of patients, thus intensifying dependency problems. According to the Cartwrights the patient with a strong expectation of improvement based on belief in the procedures or techniques may be someone with a generalized strong belief in the curative powers of techniques alone divorced from interpersonal dynamics and personal responsibility. Such a person's behaviour in psychotherapy is likely to be impersonal and he is unlikely to progress unless his expectancies are modified. It is only with regard to the last belief, namely the patient's belief in himself as the major source of help, that we are likely to find a correlation with improvement. If this expectancy is not simply a reflection of a counter-dependency, or rejection of the therapist, then the patient is likely to prove to be a serious therapeutic worker in his own right.

Frank (1959) lists a number of influences which affect a patient's expectancies. These include the sanctioning of psychotherapy as the method of choice by the culture, positive and understanding attitudes on the part of the referring 'intake professionals', the therapist's faith in his method of treatment for the patient, and the degree of the patient's distress as a motivating factor.

From the limited number of experiments reported on the effects of patients' expectancies on treatment outcome it is impossible to draw firm conclusions. Much of the work has not been cross-validated, small samples and dubious measuring instruments have been employed, and the psychotherapy and the psychotherapists investigated have not been well described. In spite of this, Goldstein considers that there is increasing research evidence to support the view that patient prognostic expectancies are related to subsequent improvement in psychotherapy.

The exact nature of this relationship, however, remains obscure. In his view the evidence so far indicates that expected and perceived improvements in psychotherapy are not related in a linear manner, but point toward curvilinearity. Thus 'level of aspiration' in the patient or the degree to which improvement is anticipated seems to be related to expectancies. Patients with moderate expectations of improvement reported the greatest symptom reduction following psychotherapy (by medical students as part of the training curriculum). Overoptimistic and pessimistic patients reported minimal symptom reduction. Degree of reported stress (considered by Goldstein to be a measure of motivation) was also found to be related to expectancies with more favourable expectations being related to the number and intensity of the symptoms which the patient attributed to himself before therapy. This finding fits in with our own data to be presented later. Our argument is, however, that the number of symptoms or problems complained of is not necessarily an indication of the amount of distress subjectively experienced. Mono-symptomatic conditions, or a single delusion, can be as crippling and distressing as more generalized conditions. We feel, rather, that the way in which the patient presents his problems depends upon underlying personality factors. This is closer to Frank's (1959) suggestion that the generalization of symptom and problem areas may indicate a willingness on the part of the patient to emphasize aspects of himself which show his vulnerability or weakness. This reflects a faith in the therapist and the therapy which in itself is a favourable prognostic indicator. When Goldstein was writing, behaviour therapy was not practised as widely as it is now, and no doubt a number of the patients reporting a smaller number of symptoms would have been recommended for behaviour therapy which, for them, might have been a more acceptable form of treatment.

In addition to expectancies concerning prognosis, patients have expectancies concerning the therapist and the therapist–patient relationship. Both the patient and the therapist play certain roles in the treatment process. These roles will be determined by their assumptions about illness and treatment and their conception of the nature of the doctor–patient relationship. The influence of such role anticipations on behaviour and personality has been a central object of study by social psychologists and sociologists for many years. At the most profound level the attitudes and expectations of parents, siblings and peers towards him provide the basic elements of the child's developing self-concept. The modification of internalized, negative expectations (such as the tragic belief of many psychiatric patients that they are unloveable) is the function of much psychotherapy. It is well recognized by psychotherapists that much of a patient's destructive behaviour is simply an attempt to justify this deeply held belief.

Goldstein has listed research evidence indicating the major influence of role expectations on behaviour in such widely separated areas as reactions to painful stimuli, group productivity, post-hospitalization adjustment of mental patients, adjustment to age and sex roles, post-disaster behaviour, and psychotherapy. In discussing the latter Kelly (1955) has observed that there are many different ways in which a patient may initially conceptualize his treatment. As his initial conceptualization changes, behaviour in the treatment sessions will change correspondingly:

> From the client's conceptualization of psychotherapy comes the role he expects to play and the role he expects the therapist to play. His behaviour as a patient should be seen in this light. Patients may have any of the following expectations concerning the therapist's role as: parent, protector, absolver of guilt, authority figure, prestige figure, a possession, a stabilizer, a temporary respite, a threat, an ideal companion, and a representative of reality.

Goldstein has examined the research findings with regard to patient expectancies of the therapist and finds a consistent basic triad of expectancies concerning the therapist:

1 *Nurturant* Patients falling into this group anticipate a guiding, giving, protective therapist who is neither businesslike, critical of the patient, nor expecting the patient to shoulder his own responsibilities.
2 *Model* This group of patients expects a well-adjusted, diplomatic, non-judgmental, permissive listener. The therapist is not expected to be either protective or critical.
3 *Critic* The third group is composed of patients who expect the therapist to be critical and analytical. It is thought that he will want the patient to assume considerable responsibility, and it is anticipated that he will be neither gentle nor indulgent.

The importance, in the treatment process, of the mutuality of role expectations on the part of the patient and therapist has been emphasized by a number of writers including Chance (1959), Gleidman, Stone, Frank, Nash and Imber (1957) and Goldstein (1962). Important suggestions arising out of these studies include the following:

1 Mutality of expectation may be one of the prerequisites to therapy;
2 The degree of strain and disequilibrium in the therapeutic relationship is related to the degree of dissimilarity of the expectations of
   patient and therapist in terms of the role each is to play.
3 If treatment is to proceed, where the patient's expectancies are
   widely divergent from those of the therapist, a shift in the direction of the latter's frame of reference on the part of the patient is
   essential.
4 Cultural factors and social conditioning underlie the formation and
   expression of these treatment expectations. We would include, also,
   certain basic personality attributes.
5 Duration of therapeutic contact may well be related to the degree
   of congruence with regard to patient and therapist expectancies
   concerning the purpose and method of the treatment process. To
   quote Frank (1959):

   length of treatment probably reflects in part the therapist's and the
   patient's expectancies. Those who practise long-term psychotherapy find that their patients take a long time to respond; those
   who believe that good results can be produced in a few weeks claim
   to obtain them in this duration of time. There is no evidence that
   a larger proportion of patients in long-term treatment improve,
   or that the improvements are more permanent than in patients
   treated more briefly. On the other hand, there is some experimental evidence that patients respond more promptly when they
   know in advance that therapy is time-limited.

An important study by Tollinton (1973) has reviewed recent research
findings and theories in the area of patient expectancies. He points out
that Goldstein's theory has two facets, namely the importance in treatment of a close match between patient and therapist expectancies and
the importance of a 'realistic' level of expectancies. Too high or too
low a set of expectancies, which Goldstein suggests are based on a low
level of ego strength, carry an unfavourable prognosis.

Thus Goldstein and Shipman (1961) found that symptom improvement during the initial psychotherapeutic relationship was directly
related to the patient's expectations of improvement with therapy. The
apparent curvilinear relationship between expectations and outcome
suggested to them the weak ego theory as a possible explanation.
Lipkin (1954), Lennard and Bernstein (1960) and Uhlenhuth and

Duncan (1968) found, in subsequent psychotherapy, that patients with positive anticipations did better than those with more negative anticipations. Friedman (1963) found that the prognostic anticipations of his patients in a cross-cultural study were directly related to the improvement obtained at the end of the initial consultation. He found no evidence of the curvilinearity described by Goldstein and Shipman, and he suggested that their results might be explained by their use, in measuring expectations, of raw scores rather than scores adjusted for degree of initial distress. Tollinton points to a number of such discrepant research findings. Brady, Reznikoff and Zeller (1960) failed to find any relationship between expectancies measured by a projective test and an open-ended questionnaire and therapists' rating of outcome in a large group of hospitalized patients with mixed diagnoses. Goldstein (1960) himself failed to find any relationship between expectancies of personality change and outcome measured by self-ideal-self discrepancy on a Q-sort.

As Tollinton points out, failure in replication of results may stem from a number of causes. The studies themselves differ in a number of important aspects. The techniques of expectancy measurement, the changes investigated and the initial population all differed greatly as did the therapeutic experiences that the patients underwent. Until these variables can be brought under a measure of control no realistic comparison of results can be made.

His own study is a methodologically sound one involving the formulation of specific hypotheses based on the previous research findings, two fairly large groups of patients undergoing specified treatment programmes and well known standardized psychological tests of distress, neuroticism and personality factors including ego strength. In the main his results support Goldstein's (1962) suggestions of an important relation between a patient's initial expectancies and outcome but his results indicate that personality difficulties tend to dissipate this relationship. The evidence suggests to Tollinton that the factors measured by his expectations questionnaire are 'as important, if not more so, in determining the initial outcome of treatment than the factors measured by the distress questionnaire'. The curvilinear relationship between expectancies and outcome postulated by Goldstein was again not supported, and the measures of ego strength and neuroticism failed to show a significant relationship to the expectation outcome discrepancy in the single out-patient interview. However, 'a definite trend in this direction is apparent by the end of a first month of treatment in a psychotherapeutic community'.

Speculation about the underlying process responsible for the expectancy phenomenon has centred around the concept of level of aspiration (Lewin, Dembo, Festinger and Sears, 1944) and its possible mediation of the effect of hope, or achievement motivation (Atkinson, 1957; De Charms, 1968). Those who were able to hope for considerable improvement in the face of illness, when interacting with the 'symbols' of healing, obtained relief whereas those without hope were unaffected by the symbolic nature of the experiences undergone.

Tollinton considers that in these arguments, distress and expectancies are seen as measures of internal processes within the patient that are accessible to external symbolic interaction. An alternative view, based on a more molecular level of analysis, is that put forward by Helson (1964). In this theory expectancies play a secondary role in which they form part of an adaptive response to the environment, which, in this context, includes past experience, present distress, and treatment. This is very much the argument of Frank (1968), Balint (1964) and the present authors. Tollinton points out that neither view necessarily excludes the other, but they emphasize different aspects and levels of a postulated causal sequence, none of which has yet been tied down by empirical research.

A number of investigations of patients' expectancies have concentrated on attempting to modify them in a more realistic direction and have shown a degree of benefit obtained from the effort expended but have not shed direct light on the questions raised by Goldstein (Orne and Wender, 1968; Sloane, Cristol, Pepernik, and Staples, 1970). According to Tollinton a difficulty in assessing the results of these two reports lies in the question of the meaning of the correlations observed. In general, they may be interpreted in terms of changes in the patient's experience of distress, or as a change in his willingness to report distress. The first interpretation is favoured by Goldstein, who discusses the changes that occur in terms of a patient's aspirations, and the second is discussed by Friedman (1963), who attempted an explanation in terms of cognitive dissonance. A more radical interpretation of the second kind might be provided by sensory decision theory (Clark, 1969). Finally, Kiesler (1973) has described a number of studies and measures of patients' conceptions and preferences regarding psychiatric treatment and mental illness. The studies reported, however, are very general in nature and seem to have been carried out on student or general public rather than patient samples. A study by Fischer and Turner (1970) is of particular relevance since they found that subjects high on authoritarianism and high on dependence on 'external' control of behaviour tended to express negative attitudes to seeking professional psychological help. In their female subjects only those tending to respond in a 'socially desirable' manner on their measure and those indicating high interpersonal trust expressed favourable attitudes to seeking such help.

The Treatment Expectancies Questionnaire

In a series of some forty pre-treatment interviews conducted in our Psychology Department an attempt was made to elicit patients' treatment expectancies. The response to such direct questions as 'what sort of treatment do you think you should get?' or 'how do you think treatment should help you?' were too limited to be of much help. Patients were unable to verbalize very precisely how they felt about treatment and they had apparently only a very hazy general idea of either psychotherapy or behaviour therapy. For this reason we decided to formulate statements ourselves.

In formulating these questions we were governed by the findings of previous work (Caine and Smail, 1969). The evidence is that both staff and patients differ sharply amongst themselves about the nature of 'psychiatric illness' and about how the treatment should be approached. On the one hand, staff and patients may see the problem in very similar terms to traditional physical medicine: physical treatments are seen as most effective; the relationship between staff and patient should be formal; knowledge and skill are more important for the therapist than personality; and hygiene, cleanliness and discipline are important factors to be considered in the nursing care of psychiatric patients. On the other hand staff and patients may adopt the very opposite view, regarding the quality of the relationship between staff and patients and between the patients themselves as fundamental in the treatment process. Physical treatments are seen as less important than the discussion of interpersonal problems, and freedom of expression in this respect is regarded as more important than control. On the basis of findings of this kind we have argued, as has Lillie (1973) in his review of the work in this field, that two broad approaches seem to be operative, namely, the organic and the psychological. The former is seen by its protagonists as requiring a traditional physical treatments approach, and the latter as requiring a revolutionary one in terms of how the 'illness' is viewed and how treatment is applied.

In our view behaviour therapy in its classical application stands close to the organic approach in that the emphasis is on symptoms only, the therapist is very much in charge as the expert, the technique in terms of knowledge and skill is seen as more important than the personality of the therapist, and the relationship is very similar to the traditional doctor–patient relationship. In group therapy, on the other hand, the emphasis is on attitudes and relationhips rather than symptoms; it is in the main a more democratic process in that patients may challenge the therapist's leadership and knowledge, personality is seen as important, and free discussion about feelings is encouraged.

With these alternatives in mind a number of questions which might reflect a preference for an organic or psychological approach were framed. This list of statements was then submitted to five practising group therapists and five practising behaviour therapists who were asked to sort them into favourable or unfavourable attitudes as far as their own particular treatment was concerned. Only those statements (twenty-eight in number) where there was complete agreement amongst the therapists were used in the construction of the Treatment Expectancies Questionnaire (TEQ). In scoring the questionnaire a four point rating scale for each item was used, running from disagree to agree.

The patient sample employed in the construction of the TEQ was drawn from 182 patients referred to the psychotherapy clinic at Claybury Hospital for analytic-type group psychotherapy or desensitization behaviour therapy. In the main, this was a middle class or lower middle class group of at least average intelligence and verbal ability. There were no significant differences in these respects between those allocated to group psychotherapy and those allocated to behaviour therapy. Age and sex distributions are shown in Table 3.1.

Table 3.1 Mean ages of neurotic patients entering a psychotherapy clinic[*]

	n	Mean	sd
Behaviour therapy (males)	38	31.63	10.29
Behaviour therapy (females)	44	30.70	10.82
Small group therapy (males)	50	24.60	4.94
Small group therapy (females)	50	26.92	7.10

[*]See Caine and Wijesinghe (1976).

From Table 3.1 it can be seen that the sex factor is balanced, but patients allocated to behaviour therapy tended to be somewhat older.

Allocation to either of the treatments involved was made by the consultant psychiatrist in charge of the clinic, in consultation with the therapist likely to carry out the treatment, without reference to the psychological test results beyond exclusion on the grounds of below average intelligence or verbal ability. In addition to the TEQ and the measures reported in Chapters 1 and 2, a number of standard diagnostic and attitude tests were also administered, but not all patients completed these.

A principal components analysis was carried out on the first 135 completed questionnaires and the results were analysed in relation to clinical and test data involving the larger sample. An item was allocated to a component when it loaded most highly on that component in relation to the others. Only the fifteen such items making up component one of the analysis were found to relate significantly to the other data. An inspection of these items showed that they could be associated with a number of different but apparently related beliefs with which the patients agreed or disagreed:

- a denial of interpersonal difficulties;
- believing in treatment by a specialist who should take a directive and controlling role;
- believing that talking about emotional problems is of little value;
- believing that other patients would be of no help; seeing mental illness as a matter of self-control;
- believing that treatment consists of being taught what to do in order to be able to cope;
- believing that it is the doctor's knowledge rather than his personality which is the effective ingredient of treatment.

In the opinion of the therapists performing the allocation of items, agreement with these beliefs would indicate a favourable set towards behaviour therapy whereas a rejection of them would suggest a group psychotherapy orientation.

These orientations to treatment were examined in a number of ways. It is essential to our argument that pre-treatment expectancies be shown to be reflected in subsequent treatment behaviour and experience. In the first place expectancies should affect the way patients present their difficulties which in turn will affect the treatment allocation. The pre-treatment expectancies of patients actually assigned to group therapy on clinical grounds are compared with those assigned to behaviour therapy in Table 3.2 for three independent samples. Table 3.2 shows that the Treatment Expectancies Questionnaire is a highly effective instrument for distinguishing patients allocated to group or

Table 3.2 Treatment Expectancies Questionnaire scores of three samples of neurotic patients entering a psychotherapy clinic

Sample	n	Mean	sd		
1* Behaviour therapy (males)	38	37.34	7.37	n.s.	F = 16.82
Behaviour therapy (females)	44	38.88	6.96		p < 0.001
Small group therapy (males)	50	33.66	6.72	n.s.	
Small group therapy (females)	50	34.24	6.31		
2 Behaviour therapy (mixed)	25	38.08	6.55		t = 4.04
Small group therapy (mixed)	30	30.90	6.56		p < 0.001
3 Behaviour therapy (mixed)	100	38.01	—		F = 10.52
Small group therapy (mixed)	153	32.09	—		p < 0.001

*See Caine and Wijesinghe (1976).

behaviour therapy. This has held true in three independent samples, two of which are of substantial size. The treatment allocation was based on a psychiatric, symptom orientated assessment. The implication is that the symptom pattern revealed in the interview is related to the more general treatment expectancies of the patients.

In addition to patient samples, it has been possible to obtain two non-patient groups, whose mean scores are shown in Table 3.3. The correlation between the Treatment Expectancies Questionnaire, the Direction of Interest Questionnaire and the Conservatism Scale for the various samples are shown in Table 3.4. These data indicate that a relatively low treatment expectancies score is associated with allocation to group psychotherapy rather than behaviour therapy as far as patients are concerned and that professionals attending an introductory course in group psychotherapy tend to score particularly low on the

Table 3.3 Treatment Expectancies Questionnaire scores of non-patient groups

	n	Mean	sd
Voluntary helpers at a general hospital	38	31.29	6.8
Professionals attending an introductory course in group psychotherapy			
Females	109	22.89	3.9
Males	27	23.22	4.0

Table 3.4 Correlations between the Treatment Expectancies Questionnaire, the Direction of Interest Questionnaire (DIQ) and the Conservatism Scale (C Scale) in various samples (age partialled out as appropriate)

	n	DIQ	C Scale
Neurotic patients	182*	-0.36^{***}	0.30^{***}
	181	-0.30^{***}	0.20^{***}
	64	-0.35^{***}	0.44^{***}
Non-patients			
Voluntary helpers at a general hospital	38	-0.47^{***}	–
Professionals attending an introductory course in group psychotherapy	136	-0.19^{**}	–

* See Caine and Wijesinghe (1976).
** $p < 0.05$.
*** $p < 0.01$.

questionnaire. In both patient and non-patient samples the Treatment Expectancies Questionnaire is associated with direction of interest, with an inner direction being associated with a psychological set to psychiatric treatment. Only the patient samples completed the Conservatism Scale and in these a more radical attitude is associated with a psychological set.

Summary

In order to link neurotic patients' psychiatric treatment expectancies with specific treatment regimes, a questionnaire was devised expressing attitudes favourable to group psychotherapy and attitudes favourable to behaviour therapy as seen by therapists committed to one or other approach. A factor analysis of the attitude questionnaire revealed a component which successfully differentiated patients allocated on clinical grounds to group psychotherapy on the one hand and to behaviour therapy on the other. The component was also found to be significantly related to the Direction of Interest Questionnaire in both patient and non-patient samples and to be correlated with the Conservatism Scale in a number of neurotic patient groups.

Chapter 4
Staff expectancies and attitudes to patient care

Enquiries into the question of the attitudes of professional staff to the treatment and care of psychiatric patients have suggested two facets with a presently increasing cross-fertilisation between them. On the one hand interest has centered on the nature of the therapeutic relationship between patient and therapist in formal psychotherapy. On the other the interest has been focused on the effect on patient and staff morale of ward atmospheres in psychiatric and general hospitals.

With regard to the nature of therapeutic relationships the research initiative has developed within the schools of psychotherapy rather than from behaviour therapy. Traditionally, behaviour therapists emphasize technique, although there are signs that this attitude is softening and some attention is being paid to the therapist–patient relationship (Kanfer and Saslow, 1965; Meyer, Liddell and Lyons, 1977). The concern, however, seems to be limited to developing an action-orientated approach 'whereby the therapist and the patient develop and maintain a mutual relationship with the ultimate aim of developing, guiding, and encouraging the patient's self-control and understanding' (Meyer, Liddell and Lyons, 1977).·

With regard to psychotherapy, with the increasing recognition of the vital part played in the treatment process of the personality by the therapist regardless of the theoretical school to which he belongs, discussion and research has been directed towards elucidating the personality attributes or attitudes most likely to promote a psychotherapeutically effective relationship with patients. Unfortunately, among the experts there is little agreement as to what is an effective relationship with opinion varying from proponents of a detached, neutral, scientific attitude (Freud, 1958; Mowbray and Roger, 1963; Chertok, 1966), to proponents of an involved, warm, empathic, genuine,

53

trusting and spontaneous approach (Jung, 1954; Jourard, 1964; Rogers, 1957; Dyer, 1974; Smail, 1978; Truax and Wargo, 1966).

Kiesler (1973) has produced an exhaustive review of the research in the field of individual psychotherapy and he quotes evidence to show that these wide differences in therapists' attitudes and behaviour exist even among psychotherapists subscribing to the same theoretical orientation. Similarly, Meehl (1960) reports a study in which 168 psychotherapists completed a questionnaire dealing with 132 aspects of therapeutic technique. The therapists included both medical and nonmedical practitioners representing a range of orientations including Freudians, neo-Freudians, Radovians, Sullivanians, eclectics, and 'mixed'. From an analysis of the questionnaire responses it emerged that approximately half the therapists regarded warmth and empathy as more important in the treatment process than accurate insight into the client's difficulties. Four out of five believed the personality of the therapist to be of greater importance than the theory of personality he holds and about half believed that 'interpretation' is a greatly overrated therapeutic tool. Of direct significance for our own research is the belief of over one third of their sample that 'literary, dramatic, aesthetic, or mystical people are likely to be better therapists than people of a primarily scientific, logical, or mathematical bent'. Just how 'correct' attitudes are to be inculcated in the budding psychotherapist is very much a matter of debate. According to Dent (1978) Freud and Rogers rely on their psychotherapeutic technique to reduce the influence of the personal needs and conflicts of the therapist. In the case of the analytical school a personal analysis is also essential. Other therapeutic schools consider that training in the social skills of warmth, genuineness, spontaneity and empathy is possible and desirable, although Smail (1978) has questioned the authenticity of such acquisitions.

Smail's analysis of the nature of empathy is instructive since he quotes social psychological research suggesting that accurate judgment of one person by another is facilitated by actual similarity in personality between those involved. This is close to Dent's (1978) view that the outcome of therapy is determined not by what is said and done, but by what is meant and understood. Meaning and understanding are the result of a complex subliminal interaction of personalities. For Dent this places the study of the personality of the therapist as central to psychotherapy issues. In his opinion, since personality is more easily measured than specific behaviour patterns, it can tell us a good deal about what the therapist does in fact do, and an understanding of the personality will give us an understanding of the meaning

of behaviour. However, as to the other aspect of the interpersonal process, we would give equal if not more weight to the personality of
the client.

Dent's research has involved the A–B Scale developed from the
Strong Vocational Interest Blank by Whitehorne and Betz (1960). In
earlier work, on the basis of doctors' records concerning their schizophrenic patients and their treatment, Whitehorne and Betz (1954) had
been able to distinguish between two types of doctor–patient relationship, called A vs. B, with A doctors treating their schizophrenic patients
more successfully. The A therapist:

1   indicates in his personal diagnostic formulation some grasp of
the personal meaning and motivation of the patient's behaviour,
going beyond the mere clinical description and narrative biography;
2   in his formulation of strategic goals in the treatment of a particular patient, selects personality orientated goals, i.e. aims at assist-
ing the patient in definite modifications of personal adjustment
patterns rather than the mere decrease of symptoms;
3   in his day to day tactics makes use of 'active personal participation', rather than the patterns 'passive permissive', 'interpretations
and instruction', or 'practical care'.
4   There is a similarly high association between an improved
condition at the time of a patient's discharge and the development
by the patient, while in treatment, of a trusting, confidential relationship to the therapist.

It is of considerable interest for our own work that roughly half the
items of the A–B Scale have to do with a preference for manual and
mechanical activities which the A therapists tend to dislike. In his own
work involving hospitalized psychiatric patients, juvenile delinquents
and health care staff, Dent extends the areas of interests and attitudes
to include a number of those used by Walton (1969) and, in another
context, by Coan (see Chapter 5). Of particular relevance for our work
are his measures of 'regression in the service of the ego', 'tolerance of
"unrealistic" experiences', 'need for order', and 'tolerance of complexity'. An empathy study is also included in his report. In our
opinion this represents a considerable convergence by a number of
research workers on the same areas of personality functioning. In his
summary of his findings he concludes that

there is little that defines the effective therapist in a *general* sense

in these studies. Instead, specific personal tendencies and interests
define effectiveness with particular types of mental or behavioural
problems. There is therefore no support for the 'generalist approach',
but there is a great deal of support for the differential hypothesis
that different disorders require different treatments . . . . if future
studies continue to confirm the differential hypothesis, the implications of the findings are widespread. For one thing, diagnosis is a
critical variable. Evaluation of services is impossible unless consideration is given to the type of problem the client presents. As we learn
more and more about the specific needs of particular kinds of
clients, we must also learn the extent to which therapists can and
will adapt to different kinds of patients. And indeed, there is some
evidence that opposite kinds of milieus are needed for some kinds of
disorders (e.g. schizophrenics vs. sociopaths). It seems likely that
milieus will have to specialize in particular disorders.

Amongst other findings his own research confirms previous work
suggesting that 'neurotics are *not* well served by therapists who like
to solve problems' and that 'schizophrenics are best served by a therapist who is active and personally involved with the patient'.

The second facet of the problem of staff attitudes to patient care
involves the gradual invasion of general and psychiatric hospitals by
psychotherapeutic ideas, promoted largely by the development of
therapeutic communities with the acceptance of all grades of staff as
possible psychotherapeutic agents. Marks (1973) and Peck (1973) have
argued for a massive extension of the nurses' role as therapists, involving a new look at training and selection. In this respect, nursing staff
have become increasingly concerned with the relationship aspect of
patient care. Altschul (1972) has documented the literature regarding
the therapeutic use of nurse–patient relationships, most of which has
been published in the last twenty years. Similar issues to those of professional psychotherapists have been raised and similar disagreements
are reflected with regard to the relative virtues of adopting a personal
versus an impersonal approach to patient care, the degree of personal
involvement advisable, and authoritarianism, etc.

In this regard the well known works of Stanton and Swartz (1954)
and Goffman (1971) have pointed to the anti-therapeutic ethos of
many traditional mental hospitals. In such institutions the staff have
certain characteristic assumptions about the patient's role in the social
organization. He may no longer be looked upon as a member of a
family, a friend, an employee, or a customer but rather as a diagnostic

category, a chronic, my patient or simply as clinical or research material. Emphasis may be placed on maintaining psychological and social distance from the patient with emotional involvement being seen as dangerous. Decisions about admission and discharge are made by the staff only, with patients having little or no say in them. Contact with the outside world may be kept to a minimum and may be looked upon as a privilege. The patient may be required to sleep, work and play in one place and even the smallest detail, such as when he may wash and shave, may be decided for him. His clothes may not be his own and they may be shared with other patients. Social experience and responsibility may be reduced to a uniform, dehumanized level. Wing (1962) maintains that it is probably safe to say that most patients who have been continuously resident for more than two years in a mental hospital will have been exposed to many of the general features of 'total institutions', to use Goffman's term. Persons subjected to such regimes exhibit certain recognizable features, namely apathy, lack of spontaneity, lack of interest in outside activities, inability to adjust to or make decisions about relatively commonplace life situations, and an increasing dependence upon the institution.

The recognition of the anti-therapeutic nature of such all too prevalent attitudes in both psychiatric and general hospitals has led to the development of the revolutionary approach of milieu therapy and the therapeutic community (Clark, 1964; Jones, 1952; Martin, 1955; 1962; Barton, 1959).

Rapoport (1960) has described three basic beliefs of the staff of the therapeutic community he studied, which seem to us to be of a very different order from those held by staff in total institutions. Thus (a) every activity, every relationship that develops in the unit is treatment; (b) all treatment is rehabilitation, involving both reorganization of personality and adjustment to the unit's social system and ultimately to life outside the unit; (c) all patients should get the same treatment. He has abstracted four operative treatment processes, namely 'democratization', 'permissiveness', 'communalism' and 'reality confrontation'. The emphasis in the treatment process is on the quality of the relationships and communications developed within the community.

This work in psychiatric institutions can be paralleled by the work of Revans (1964) in the general hospital field. Revans and his colleagues at the Manchester College of Science and Technology spent four years studying the staff and patient turnover in a number of general hospitals in the North of England, and they were able to relate staff turnover and length of patient stay in hospital to hospital ethos. Hospitals with higher morale had less staff turnover and quicker patient discharge than did hospitals with lower morale. As with Rapoport, the locus of morale, in Revans's opinion, lies in the communication system of the hospital and, in this respect, each hospital studied revealed a character of its own which was largely the expression of its internal stresses and anxieties. In some cases this ethos militated against the easy assimilation of a new member of the staff (whether student or senior nurse), and the discharge of patients.

Interest in this area has greatly increased in recent years and a large number of authors have devised measures of hospital or ward atmospheres. A comprehensive list of such instruments has been compiled by Comrey, Backer and Glaser (1973). Of particular relevance for us in demonstrating the use of such measures of ward atmospheres is a study reported by Kennard (1973). Kennard administered the Ward Atmosphere Scale (Moos and Swartz, 1972) to the staff and patients of a therapeutic community ward (Phoenix Unit, Littlemore Hospital, Oxford) which admits a largely unselected patient population. Physical treatments are administered as considered appropriate within the therapeutic community ethos. Compared to the average score for 32 British psychiatric wards both patients and staff at the Phoenix scored more than one standard deviation lower on 'order' and more than one standard deviation higher on 'insight', 'autonomy' and 'aggression'. In addition, the staff were lower on 'clarity' and 'submission'.

The present investigations have been based on the work of Caine and Smail (1969). This was an intensive study of a therapeutic community set up in the late 1950s (Martin, 1962) for the treatment of chronic neurosis on an in-patient basis. The effectiveness of the method was assessed by means of the serial testing of patients using tests directed at different levels of psychological functioning, follow-up, and the use of a comparative 'conventional treatment' sample. The main findings of the treatment comparison were that test score changes at 'deeper' levels of psychological functioning were indicated in the therapeutic community sample which were not present in the conventionally treated group and significantly more of the latter were still on drugs at follow-up. The reasons given for improvement by a small sample of the two groups investigated are illuminating, as Table 4.1 shows. Clearly the perceptions of their treatment experiences were very different for the two groups, and this must have had a profound effect on their subsequent adjustment and response to further emotional crises. At follow-up it was obvious from our interviews that the two groups of patients had indeed learned to cope with their symptoms

Table 4.1

Reasons	Therapeutic community (n = 20)	Conventional treatment (n = 29)
Drugs	0	19
Rest in hospital	0	19
Change in life circumstances since leaving hospital	0	5
Shock of seeing other patients	0	2
Loss of weight	0	1
Dislike of hospital	0	1
Own will power	2	4
Relationships formed within the hospital	15	6
Hospital treatment of little value	3	12

and problems in different ways. The therapeutic community patients had learned to search for the dynamics of their situation whereas the conventional group simply resorted to a further supply of pills for relief.

On the basis of this evidence, which is encouraging as far as the therapeutic community approach to treatment goes, it was decided to see if we could go some way in determining the nature of the therapeutic processes or relationships involved. The therapeutic community builders and previous research reports have suggested a number of general attitudes and beliefs to be found amongst the staff of such communities. For example, Stanton and Swartz (1954) describe the conflicting attitudes to formal organizational procedures of the hospital staff, with some personnel inclining to emphasize the importance of formality and organization on the one hand and others insisting that these aspects are not the business of psychiatry on the other. The staff were divided according to whether they favoured intuition rather than 'research', feelings rather than thoughts, and spontaneity rather than planning. Stanton and Swartz noted that these attitudes were maintained with considerable emotional investment and they seem clearly related to Jungian concepts of personality. A remarkably similar pattern of 'job preferences' on the part of supervisors has been found in industry by Fleishman (1969). His Leadership Opinion Questionnaire is a factor analytically derived scale tapping two approaches to work efficiency, namely Consideration (an emphasis on feelings, warmth of communication, and rapport) and Structure (an emphasis on planning, scheduling and directing).

As far as we are aware no detailed attitude survey had been carried out on both staff and patients simultaneously. The method adopted for the study of the therapeutic community with which we were concerned was to carry out non-directive, tape recorded interviews of all the staff and all the patients about their experiences, roles and relationships within the community. On the basis of this information the Attitude to Treatment Questionnaire (ATQ) was constructed, which was then circulated to a large number of psychiatric hospitals and therapeutic communities within the United Kingdom. In all, eighty-two patients, seventy-nine doctors and one hundred and twenty nurses completed the questionnaire, and principal component analyses were carried out for the three groups separately.

The first components for doctors, nurses and patients are very similar. In all three groups there is an emphasis on physical treatment, discipline, formal impersonal relationships between staff and patients and an avoidance of emotional problems, and an emphasis on the absolute power of staff, particularly of doctors. The first component for patients has now been cross-validated by Trauer (1977), using a sample of 191 patients with the whole range of functional disorders (psychotic, neurotic and personality disorders) represented in the sample. In addition to finding a significant correlation with age he found that patients elected as chairmen of the community meetings on the ward had significantly lower scores on Component I than did the rest of the patients. In other words they saw their treatment in less organic terms and they saw the value in the treatment process of informal relationships, personality, and a flattening of the authority structure.

In the Caine and Smail studies Component I was validated against hospitals with a known treatment orientation and highly significant differences in attitudes to patient care were found between physical treatment and therapeutic community orientated hospitals in both the doctor and nursing samples. Differences emerged in the patient samples too, but these differences were harder to interpret since some of the patients involved were actually receiving physical treatments albeit in a therapeutic community orientated ward or hospital, and there were diagnostic differences between samples. The relationship between Component I scores and diagnostic category is presently being examined by Trauer at St George's Hospital.

Panayotopoulos and Stoffelmayr (1972) found differences in the expected direction on Component I between psychiatrists trained in psychotherapy and psychiatrists untrained in this approach. In a further study Pallis and Stoffelmayr (1973) again found similar differences on the ATQ between psychiatrists who used psychotherapy and those who did not or who were uncommitted. Conservatism and tough-mindedness were found to be related to a preference for physical methods in treating psychiatric patients. Length of training in psychiatry or in any branch of medicine was not related to treatment attitudes as measured by the ATQ. Pallis and Stoffelmayr emphasize the importance of social attitudes in determining psychiatric treatment preferences and warn us to be aware of such influences in debates concerning the efficacy of treatment approaches. In reviewing these researches Lillie (1973) considers that the ATQ may be considered to distinguish between two broad approaches to psychiatric treatment, namely the psychological and the organic.

A number of studies comparing different nursing groups on the ATQ have been completed. Caine (1970) found differences between general, psychiatric and therapeutic community nurses which were not related to age or nursing status. Following a series of meetings over a period of a year for the explicit purpose of discussing attitudes to patients and to colleagues, both the general and psychiatric nurses indicated a shift in the direction of the therapeutic community nurses.

The studies of staff and patient attitudes reported in Caine and Smail, *The Treatment of Mental Illness* (1969) involved the use of scores derived from the principal component analyses of the data. The use of the scores in this form, although providing an element of statistical sophistication, is very time-consuming, so we have reverted to the simple five point scoring system for each questionnaire item in our subsequent investigations. In the initial studies, too, although similar items loaded on the first component for patients, nurses and doctors the saturations were not identical. It was therefore decided to concentrate on the items making up Component I for the nurses since they have provided most of the material in subsequent investigations.

In analysing the available records of the original doctors' sample in this regard it was found that approximately 50 per cent of the items overlapped those of the nurses and a correlation of 0.71 was obtained between the records scored for Component I of the doctors' analysis and rescored for Component I of the nurses' sample (n = 75). From the records it was possible to obtain samples of doctors subscribing to different psychiatric treatment orientations and the means and standard deviations of their scores on the ATQ Component I (nurses) are shown

Table 4.2 Scores on ATQ Component I (nurses) of doctors subscribing to different psychiatric treatment orientations

Orientation	n	Mean	sd
Therapeutic community	22	37.23	7.00
Psychotherapy (group or individual)	10	48.80	7.05
Eclectic	40	49.80	9.88
Organic	6	54.17	6.41

in Table 4.2. There is a highly significant difference between the primarily therapeutic community orientated doctors and other groups, with the organically minded indicating the most traditional attitudes to patient care. The mean scores and standard deviations of a number of nursing samples obtained from different studies are shown in Table 4.3. The mean score of the total staff of a highly developed therapeutic community is shown for comparative purposes. No significant correlation with age was found in three large groups of nurses (n = 73, 94, and 72). A reliability coefficient for the ATQ of 0.79 in a sample of 52 psychiatric and general nurses retested after about a year interval has been reported by Caine (1970) and a coefficient of 0.76 reported by Hall (1974) for 21 student psychiatric nurses retested after three months. As we have noted, the Caine retest investigation indicated a significant shift in attitudes in a more therapeutic community direction following a series of monthly meetings on attitudes to patient care.

In confirmation of our own studies, Robertson (personal communication) and Abbati (1974) have found the ATQ to distinguish successfully between psychiatric and general nurses. Thus Abbati reports: 'it was shown that the ATQ did effectively discriminate between samples of psychiatric and general nurses both at outset and later on in training, and that for both samples attitudes change in the course of training'. This change involved a drop in score suggesting a movement in a more psychotherapeutically orientated direction. Tutt (1969; 1970) found that trained psychiatric nurses scored considerably lower on the ATQ than did untrained staff. In his view the two groups of nursing staff may well have experienced different aims in their induction and training and this is reflected in their attitudes.

In another of our studies at Claybury Hospital (Caine, 1975) the effects of experience in a therapeutic community orientated hospital were examined in a group of occupational therapy students. Forty-one students were given the ATQ on their arrival at the hospital for a period of practical training; they were retested on their departure three months later, and again after they had held a job for one year

Table 4.3 Scores on ATQ Component I (nurses) of various nursing samples

Samples	n	Mean	sd
Specialized therapeutic community staff	18	31.83	5.68
Trained psychiatric nurses working in therapeutic communities	59	41.86	9.67
Psychiatric nursing staff working in traditional psychiatric hospitals (32 trained; 5 students)	37	54.70	8.30
Psychiatric nursing staff attending a meeting on staff attitudes (status unreported)	36	58.94	10.11
Trained psychiatric nurses from three traditional psychiatric hospitals	40	62.60	10.82
Psychiatric nurses attending a conference (status not reported)	72	51.18	10.65
General hospital nurses attending a meeting on staff attitudes (31 trained; 8 students)	39	61.72	7.51
General hospital nurses attending a meeting on staff attitudes (status unreported)	45	58.24	7.64

on finishing training. For comparison the Hysteroid-Obsessoid Questionnaire (HOQ), a measure known to be relatively stable, was similarly administered. The results are shown in Table 4.4.

Table 4.4 Test and retest means and standard deviations of the ATQ and the HOQ in a sample of 27 occupational therapy students

Occasion	ATQ		HOQ	
	Mean	sd	Mean	sd
Test 1	54.22	9.96	25.92	5.85
Test 2	46.26	8.33	26.00	6.41
Test 3	45.00	8.89	25.89	6.74

An analysis of these results indicated that the students shifted to a significant degree in the direction of the hospital orientation and that this change in attitude to patient care persisted on completion of training and into their first job. On the other hand, virtually no change was indicated in basic personality structure as measured by the HOQ. In addition, no correlation was found between the hysteroid/obsessoid dimension of personality and attitudes to patient care.

As we have indicated, Component I of the doctors', nurses', and patients' analyses centres on the same attitudes, but the actual items going to make up the component for the three groups are different. In order to make direct comparison between staff and patient attitudes possible, we have rescored the available questionnaire data for the patients using the items composing Component I for the nurses. The correlation between the scores on patient Component I and nurses' Component I was found to be 0.94 (n = 73). The means and standard deviations of Component I (nurses) for various patient samples are shown in Table 4.5. Thus as with nurses and doctors, a low score is

Table 4.5 Scores on ATQ Component I (nurses) of various patient samples

Samples	n	Mean	sd
Therapeutic community (neurosis unit, no physical treatments)	18	39.94	7.38
Neurosis unit (eclectic, physical treatments, therapeutic community to a limited extent)	13	64.69	4.00
Traditional mental hospital admission unit	15	57.18	1.95
Acute admission until run on therapeutic community lines but using physical treatments	22	52.00	3.08

associated with a therapeutic community approach to patient care, whereas a relatively high score is found in association with a more traditional, physical approach.

The ATQ Component I scale has been correlated with direction of interest, conservatism and treatment expectancies in a number of studies and these correlations are shown in Table 4.6.

Summary

The Attitudes to Treatment Questionnaire successfully differentiates between two broad approaches to patient care, namely a 'psychological' approach versus an 'organic' one, represented institutionally at the extreme ends by the therapeutic community approach on the one hand

Table 4.6 Correlations of the ATQ with Direction of Interest Questionnaire (DIQ), Conservatism Scale (C Scale) and Treatment Expectancies Questionnaire (TEQ) in various samples

Sample		n	r	p <
DIQ	General, psychiatric and mental handicap nurses of various grades attending an 'attitudes' course	94	−0.32	0.01
	General, psychiatric and mental handicap nurses (trained staff only) attending an 'attitudes' course	36	−0.33	0.05
	Nurses attending a psychiatric nurses' conference:			
	student nurses	63	−0.33	0.01
	trained nurses	52	−0.52	0.01
	General hospital student nurses	64	−0.26	0.01
	General hospital trained nurses	29	−0.20	–
	Pre-clinical medical students	98	−0.24	0.05
C Scale	General, psychiatric and mental handicap nurses of various grades attending an 'attitudes' course*	75	0.50	0.01
	General, psychiatric and mental handicap nurses of various grades attending an 'attitudes' course*	94	0.22	0.05
	Nurses attending a psychiatric nurses' conference (various grades)*	72	0.44	0.01
	Psychiatric nurses (students)**	21	0.41	–
	Psychiatric (trained)***	42	0.44	0.01
TEQ	Various professionals attending an introductory course in group psychotherapy (n = 117) and sundry volunteers (2)	119	0.40	0.01

* Caine, T. M. and Leigh, R. (1972).   ** Hall, J. N. (1974).   *** Pallis, D. J. and Stoffelmayr, B. E. (1973).

and the general hospital on the other. Traditionally orientated psychiatric hospitals tend to fall in between. From the attitudes point of view the differentiation is in terms of an emphasis on the physical aspects of care — an impersonal approach towards patients emphasizing the need for formal discipline, control and physical hygiene. This difference in approach is reflected in different grades of staff and in patient samples. No correlation with age was found amongst nurses, but older psychiatric patients tended to express the more 'organic' attitudes. Retest reliability is high, but the attitudes are seen to be affected by training and experience in nursing and occupational therapy samples. The evidence is consistent over a number of studies, demonstrating that the attitudes to psychiatric treatment of various staff groups are related to the adjustment strategies of direction of interest and conservatism. One study indicates an overlap in attitudes between the Attitude to Treatment Questionnaire and the Treatment Expectancies Questionnaire.

Chapter 5
Thinking styles, creativity, and adjustment strategies

In the ancient Chinese text, the *I Ching*, the universe is considered to be guided by two opposing principles, which in turn have become embodied in human consciousness. These two principles are identified as Yang and Yin, and they work towards a balanced universe. In this phenomenal world Yang appears as the active, masculine principle and 'stands for heat, hardness, expansion and dryness'; Yin, the passive feminine principle, represents 'cold, softness, contraction and wetness' (Van Over, 1971).

In more recent times Koestler (1976), quoting Kepes (1956), has expressed this dualism in less symbolic terms:

There are two morphological archetypes, expression of order, co-herence, discipline, stability on the one hand; expression of chaos, movement, vitality, change on the other. Common to the morphology of outer and inner processes these are basic polarities recurring in physical phenomena, in the organic world and in human experience.

These contrasting principles could be seen to play an important role in all activities which involve growth and development. In Darwin's (1928) theory of evolution he identified a process of variation which leads to an increase in living forms, and a process of natural selection, whereby only the fittest were retained for survival. A similar two process idea has been applied to the biological development of the individual organism by Coghill (1929), who showed that growth takes place by successive stages of differentiation and integration. These concepts have since been used to describe psychological development by Lewin (1936), Werner (1947), Jung (1933) and several others. Jung identifies differentiation and integration as the two basic components of the process of individuation.

In studies on the structure of the intellect two contrasting styles of thinking which parallel these principles have been noted. Ornstein (1975) has marshalled evidence to show that there are two forms of consciousness which may have a physical basis in the brain. He contends that the left hemisphere is predominantly involved with analytic thinking, and processes information in an ordered, sequential manner. The right hemisphere, by contrast, is more concerned with integrative functions, spatial orientation and intuitive activity. However, as pointed out by Gazzaniga (1967), in the young child each hemisphere is about equally developed with respect to language and speech function, which suggests that the differences in the two hemispheres are largely brought about through the processes of maturation, where social learning is likely to play an important part.

Whether these thinking styles have a biological basis or not, studies such as those of Getzels and Jackson (1962) have shown that one type of thinking may have a consistent bias in the intellectual functioning of the individual. Amongst their intelligent adolescent population they identified two contrasting groups, namely a 'high IQ' group consisting of the top 20 per cent on IQ but not in the top 20 per cent on 'creativity', and a 'high creativity' group who were in the top 20 per cent on 'creativity' but not on IQ. Hudson (1966) has pointed out that the use of the terms creative and creativity in this context may be misleading and, alternatively, refers to the 'high IQ' as the convergent group and the 'high creative' as the divergent. Convergent thinking implies the narrowing down of possibilities to produce the right answer. It is the type of thinking required by the conventional intelligence test and is heavily biased towards the deductive type of reasoning. Divergent thinking, in contrast, is characterized by the production of as many answers as possible, thinking in different directions, and seeking variety. As such it is not completely determined by the information provided and is the factor necessary for success in 'open-ended' tests.

The dichotomy evinced on the basis of the study of intellectual ability has been sharply accentuated by the emergence of contrasting personality styles. In perusing the descriptions of convergent and divergent thinking types we have found a link with our own particular interest in conservatism and direction of interest. The converger has been described by Barron (1968) as conforming, tending to do the things that are prescribed, respecting authority, submissive, compliant and overly acquiescent; by Hudson (1968) as having conventional attitudes, pursuing technical and mechanical interests in his spare time, and being emotionally inhibited. On the other hand, the diverger is seen by Barron as being verbally fluent, conversationally facile, and interested in philosophical problems and the meaning of life; Hudson sees him as holding unconventional attitudes, having interests which are connected in one way or another with people, and — emotionally speaking — as uninhibited. There seems to be commonality here with the two types we have discussed in earlier chapters. The converger fits in well with the outwardly directed person who considers himself to be realistic, who prefers engineering or domestic science to philosophy, who in general has a conservative attitude to life and a control attitude which influences the imposition of structure, order and meaning. The diverger finds common ground with our inwardly directed person, with his emphasis on ideas, concern with abstract problems such as the meaning of life, his liberal social attitudes and an openness to inner feelings, fantasy and dream material. Guilford (1956) has suggested that divergent production is an important factor in creative thinking. However, the relationship between divergence and creativeness has not been made explicit. The evidence is often conflicting, even when studies have been confined to those who have achieved a level of excellence in their selected field (Roe, 1951; Mackinnon, 1962). The confusion of creativity with divergent thinking comes from the rather loose usage of the former term. Even though the divergent process has been associated more particularly with the arts (Hudson, 1966), the components of creativity as identified by Jackson and Messick (1965), i.e. novelty, appropriateness, transformation and condensation, will apply equally to science. Nevertheless, it would seem that there are obvious differences in the manner in which convergent and divergent processes are used in realizing the aims of creative arts and science and, in general, the life styles of creative artists and scientists. Libby (1970) has stated: 'Science is the study of scientific method to discover new facts and truths eventually to be formulated as natural law. The scientific method is a disciplined procedure in which objectivity is the main aim.' Thus, whatever the essential process, scientific creativity at least in terms of its products must measure up to 'reality'. As Mackinnon (1970) has argued, the question for science is not so much whether creativity springs from a neurotic motive or a visionary experience, or appears as the end result of a long train of empirical studies, but rather, whether the end product is adaptive to reality and can be evaluated, elaborated and communicated to others.

Artistic creativity, by contrast, is predominantly subjective, permitting a rather more obvious personal impingement upon the creative process. Individualistic art may have the quality of novelty and originality in its conception, but it is doubtful if communication is a high priority. As Comfort (1961) has argued:

> In our culture most, if not all works of art have their origin in compelling ideas — situational, verbal, formal, symbolic — which occur to the artist's mind. The distinguishing mark of these ideas is that they seem significantly out of proportion to the rational scale of values, and that they produce at the same time emotion and a desire to develop them. The experience, which used to be called inspiration, is the basic unit, as it were, of the individualistic art of modern societies — it is the answer to the question which is sometimes asked whether the artist intends or aims to communicate, whether he has an audience in mind.

There has been a great deal of controversy as to whether the divergent and convergent processes are specific to creative art and creative science respectively, or whether divergence is common to both. While MacKinnon (1962) tends to support the latter point of view, Roe (1951) argues that scientific creativity involves the formulation of specific hypotheses and is dependent on the restrictions of the scientific method. As such, the dominant process will be convergent thinking, as it involves the selective narrowing down to only those stimuli having to do with concrete, practical 'reality' and the suppression of those having to do with impulsive inner life.

In the absence of convincing evidence one way or the other, Kuhn (1962) has postulated a two factor theory which argues that in scientific creativity extended periods of convergent activity are followed by a divergent shift before a creative or original solution is produced:

> Almost none of the research undertaken by even the greatest scientists is designed to be revolutionary, and very little of it has any such effect. On the contrary, normal research, even the best of it, is a highly convergent activity based firmly upon a settled consensus acquired from scientific education and reinforced by subsequent life in the profession. Typically, to be sure, this convergent or consensus-bound research is the necessary preliminary to them . . . only investigations firmly rooted in the contemporary scientific tradition are likely to break that tradition and give rise to a new one. That is why I speak of an 'essential tension' implicit in scientific research . . . . Very often the successful scientist must simultaneously display the characteristics of the tradionalist and of the iconoclast.

Broadly speaking, the fields of science and art represent particular traditions: empirical in the former, more intuitive in the latter. It is likely that individuals enter a field due to characteristic interest dispositions, so that the personal styles of creative scientists and artists are likely to show broad differences. Thus we feel that Mackinnon's (1962) claim that 'in scientific creativity, the creative product is unrelated to the creator as a person, who in his creative work acts largely as a mediator between externally defined needs and goals', may well be an oversimplification of the relationship between the creative scientist and his product. Our view is supported by the work of McClelland (1962), who found that the successful physical scientist had a puritanical or conservative family background, withdrew from people, and invested his energy and interest in natural phenomena, with an early preoccupation with the control and analysis of things.

The life style of the creative artist, unlike his scientist counterpart, has received much more attention due to the often noted association between psychological instability and those who have reached the pinnacle of artistic creativity. The lives of Beethoven, Van Gogh, Shelley and many other men of genius would appear to validate Barron's (1958) claim that 'if adaptation and maturity in human relations are the essentials of psychological health then the creative genius is frequently not healthy.'

Although Freud's (1922) view on the scope of irrational unconscious forces in creativity was confined to the artist, Barron (1968), in developing his arguments from a Freudian base, has applied them to all creativity:

> The creative individual in his generalised preference for apparent disorder, turns to the dimly realised life of the unconscious, and is likely to have more than the usual amount of respect for the forces of the irrational in himself and others. This respect consists in a faith that the irrational itself will generate some ordering principle if it is permitted expression and admitted conscious scrutiny. To put the matter more strongly, I believe that the creative individual not only respects the irrationality in himself, but counts it as the most promising source of novelty in his own thought.

The use of the Freudian concept of the unconscious to explain creativity has resulted in the reduction of all such activity, banal or inspired, to the level of pathology. Also, in the uninhibited emotionality of the artist and its relation to creativity lies a profound Freudian paradox. On one hand the expression (rather than repression) of emotional impulses is seen as a sign of psychological health, whilst on the other the products of such emotionality which form the basis of artistic creation are seen as being significant of neurosis.

The confusion between artistic creativity and neurosis largely springs from Freud's conception of the unconscious, which is limited to repressed emotional experiences and the primary process representing the id or instinctive drives, which are considered to be irrational and perverse. As such, the permeation of fantasy into expressed activity, which is the prerogative of the artistic mode, is bound to be labelled pathological. Although there may be some reservations about the genuineness of the artist's emotional freedom, issue can be taken with the Freudian equation of neurosis and artistic creativity. Jung (1959), on the other hand, in dealing with artistic creativity, makes a distinction between a psychological and a visionary mode of action. The former takes its material from conscious experience and in no way transcends the boundary of psychological intelligibility. In contrast, the visionary mode is accounted for by Jung as the emergence of the collective unconscious which he characteristically describes as:

> a certain psychic disposition shaped by the forces of heredity; from it consciousness has developed. In the physical structure of the body we find traces of earlier stages of evolution, and we may expect the human psyche also to conform in its make-up to the law of phylogeny. It is a fact that in eclipses of consciousness — in dreams, narcotic states, and cases of insanity — there come to the surface psychic products or contents that show all the traits of primitive levels of psychic development. The images themselves are of such primitive character that we might suppose them derived from ancient esoteric teaching.

Thus Jung sees the artist's vision as transcending the personal and reaching a higher plane:

> The artist is not a person endowed with free will who seeks his own ends, but one who allows art to realize its purposes through him. As a human being he may have moods, a will and personal aims, but as an artist he is a 'man' in a higher sense — he is 'collective man' — one who carries and shapes the unconscious psychic life of mankind.

Although there are notable differences in artistic and scientific creativity there are common features which they share with the process of growth, including growth through psychotherapeutic change. To grow, we must be willing to relinquish the security afforded by habitual modes of behaviour and experience. We must permit the emergence of new ways of thinking, feeling and expressing, and the disorganization of non-adjustive patterns and defences (a divergent process). This process is likely to be followed by a new awareness of the capacities, resources and impulses within the individual. These may then be channelled and integrated into new adaptive strategies (a convergent process). Similar ideas are contained in the principles or strategies of openness to experience and control, which Coan (1974) has considered to be central to personality development (Chapter 6).

Our initial interest in convergent and divergent thinking was due to the observed similarities between the personal styles associated with these thinking types and the personal adjustment strategies with which we were concerned. We have since identified them in relation to broad underlying principles which incorporate intellectual and personality factors and have a common basis with creative activity, personality development and psychotherapeutic change.

Our initial attempt to relate convergent-divergent thinking to our other measures was carried out on a small sample of sixteen patients referred to an out-patient clinic for group psychotherapy or behaviour therapy. There were equal numbers of men and women in the group. They tended to be in their early adulthood, to be of average verbal ability but to be above average in intelligence (Table 5.1).

Table 5.1 Means and standard deviations of age and intelligence measures for Sample 1 (n = 16)

	Mean	*sd*
Age	29.87	17.77
Mill Hill Vocabulary (percentile score)	50.69	23.80
Progressive Matrices (percentile score)	80.38	18.25

Our hypotheses were that patients with an outward direction of interest and conservative social attitudes were more likely to be convergent in thinking, while patients with an inward direction of interest and a liberal social orientation were more likely to be divergent in thinking. The former group, we argued, were likely to focalize their distress and express treatment expectancies in line with behaviour therapy. The latter group were likely to present more diffused complaints, explore a range of possibilities for their distress and have expectancies which favoured small group psychotherapy.

In addition to the vocabulary and intelligence tests the following personality and attitude tests were administered:

The Personal Disturbance Scale (PD/SSI)
The Direction of Interest Questionnaire (DIQ)
The Conservatism Scale (C Scale)
The Treatment Expectancies Questionnaire (TEQ)
The Hostility and Direction of Hostility Questionnaire (HDHQ)
The Hysteroid-Obsessoid Questionnaire (HOQ)

For our measure of convergent-divergent thinking two widely used open-ended tests were employed. The first — the Uses of Objects Test — is simply the following:

Below are five everyday objects. Think of as many uses as you can for each.
1   a barrel
2   a paper clip
3   a tin of boot polish
4   a brick
5   a blanket

The second — the Meanings of Words Test — is similar:

Each of the ten words below has more than one meaning, write down as many meanings for each word as you can.

bit	pink
bolt	pitch
duck	port
fair	sack
fast	tender

These open-ended tests were administered without a time-limit and were introduced at an early stage in the administration of the battery to avoid a possible flagging of interest and motivation.

Different authors have used different indices in the scoring of these tests. Hudson (1966) has used fluency (the total number of responses). Torrance (1962) has suggested a scoring system based on fluency, flexibility, originality and elaboration. Vernon (1971) has pointed out that these four scores intercorrelate so highly that the effort of differentiation is a waste of time. Vernon, himself, has used an unusualness score based upon the statistical frequency of a response occurring, but our sample was too small to apply this procedure.

Bearing in mind Vernon's findings with regard to fluency, flexibility, originality and elaboration, we decided to score as divergent any response reflecting a tendency to move away from the practical, fixed use of an object. Three psychologists scored each protocol independently, using this principle of allocation. Generally there was a high measure of agreement but when there was a discrepancy the item was discussed and common agreement was obtained. Since many of the responses were recurring it was possible to build up a table of convergent and divergent items. Since the responses to the Meanings of Words test did not appear to involve the factors of flexibility and originality, we based our scoring system on fluency only, i.e. the total number of responses given by the subject.

The correlations between the Uses of Objects, Divergence or D Score, and the other test material are shown in Table 5.2. Although failing to reach a statistically significant level, the correlations in the

Table 5.2 Correlations between the Uses of Objects Divergence Score and other psychological measures for Sample 1 (n = 16)

Tests	r	p
Mill Hill Vocabulary	0.19	n.s.
Progressive Matrices	0.09	n.s.
Personal Disturbance Scale (PD/SSI)	0.05	n.s.
Direction of Interest Questionnaire (DIQ)	0.36	n.s.
Conservatism Scale (C Scale)	—0.31	n.s.
Treatment Expectancies Questionnaire (TEQ)	—0.23	n.s.
Total Hostility Score of HDHQ	0.50	<0.05
Direction of Hostility Score of HDHQ	—0.03	n.s.
Hysteroid-Obsessoid Questionnaire	0.17	n.s.

expected direction between the D Score and the DIQ, the C Scale and the TEQ were of a sufficiently high order to warrant further investigation. Factors militating against a higher level of correlation we felt were the limited size of the sample and the response set to the Uses of Objects Test. Kogan and Morgan (1969) have suggested that, like other psychological tests, divergent measures are affected by situational and motivational factors such as administrative set, anxiety and defensiveness. Vernon (1971) has reported that 'divergent thinking scores obtained under relaxed conditions have generally richer psychological meaning than those obtained under more formal test-like conditions'. We thought it reasonable to assume that the inclusion of the open-ended tests in a battery of intelligence and diagnostic tests would suggest to the patients that they were contributing to their pre-treatment assessment. With this in mind their responses might well be unduly guarded. We therefore decided to repeat the study, using a larger sample of patients and altering the administration of the open-ended tests.

A further sample of fifteen female and ten male out-patient neurotics were tested on the battery. They were very similar in age, vocabulary and intelligence level to the first sample (see Table 5.3). In order to

Table 5.3 Means and standard deviations of age and intelligence measures for Sample 2 (n = 25)

	Mean	*sd*
Age	27.40	8.89
Mill Hill Vocabulary (percentile score)	51.88	31.44
Progressive Matrices (percentile score)	80.00	17.28

separate the open-ended tests from the pre-treatment assessment battery the following instructions were given. For the Uses of Objects:

> This test is just for research and is a test of imagination and creativity. You have to think of as many uses as possible for each of the objects listed here. The more you can think of the better. You have fifteen minutes to finish the test. Use your imagination and try to think of a number of uses for each of the objects.

For the Meaning of Words Test the instructions were:

> This test is just for research and is a test of imagination and creativity. Each of the ten words below has more than one meaning. Write down as many meanings for each word as you can. You have fifteen minutes to finish the test.

Under the new administration the mean D score rose from 9.75 (sd = 5.38) for the first sample to 16.40 (sd = 12.33) for the second — a statistically significant rise (t = 2.34, p < 0.05).

Table 5.4 shows the relationship between the D score and the other test material for the second sample. These results show that the DIQ, C,

Table 5.4 Correlations between the D Score and the other psychological measures for Sample 2 (n = 25)

	r	p
Mill Hill Vocabulary	0.27	n.s.
Progressive Matrices	0.40	<0.05
Personal Disturbance Scale (PD/SSI)	0.22	n.s.
Direction of Interest Questionnaire (DIQ)[*]	0.50	<0.01[**]
Conservatism Scale (C Scale)[*]	−0.35	<0.05[**]
Treatment Expectancies Questionnaire (TEQ)[*]	−0.48	<0.01[**]
Total Hostility Score of HDHQ	0.29	n.s.
Direction of Hostility Score of HDHQ	−0.28	n.s.
Hysteroid-Obsessoid Questionnaire	0.13	n.s.

[*] One-tailed.
[**] See Caine, Wijesinghe and Wood (1973).

and TEQ are significantly correlated with the D Score. When the correlations with the Progressive Matrices and Mill Hill Vocabulary are partialled out the correlation of the D Score with DIQ is 0.46 ($p < 0.02$), with C is 0.33 ($p < 0.05$) and with the TEQ is −0.46 ($p < 0.02$).

Changing the instructions for the Meaning of Words Test did not appear to affect the results. The mean for the first sample was 25.12 and for the second 25.52. It was therefore possible to combine the data for the two samples in determining the relationships with the other test data (Table 5.5). Not surprisingly, high correlations were found

Table 5.5 Correlations between the Meanings of Words Test and the other psychological measures for the two samples combined (n = 41)

	r	p
Mill Hill Vocabulary	0.61	<0.01
Progressive Matrices	0.55	<0.01
Personal Disturbance Scale (PD/SSI)	0.14	n.s.
Direction of Interest Questionnaire (DIQ)	0.41	<0.01[*]
Conservatism Scale (C Scale)	−0.25	n.s.
Treatment Expectancies Questionnaire (TEQ)	−0.40	<0.01[*]
Total Hostility Score of HDHQ	0.14	n.s.
Direction of Hostility Score of HDHQ	0.20	n.s.
Hysteroid-Obsessoid Questionnaire	0.25	n.s.

[*]One-tailed.

between the Meaning of Words Tests and the abilities tests, with a rho coefficient of 0.61 (p < 0.01) with the Mill Hill Vocabulary Test and 0.55 (p < 0.01) with the Progressive Matrices. Even though a similar pattern of connections emerged with this test and the questionnaire material as for the Uses of Objects Test, when the correlations with the abilities tests were partialled out, the values of the correlations were much reduced. The only measure to hold statistical significance was the TEQ (r = −0.45, p < 0.05).

Claims that convergers and divergers were none other than extraverts and introverts have been repudiated by Hudson (1968). This repudiation is supported in our study by the lack of relationship between the HOQ (which correlated highly with the Extraversion Scale of the Maudsley Personality Inventory) and the D Score. The low correlations obtained are not in line with the predictions made by the proponents of Eysenck's theory of extraversion and introversion. The absence of a relationship between the D Score and the HOQ together with the consistent relationship with the DIQ adds further weight to our contention that the direction of interest dimension, and not social extraversion, is of relevance here.

Of the open-ended tests, the highest relationships were obtained with the Uses of Objects − a test which has been shown to be less dependent on abilities but to be easily affected by administration and motivational factors.

By contrast, the Meaning of Words Test seems to be dependent on ability, but not to be affected to the same extent as the Uses of Objects Test by administration and response set. Despite these differences, the D Score correlates highly with the Meaning of Words Test. The correlation between the two tests in Sample 1 was r = 0.62 (p < 0.01) and in Sample 2 was r = 0.64 (p < 0.01). This suggests an important verbal bias on the part of the divergent thinker. It would appear that interest in abstract, theoretical concepts reinforces their natural ability.

It has been previously demonstrated that the converger is the person with conventional attitudes and respect for authority and that the diverger is the liberal non-authoritarian (Hudson 1966, 1968). Hudson's work in this respect is supported in that the relationships between the open-ended tests and the Conservatism Scale are in the predicted direction, although falling short of statistical significance. Earlier studies, particularly those of Getzels and Jackson (1962) and Hudson (1966), have shown that divergers tend to express more aggression and humour in their responses to tests such as the Uses of Objects than do convergers. This leads them to describe divergers as being emotionally uninhibited and, in contrast, the converger as emotionally inhibited. Austin (1971) has come to similar conclusions on the basis of the number of dreams recalled during equivalent REM periods. It is of relevance to note with our patients that whilst violence and humour were nearly absent in their responses to the Uses of Objects, the divergers admitted to a significantly higher proportion of hostility items on the HDHQ than did the convergers. The way in which hostility is expressed, in an inward or outward direction, was found to be unrelated to type of thinking.

The finding that is both new and particularly relevant as far as neurotic patients are concerned is the consistent relationship between both the Uses of Objects and the Meanings of Words and the Treatment Expectancies Questionnaire. This indicates that the diverger, who has been identified as the inwardly directed type, has treatment expectancies favouring a group therapy approach. By contrast, the converger with his outwardly directed interests has expectancies more in line with behaviour therapy.

Summary

Convergent and divergent processes have been identified in relation to two broadly differentiated personal styles on the basis of previous personality descriptions, as well as the empirical evidence from our own investigations. We have argued that scientific and artistic creativity in many ways epitomize these two processes just as they are reflected in the life styles of creative scientists and artists. These processes may also be related to particular treatment strategies so that patients with a convergent bias may favour behaviour therapy while those with a divergent bias may favour group psychotherapy.

Chapter 6
Openness, control, and neurosis

In collaboration with Susan J. White, M.A., M.Sc.
(M.R.C. Statistical Research and Services Unit, University
Hospital Medical School, London)

Our research has been mainly with psychiatric patients in the areas of neurotic malfunctioning and treatment. It is therefore of great interest to us to discover a considerable degree of convergence with Coan's (1974) work on optimum psychological functioning involving normal samples of a very different order from ours. Coan's main purpose was to define optimum functioning in terms of the fundamental personality variables involved, and he has described what he considers to be 'a major attempt to apply techniques of multivariate analysis to the domain of the optimal personality and to examine the theoretical implications of the findings involved'. Since his treatment of this assignation is profound, wide-ranging, and expert in terms of the use of multivariate statistical techniques, we make no apology in reporting his work in some detail.

Coan points out that the nature of the ideal structure and development of personality has been the subject of much speculation but of little systematic research. Freud referred to ego strength and the genital character, Adler to mastery or control, Jung emphasized individuation, Rank described the creative artist, and Fromm the productive character. In recent years, in defining the optimal personality, the terms adjustment, normality, maturity, self-actualization, self-consistency, special awareness, openness to experience, and mental health have all been invoked.

Coan considers these definitions in detail, noting that although some of them are deeply embedded in both Western and Eastern philosophic and religious thought, they involve many contradictions. Regarding the phenomenon of special awareness, for example, Western thought has characteristically emphasized a symbolic, analytical comprehension of reality that can be verbalized. Eastern thought, on the other hand, has traditionally emphasized a non-analytical, non-symbolically mediated immediate awareness of a reality that cannot be directly expressed in words. Again, the orderly, predictable state of being implied by the concept of self-consistency cannot be maintained if spontaneity and openness to new experience are to be invoked. Social adjustment may be incompatible with social concern and self-awareness may preclude a high level of self-esteem. In view of these difficulties, Coan suggests that the optimum state of being probably involves a number of fairly distinct dimensions. In order to define these more precisely his approach has been to examine the relationships between a very large conglomeration of possibly relevant personality attributes within a large common population — a task which would have been impossible before the advent of modern statistical techniques and computers.

Coan administered this extremely extensive battery of psychological tests to several hundred psychology and liberal arts students at the University of Arizona, on a group basis. Complete sets of test battery scores were finally available for analysis for 170 men and 191 women. In all, 135 personality attributes were measured, including:

> openness to various aspects of experience, including 'regression in the service of the ego' (Kris, 1952)
> early memories
> miscellaneous activities
> attitudes to various aspects of control
> general beliefs
> reality contact
> Cattell's 16 personality factors
> independence
> manifest anxiety
> rigidity
> ego strength
> conformity
> dogmatism
> cognitive functioning
> temporal orientation
> the self concept
> art preferences
> consistency of interests and self ratings
> projective test material
> closure flexibility
> creativity
> social extraversion, etc.

His summary of the results of the factor analysis of the battery entailed the following points:

1   No common general dimension of phenomenal organization emerged.
2   Reality contact, logical consistency of the attitude-belief system, and uncoventionality of thought were interrelated, but they seemed to bear little relationship to most of the other aspects of adjustment that were studied.
3   Self-insight was related to openness to experience and feelings of subjective distress.
4   Several semi-dependent patterns of openness to experience were identified and there was some evidence of a weak general factor of openness.
5   Various forms of openness were related positively to subjective distress.
6   The idea of a general factor of experienced control was not supported. The control experience in one area of life may be unrelated to control in another.
7   There was a general tendency for various forms of experienced control to correlate negatively with both openness and subjective distress.
8   The ability measures correlated much more highly with each other than with the non-ability measures.
9   Two measures of impaired intellectual functioning were found to be unrelated to other measures in the battery.
10 An originality score was found to be related to personality variables involving a willingness to speculate and to entertain unusual ideas.
11 For the battery as a whole, nineteen obliquely rotated factors emerged. The factors most relevant to theories of optimum personality functioning include:
     distress proneness
     object orientation vs. personal orientation
     openness to experience
     acceptance
     pessimism vs. optimism
     deliberateness vs. spontaneity
     responsibility
     self-dissatisfaction vs. self-satisfaction
     scope of early memories

12 There was no evidence at the first-order level of statistical analysis of a unitary dimension that could be identified as a general factor of personality integration, self-actualization, or positive mental health.

13 Sex differences were found in a large number of variables, many of them central to various concepts of the optimal personality. To quote from Coan:

> Men were more object-orientated than women, women more person-orientated. This and a number of related differences seemed to involve the thinking-feeling and logos-eros dichotomies of Jung. Men reported greater personal control, perhaps because they had a greater need to maintain a self-image of mastery. They tended to emphasize independent and individualized action, while women were likely to be more orientated to harmony and relatedness. Women tended to be more open to experience, most notably in the realm of feeling and thought. Men were more open to experience regarding action. Men scored higher on the measure of reality contact employed, but women scored higher on self-realism. Women reported much more subjective distress in various forms than did men. Characteristic differences in intellectual performance were also found.

Coan's evaluation of his findings suggests to him that we should abandon the attempt to identify one optimal personality pattern and that we should think, instead, in terms of a variety of patterns that are desirable for a variety of purposes.

The somewhat contrasting patterns which seem most relevant to Coan can be summarized:

1 openness to experience vs. stability and freedom from distress
2 an orientation towards harmony, relatedness, unity vs. a sense of clear differentiation, autonomy, individual achievement
3 relating to oneself and others as persons vs. an objective orientation
4 spontaneity vs. planning and order
5 self-confidence vs. realistic appraisal of one's limitations
6 optimistic attitude towards the world vs. a realistic appraisal of world conditions.

He emphasizes that these polarities are not totally independent of one another and that is possible to recognize two broad classes. On the one hand, there are potential modes of being that require a kind of openness, fluidity, permeability, or accessibility. For these to appear we must relax control over ourselves and the world around us. On the other hand there are potential modes of being which require deliberate control, restriction of attention, and systematic thought and action. The open attitude permits a more spontaneous and direct response to all events. It facilitates a genuine, uncalculated relationship with others which can involve both supreme joy and deep hurt. A broad awareness of ourselves, of life, and of the world is possible since nothing is deliberately excluded, restricted, or overstructured in the flow of impressions. The second basic attitude of order and control is necessary to impose meaning on the experience of the moment. Through this more deliberate, analytical, or reflective attitude the immediate reactions to things that have occurred in the past and may develop in the future can be related. We thereby can arrive at a relatively well ordered view of ourselves and our world. We can relate each action to an overall system of values or philosophy and we can achieve the measure of self-consistency necessary for the achievement of long-term goals. We can develop various abilities and skills, a sense of control and degree of self-esteem which make it easier to withstand stress and frustration. Seeing beyond immediate difficulties, we can work more positively and effectively toward future resolutions and maintain more stable relationships.

Coan's research suggests to him that the second basic attitude of order and control makes for greater stability and adjustment with a greater freedom from distress and the greatest self-satisfaction over time — at the expense of the spontaneity, genuineness, and intensity represented by a greater openness. He recognizes the need for some balanced combination but his results indicate that, by and large, the people who best represent the first attitude are not, at the same time, the people who best represent the second.

Although this may be true, both attitudes are essential for constructive growth. For Coan, personality development is a creative process depending on a balance of two kinds of subprocesses. On the one hand there are those subprocesses that lead to the breakdown of existing adjustive patterns involving change, variety and disorder and on the other hand there are those subprocesses that lead to the emergence of an overall ordering, unifying, or integrating of the patterns of adjustment. These two processes and their implications for growth, development and creativity have been discussed in relation to convergent-divergent thinking in Chapter 5.

In this theory of personality development, flexibility is a key require-
ment of growth, both as a pre-condition and as a consequence. Coan
points to Jung (1933) as the foremost protagonist of this view. As discussed in Chapter 1, from the Jungian standpoint, the introvert attaches
greater value to the inner world, and in him the psychological functions
of thinking, feeling, sensation and intuition are governed by internal
conditions. The extravert is the opposite, attaching greater value to the
external world, and his psychological functions are governed by outside
conditions. It is possible to utilize one orientation or attitude to the
virtual exclusion of the other. For Jung, the state to be desired is that
in which the individual can utilize constructively both the inner and the
outer attitude as the existential situation demands. A similar flexible
use of the four functions of thinking, feeling, sensation and intuition
is required for optimum personal development.

Coan's measure of openness to experience was based on that of
Fitzgerald (1966a, 1966b), who had drawn heavily on the concept of
'regression in the service of the ego' used by Kris (1952) in his psychoanalytic explorations in art. Such regression is seen by Kris as fundamentally constructive in its use of unconscious dream and fantasy
material for creative purposes. Coan added test items reflecting Jung's
attitude-function system to those of the Fitzgerald openness to experience inventory. The original factor analysis of the Coan measure
revealed sixteen factors. In further work (Coan, 1972) the first seven
factors have been replicated and these provide the basis for the present
Experience Inventory:

1   *Aesthetic sensitivity vs. insensitivity* The high scorer reports a
    variety of aesthetic experiences. The low scorer expresses a more
    prosaic orientation, which emphasizes clear representation and
    denotation.
2   *Unusual perceptions and associations* The high scorer reports
    various unusual ways of experiencing himself, his body, and his
    physical surroundings.
3   *Openness to theoretical or hypothetical ideas* The high scorer
    enjoys abstract, novel, and unusual ideas and intellectual puzzles,
    while the low scorer is repelled by such things.
4   *Constructive utilization of fantasy and dreams* A number of items
    suggest an access to unconscious processes or a willingness to rely
    on them for creative or constructive ends. The high scorer reports
    the use of dreams, daydreams, and undirected thought for problem
    solving and other purposes.

5   *Openness to unconventional views of reality vs. adherence to mundane material reality* The items concern the subject's willingness to entertain a variety of specific ideas in such realms as astrology, extrasensory perception, astral projection, and reincarnation.

6   *Indulgence in fantasy vs. avoidance of fantasy* The high scorer reports that he spends a lot of time daydreaming and enjoys the content of his fantasises. The low scorer tries to avoid daydreaming and prefers to keep his thinking channelled along orderly, realistic and constructive lines.

7   *Deliberate and systematic thought* The high scorer reports a need for orderly and planned thinking and frequent indulgence in it. The item content implies most directly an openness to this kind of thought, rather than the use of it to avoid the kinds of thought embodied in other scales, but the scale shows a slight tendency to correlate negatively with the others.

With regard to the second general principle, Coan has developed his Personal Opinion Survey as a measure of experience of order, control and integration. Dissatisfied with the previous work by Rotter (1966) on the internal-external locus of control as too dependent on social learning theory, he has developed his own scale with a focus on the varieties of human experience rather than on a particular expectancy interpretation of control. As with the Experience Inventory, an original set of eighteen factors has now been reduced to seven in cross-validation work (Coan, Fairchild, and Dobyns, 1973):

1   *Achievement through conscientious effort* The high scorer espouses the view that one can accomplish many things if one tries hard enough. Success may lie in the academic, social or physical realm.

2   *Personal confidence in ability to achieve mastery* Here the high scorer expresses confidence that he as an individual has the capacity for accomplishment in various realms – mathematical, mechanical, scientific, athletic, linguistic. The areas of success with which this scale is concerned tend to be intellectual in character and tend to be deemed more appropriate for men than for women in our society.

3   *Capacity of mankind to control its destiny vs. supernatural power or fate* The items tap a general belief in man's ability to build a just society, to control both his own evolution and natural physical phenomena, and to act in a way that will permit the elimination of war.

4   *Successful planning and organization* Items refer essentially to the planning, organization and completion of tasks. The high scorer reports successful self-control in the realm of work.

5   *Self-control over internal processes* The high scorer reports control over somatic, affective, and cognitive processes. The low scorer may be afflicted with unavoidable itching, depression, ideas that run through his mind, muscular incoordination, twitching or tightening up of muscles, unexplainable cheerfulness, etc.

6   *Control over large-scale social and political events* The score indicates the extent to which the subject believes that he himself and individual people can have an effect on major societal processes.

7   *Control in immediate social interaction* The items here are all concerned with whether the subject himself is able to control social situations or secure desired responses from other people.

It seems clear that Coan's two principles of adjustment of openness to inner experience and control overlap the adjustive strategies with which we have been involved. There is a common convergence on Jung's concept of introversion-extraversion as represented by the Experience Inventory and our Direction of Interest Questionnaire and Coan's control measure may well involve a conservatism element.

In order to explore this overlap, our first task was to cross-validate Coan's measures on a British sample. We could then relate the British based scales to our own measures and to neurosis. The numbers of the various groups obtained for this purpose, together with their age ranges, are shown in Table 6.1 for the Experience Inventory (E1), the Personal Opinion Survey (POS), the Attitude to Treatment Questionnaire (ATQ), the Treatment Expectancies Questionnaire (TEQ), the Direction of Interest Questionnaire (DIQ), and the Conservatism Scale (C).

Using Coan's scoring keys, the scores on the seven aspects of openness and seven aspects of control were computed for the sample and product moment correlations between the measures were calculated. A factor analysis of all items in each questionnaire was carried out. Factor extraction was by the method of principal components, with squared multiple correlations for the initial communality estimates, followed by varimax rotation. The factors were compared with the scales distinguished by Coan.

Further composite scales for both openness and control were derived in three ways:

1   a 'total' score was obtained by summing the individual Coan scales,

Table 6.1 Subjects completing questionnaires

Source	Age range	Median age	% male (approx.)	Numbers completing questionnaires					
				EI	POS	ATQ	TEQ	DIQ	C
Medical students (pre-clinical)	18–29	19	67	98	97	98	—	98	—
Medical students* (2nd clinical year)	19–23	22	67	7	6	3	1	5	3
Institute of Group Analysis students	22–63	36	19	104	116	116	115	116	—
Sundry volunteers**	16–66	30	35	59	71	2	71	69	58
Neurotic patients	17–59	28	41	24	66	—	25	25	20
Total	16–66	27	40	292	356	219	212	313	81

* Volunteers for psychotherapy training.
** Non-clinical hospital staff, hospital voluntary workers, university students.

excluding any scale which appeared to be negatively correlated with the others;

2   a shorter form of this 'total' score was obtained using item analysis (Maxwell, 1961). This proceeded by excluding any item which failed to discriminate between subjects (i.e. an item to which more than 80 per cent of subjects gave the same reply) and by excluding items for which the proportion of affirmative replies did not increase monotonically with the 'total' score;

3   a scale was obtained from the first principal component by summing the scores of the items with high loadings on that component. For the POS, a further scale was obtained similarly from the second principal component.

The intercorrelations found between Coan's Experience Inventory scales are shown in Table 6.2. They are generally positive, with the exception of those with scale seven, which tend to be negative. This supports Coan's original findings and thus scale seven was excluded from the 'total' score of openness. The item analysis of the complete questionnaire resulted in a reduced set of fifty-nine items with scale seven virtually unrepresented. Factor analysis led to the initial extraction of twenty-seven factors with eigenvalue of at least one. These factors represented 68 per cent of the total sample variance. When all the factors were arranged in order of decreasing eigenvalue, the cumulative variance accounted for by successively including more factors increased smoothly to 100 per cent. No small subset of factors could be identified as representing a large proportion of the variance. The first factor accounted for only 12 per cent, compared with Coan's report of 25 per cent for his first factor. All Coan's original scales were here represented by items having loadings of high absolute magnitude ($\geqslant 0.30$). The least well represented scales were three (three items) and seven (one item with reversed scoring). The total number of highly loaded items was forty-eight. When an orthogonal rotation was performed, it was found that factors corresponding to Coan's scales one, four, five, six and seven could be identified with some splitting of individual scales. The most coherent factors corresponded to scale five (high loadings on thirteen of the original fifteen items) and scale one (high loadings on eight of the original set).

For the Personal Opinion Survey the intercorrelations between the seven Coan scales are also shown in Table 6.2. It can be seen that the scales are less consistently related than are the EI scales. For example, scales one and three have only one low positive relationship with

Table 6.2 Correlations between Coan's scales (n = 203–342)*

Scale	EI							POS					
	1	*2*	*3*	*4*	*5*	*6*	*7*	*1*	*2*	*3*	*4*	*5*	*6*
EI													
2	0.30**												
3	0.24	0.24											
4	0.40	0.48	0.19										
5	0.31	0.30	0.14	0.40									
6	0.29	0.42	0.17	0.40	0.26								
7	−0.13	−0.02	0.00	−0.08	−0.19	−0.19							
POS													
1	−0.13	0.12	0.03	0.07	0.00	−0.05	0.21						
2	0.06	0.06	0.42	0.00	−0.04	−0.12	0.06	0.16					
3	0.11	0.01	0.18	−0.11	−0.30	0.03	0.06	−0.02	0.13				
4	−0.08	−0.28	−0.13	−0.11	−0.10	−0.37	0.39	0.10	0.09	−0.02			
5	−0.08	−0.23	0.14	−0.27	−0.06	−0.26	0.07	0.06	0.29	0.07	0.20		
6	0.10	−0.01	0.12	−0.01	−0.05	−0.06	0.12	0.05	0.12	0.01	0.15	0.10	
7	0.08	−0.00	0.20	0.07	0.05	−0.04	−0.03	0.06	0.21	0.09	0.14	0.20	0.32

* Correlations calculated only from questionnaires having all items completed

** Correlations underlined are significantly different from zero (p ≤ 0.05).

another scale. The pattern of correlations obtained for scales three, four, and six fails to confirm that reported by Coan. The item analysis of the questionnaire led to a reduced set of 76 items drawn from all scales. Scale one was the least represented with only five items included. From a factor analysis of the 120 items forty factors with eigenvalue of at least one were found. These represented 70 per cent of the total variance. As with the EI, the cumulative variance increased smoothly to 100 per cent, and no obvious subset of factors accounting for a high proportion of the variance was distinguishable. The first and second factors accounted for 7 and 5 per cent of the total variance respectively. In the first factor forty-four items had loadings of high absolute magnitude (> 0.30). None of these items was from Coan's scales one or three, but each of the other scales was represented by six or more highly loaded items. In the second factor, scales one and three were the highest contributors, with nine and five highly loaded items respectively. Scales two, four, six and seven contributed a further six items between them, giving a total of twenty items in all. After an orthogonal rotation, seven separate factors corresponding to Coan's original scales could be identified. Each had loadings > 0.30 in absolute magnitude on eleven or more of the items from the particular scale, together with a few highly loaded items from other scales in some cases.

Table 6.2 also indicates some significant correlations between the EI and POS scales, although these tend to lack consistency. In this respect POS scales four and five are most consistently correlated with the EI scales. POS scale four is positively correlated with EI scale seven and both tend to be negatively correlated with the other EI scales, suggesting the opposition of conscious, organized planning and thinking to activities involving feelings, fantasies, dreams and intuitions.

Table 6.3 shows that the three EI composite scales are highly inter-correlated, suggesting that they are measuring much the same thing. For the POS composite scales a similar relationship pertains for the total score, the item analysis scale, and the Component 1 scale. The Component 2 scale, however, has only a low positive correlation with total score suggesting that a rather different aspect of control is involved in this scale. The intercorrelations between the EI composite scales and the POS composite scales are low and mainly not significantly different from zero, suggesting that openness and control as measured here are not necessarily dichotomously linked.

The relationships between the EI, the POS and our previously reported measures are indicated in Table 6.4, which shows the correlations obtained between the derived EI and POS scales and the

Table 6.3 Correlations between the composite EI and POS Scales* (n = 156–317)

	EI			POS		
	Total 1–6	Component 1	Item analysis	Total 1–7	Component 1	Component 2
EI						
Component 1	0.95					
Item analysis	0.98	0.97				
POS						
Total 1–7	−0.12	−0.22	−0.22			
Component 1	−0.04	−0.09	−0.14	0.89	−0.08	
Component 2	−0.02	−0.02	0.04	0.19	0.92	
Item analysis	−0.07	−0.14	−0.17	0.97	0.92	0.09

* Correlations underlined are significantly different from zero ($p \leqslant 0.05$).

Table 6.4 Correlations between the EI and POS Scales and ATQ, TEQ, DIQ and C (n = 120–275)

		ATQ	*TEQ*	*DIQ*	*C*
EI					
Scales:	1	−0.33*	−0.30	0.25	−0.25
	2	0.02	0.06	0.17	−0.08
	3	0.17	0.09	0.06	−0.10
	4	−0.14	−0.20	0.20	−0.10
	5	−0.13	−0.05	0.18	−0.23
	6	−0.10	−0.14	0.18	−0.15
	7	0.19	0.11	−0.07	0.15
Total (1 to 6)		−0.21	−0.21	0.28	−0.34
Component 1 scale		−0.25	−0.24	0.32	−0.36
Item analysis scale		−0.21	−0.19	0.31	−0.35
POS					
Scales:	1	0.22	0.22	−0.11	0.30
	2	0.24	0.06	−0.07	−0.03
	3	0.00	0.00	0.15	−0.08
	4	0.06	0.01	−0.20	0.07
	5	0.15	0.05	−0.12	−0.05
	6	−0.15	0.01	0.05	0.15
	7	−0.09	−0.13	0.04	−0.10
Total (1 to 7)		0.13	0.12	−0.12	0.10
Component 1 scale		0.01	0.04	−0.05	0.08
Component 2 scale		0.31	0.27	−0.16	0.28
Item analysis scale		0.09	0.04	−0.04	0.06

*Correlations underlined are significantly different from zero ($p \leqslant 0.05$)

Attitude to Treatment Questionnaire (ATQ), the Treatment Expectancies Questionnaire (TEQ), the Direction of Interest Questionnaire (DIQ), and the Conservatism Scale (C). As we have argued, it can be seen from Table 6.4 that the EI scales are, in fact, most consistently related to the DIQ. The negative correlations with the ATQ, TEQ and C are in line with the findings of previous studies. As the shortest measure of openness to internal events, and being relatively closely and consistently related to our previous measures, the EI Component 1 scale has advantages over the other two composite measures for further studies. There are fewer significant correlations for the POS scales. Component 2 is the only scale to be significantly and consistently correlated with our previous measures, the pattern of the relationships suggesting something of a conservatism involvement. Table 6.5 gives the mean scores obtained on the openness and control components of the various

Table 6.5 Mean scores on the EI and POS Principal Component Scales of various groups*

Group	n	EI Component 1 Mean	sd	n	POS Component 1 Mean	sd	n	POS Component 2 Mean	sd
Non-patients									
1 Medical students (pre-clinical)	75	25.8	8.4	76	24.7	5.7	83	8.7	3.7
2 Medical students (2nd clinical year)	6	39.0	5.5	4	27.2	9.8	6	8.3	4.8
3 Institute of Group Analysis Students	92	31.3	8.9	101	24.2	7.0	105	6.2	3.4
4 Sundry volunteers	41	24.9	9.8	63	23.3	8.1	63	7.4	4.4
5 Total	214	28.4	9.4	244	24.2	6.9	257	7.4	3.9
Patients									
6 UCH psychotherapy	27	27.0	8.6	27	16.3	7.9	27	9.4	3.8
7 Claybury psychotherapy	27	21.1	8.9	27	17.1	6.6	27	9.8	3.6
8 Claybury behaviour therapy	29	14.0	6.9	29	14.6	5.7	29	9.7	4.0
9 Total	83	20.6	9.7	83	16.0	6.8	83	9.7	3.8

*Statistically significant ($p \leqslant 0.05$) group differences:

EI Component 1: 1 and 4 vs. 3; 6 vs. 7; 6 vs. 8; 7 vs. 8; 1 and 4 vs 7; 1 and 4 vs.8.

POS Component 1: 5 vs. 9.

POS Component 2: 1 and 4 vs. 3; 3 vs. 9; 4 vs. 9.

groups tested. No age or sex differences were found in the data. For the non-patient samples, analysis of variance yielded a significant variation over the groups ($p < 0.001$) for the EI Component 1 scale and the POS Component 2 but no significant differences between the groups emerged for the POS Component 1 scale. The main difference on the EI Component 1 scale is probably between the non-psychotherapy groups (pre-clinical medical students and sundry volunteers) and those involved with psychotherapy (represented by the Institute of Group Analysis students as the one sizeable group) since the difference between the groups thus divided is highly significant ($p < 0.001$). This difference also holds for the POS Component 2 scale ($p = < 0.05$). Since there are age and sex differences in the composition of the groups, (see Table 6.1), we cannot be certain that the differences are due simply to psychotherapy orientation.

For the patient samples there is a significant variation between treatment groups in the EI Component 1 score only ($p < 0.001$). All three treatment groups differ from each other, with the UCH psychotherapy patients indicating the greatest openness to inner experience, the Claybury behaviour therapy the least, and the Claybury psychotherapy group intermediate. The difference between the UCH and Claybury psychotherapy group patients may be due to a number of factors such as social class, selection procedure, etc. which merit further investigation.

To determine the relationship of the EI Component 1 scale to neurosis, the pre-clinical medical students and the sundry volunteers were combined to form a non-patient group since they did not differ significantly on any of the scales. This provided a non-patient group mean of 25.5, sd 8.9 (n = 116) for the scale. The mean for the UCH psychotherapy group was not significantly different from this but that for the Claybury psychotherapy group was significantly lower ($p = < 0.02$). The Claybury behaviour therapy patients differed very significantly ($p < 0.001$) from the non-patients. For the POS Component 1 scale, comparison was made between the complete non-patient group and the complete patient group since no significant difference between the sub-samples had emerged. The mean score for the patients was considerably lower than that for the non-patients ($p < 0.001$). On the POS Component 2 scale the patients as a group scored significantly higher than did the Institute of Group Analysis students and the sundry volunteers ($p < 0.001$), but the difference with the pre-clinical medical students did not reach significance.

From these data we suggest that the following conclusions can be drawn:

1   Measures of openness and control

The Experience Inventory
Although there are some discrepancies, five of the seven original Coan scales have been identified as separate factors in our data. These are scales one, four, five, six, and seven, with scales two and three failing to separate into unitary factors. As with Coan's work, a relatively weak general factor of openness has emerged. If this factor is taken to be represented by the first principal component, the scales contributing most are scales one, four, five and six, with scales two, three and seven minimally represented. A scrutiny of the items involved indicates that this EI Component 1 scale emphasizes an openness to inner experience in terms of a rich aesthetic and mystical life, the constructive use of fantasy and dreams and an openness to the possibility of esoteric knowledge in astral projection, extrasensory perception, foretelling the future, etc. This is clearly very close to Jung's conception of introversion and William James's tender-minded type.

The Personal Opinion Survey
Seven separate factors corresponding to Coan's scales have been identified in our data, although his intercorrelations have not been entirely confirmed. Two relatively independent factors, accounting for a small per cent of the total variance, have emerged. The Component 1 scale includes items from scales two, four, five, six and seven, thus emphasizing confidence in one's intellectual activities, successful planning and organization, control over internal tensions, control over large-scale social and political events, and control over immediate social interactions. This scale was found to be uncorrelated with the EI Component 1 scale, indicating that Coan's report of a negative correlation between openness to internal events and the imposition of order on the world and on experience is not supported unequivocally in our data. Component 2 has scale one as its main contributor. The items involved consist largely of dogmatic statements to the effect that will-power and personal effort are the key to success in many areas. Some of these statements are quite unrealistic and have strong 'super-ego' qualities about them. Table 6.2 shows that the intercorrelations between the EI and POS scales are not high, nor are they entirely consistent in terms of

direction. However, EI scale seven and POS scale four are the most highly related in a positive direction and both tend to be negatively related to the other EI scales. They measure conscious, deliberate, systematic thought and organization, and as such they are at variance with the emphasis placed by the other EI scales on the unconscious, manifested by fantasies and dreams, feelings and intuitions, supporting Coan's argument.

2 Intercorrelations between the EI, the POS and our previously reported measures

The Experience Inventory

Table 6.4 indicates that, apart from the composite scales, scale one is most consistently related to the other measures, supporting the link between the artistic temperament and a propensity for psychotherapy (Meehl, 1960). The Direction of Interest Questionnaire is closely related to the Experience Inventory. This is most encouraging when one considers the diverse genesis of the two measures. As we have noted, the Experience Inventory is the offspring of psychoanalytic explorations in art and Jungian clinical observations. The Direction of Interest Questionnaire has been derived from scales held in common by three widely used psychological tests factor analytically constructed independently by psychologists differing from each other in their aims and in their conceptualizing (Caine and Smail, 1969). The conclusion is thus inescapable that permeating many different conceptual models of personality functioning is a basic, common dimension resembling closely the introversion dimension described by Jung (1933). Table 6.4 indicates that this general orientation as measured by the EI composite scales (best represented by the Component 1 scale) is consistently and predictably related to psychiatric treatment attitudes and expectancies and the general factor of conservatism. Similar findings have been reported by Kreitman (1962) and Walton (1966) in their studies of doctors and medical students.

The Personal Opinion Survey

For the Personal Opinion Survey the individual scales are not so closely or consistently related to the other measures. In this respect, the composite Component 2 scale is most closely related. Thus 'super-ego' attitudes, as reflected by this scale, tend to be accompanied by a traditional, authority-centred approach to psychiatric treatment, conservative attitudes to life, and an outward direction of interest. This constellation of attitudes is reminiscent of the authoritarian personality structure described by Adorno, Frenkel-Brunswick, Levinson and Sanford (1950).

3   *The relationship of the relevant openness and control measures to neurosis*

Table 6.5 shows that openness to inner experience as measured by the EI Component 1 scale is not related to neurosis *per se*. Non-patient and patient samples both split on this factor. However, openness to inner experience is related to psychotherapy in both non-patient and patient samples. Thus the Institute of Group Analysis students and medical students opting for psychotherapy all tend to score highly on openness in relation to other non-patient groups. Patients referred for group psychotherapy at both University College Hospital and Claybury Hospital are more introverted than are patients referred for behaviour therapy. This is good evidence that the relationships indicated by the correlational data have practical implications.

The aspects of control measured by the POS Component 1 and Component 2 scales are related to neurosis. For Component 1 no significant difference is found between the non-patient samples or between the patient samples but the difference between the non-patients and the patients as a whole is highly significant,with the patients indicating a considerable lack of control and alientation with respect to personal achievement, organising themselves, tensions and moods, political events, and immediate social interactions. With regard to the POS Component 2 scale the Institute of Group Analysis students tend to score very low but the patients as a group score high. This suggests that the experienced lack of control of the latter is accompanied by an unrealistic emphasis on the efficacy of will and personal effort which can only aggravate their condition.

In the main, our study has supported Coan's findings of differing aspects of openness and control. This would seem to be an advance on the undimensional approach to these phenomena of Rokeach (1960) and Rotter (1966). For the particular problem of selection for psychotherapy and treatment responses, the most relevant aspects of openness and control would seem to be an introverted openness to inner experience (EI Component 1), a generalized feeling of control (POS Component 2), and an authoritarian emphasis on will-power and personal effort (POS Component 2). These measures were not shown to be related to age in our data but there was a tendency for men to obtain higher POS Component 1 scores than women.

Although Coan may be right in suggesting that openness is associated with subjective distress, our data indicate that such distress is not related to psychiatric breakdown as such. Neurosis so defined is more closely related to experience of control. Perhaps the willingness to admit to anxiety, tension and depression is a feature of openness rather than evidence of an impending psychiatric collapse. The negative correlation between general openness and control reported by Coan is not supported in our group comparisons. Some of our non-patient samples tended to˙score high on both openness and control *vis-à-vis* the patients, and the correlational evidence failed to be consistent in this respect. Optimal functioning would thus seem to entail a considerable measure of both openness and control. As both Jung and Coan have already pointed out, the capacity to use both strategies flexibly in the interests of personal growth and creative effort is perhaps the important thing. However, with regard to psychiatric treatment, an obvious next step is to employ the openness and control measures in comparative treatment studies and to relate them to therapist attitudes and effectiveness. Such a framework could provide a basis for matching patient, therapist, and treatment variables as recommended by Goldstein and Stein (1976). A further intriguing problem is the relationship of openness to a patient's presenting symptomatology. What are the dynamics involved in the extremely low openness score of the phobic patients in relation to other samples?

Summary

In his search for parameters defining optimal personality functioning, Coan (1974) has focused upon two basic principles or strategies of personality functioning, namely openness to inner experience and control. In the American samples used in his research, these two strategies each sub-divided into seven different, although related, aspects of openness and control. Our own work has demonstrated very largely consistent findings in a British population. In addition, openness to inner experience and control have been found to relate in a predictable manner to psychiatric treatment expectancies and attitudes, direction of interest and to conservatism. Neurotic patient samples were found to sub-divide in terms of openness but to be distinguishable from normal samples in terms of aspects of control.

Chapter 7
The complaints of psychological distress

Following established medical practice, the individual seeking help for his psychological distress is expected to present himself to the scrutiny of a specialist observer, who then attempts to diagnose his condition. Of key importance to this procedure are the manner in which the patient presents his distress and the clinician's frame of reference. In nosological psychiatry personal complaints are objectified and referred to as symptoms and form the basis of psychodiagnosis. Psychodiagnosis is based on a supposedly objective system of classification, where symptom clusters are differentiated into a number of diagnostic categories and subcategories – a system based on the assumption that mental disorder can be understood and described like illness of the body. In this scheme diagnosis is not merely a labelling process but also implies causation and prognosis and, as such, is considered to provide a design for action.

This objective, diagnostic approach to psychological distress has come under attack for several different reasons. Firstly, there is a growing body of evidence which questions the usefulness of psychiatric diagnosis *per se*. Diagnosis based on the clustering of symptoms has been shown to be unrelated to any articulated theoretical framework (Draguns and Phillips, 1971); psychiatrists have shown a general lack of reliability in detecting symptoms or of agreeing on their importance (Kreitman, Sainsbury, Morrisey, Towers and Scrivener, 1961); diagnosis has been shown to be independent of observed symptoms (Zigler and Phillips, 1961); and diagnosis has been found to have few treatment implications (Bannister, Salmon and Lieberman, 1964). Secondly, it has been argued that nosological psychiatrists have taken insufficient account of the personal meaning of the situation to the individual seeking help. Thus, Rogers (1961) for example, has rejected diagnostic procedures since he argues that they do an injustice to the personal assumptions of the individual and he contends that all motivations and emotions that are effective and necessary for personal change are 'in the here and now'. Thirdly, as already discussed in Chapters 3 and 4, the presentation of self in an interactional situation is not a passive affair but an active process, which may involve attempts to influence the other person. Thus, by the selective disclosure of information or by the management of expressive behaviour which is designed to create a particular impression in the observer's mind, the patient can play a very decisive influence on the outcome of an interaction. This, in fact, has been demonstrated by Braginsky, Braginsky and Ring (1969) and Kelly, Farina and Mosher (1971), who have shown that psychiatric patients can manipulate their apparent levels of pathology and likeableness to obtain a desired management outcome. This, however, may well be an overstatement as to the degree of conscious control the patient has in the presentation of distress, since complaints can often become diffused, fragmented, displaced and even suppressed due to anxiety and difficulties in communication (Landfield, 1975).

Balint (1964) has made a notable contribution to the understanding of the often transitional process of presenting and elaborating complaints. We shall therefore present here his own well drawn account of the social process leading to the presentation and organization of complaints:

> particularly as a result of urbanisation, a great number of people have lost their roots and connexions, large families with their complicated and intimate interrelations tend to disappear, and the individual becomes more and more solitary, even lonely. If in trouble, he has hardly anyone to whom to go for advice, consolation, or perhaps only for an opportunity to unburden himself. He is thrown more and more back on his own devices. We know that in many people, perhaps in all of us, any mental or emotional stress or strain is either accompanied by, or tantamount to, various bodily sensations. In such troubled states, especially if the strain increases, a possible and in fact frequently used outlet is to drop in on one's doctor and complain. I have deliberately left the verb without an object, because at this initial stage we do not know which is the more important, the act of complaining or the complaints that are complained of. It is here, in this initial, still 'unorganized' phase of an illness, that the doctor's skill in prescribing himself is decisive.

Balint rather quaintly sees the doctor as prescribing himself just as he prescribes a drug. Perhaps this is to make the idea more acceptable to the traditional medical mind. On the basis of clinical case material presented at his Tavistock Clinic research seminars he later writes:

> We think that some of the people who, for some reason or other
> find it difficult to cope with the problems of their lives, resort to
> becoming ill. If the doctor has the opportunity of seeing them in the
> first phases of their becoming ill, i.e. before they settle down to a
> definite 'organized' illness, he may observe that these patients so to
> speak, offer or propose various illnesses, and that they have to go
> on offering new illnesses until between doctor and patient an agree-
> ment can be reached, resulting in the acceptance by both of them of
> one of the illnesses as justified. In some people this 'unorganized'
> state is of short duration and they quickly settle down to 'organize'
> their illness; others seem to go on offering new ones to their doctor.

In some cases, according to Balint, extensive physical examinations reveal no abnormality and the patient is informed that there is nothing wrong with him. Instead of relief, however, the reaction to this sup- posedly welcome news can be one of pained surprise, indignation and suspicion! Balint's view of illness is that it is the result of a conflict between the individual's possibilities and his environment. Everyone has some 'basic illness' or 'basic fault' in his biological structure which varies in degrees both in mind and body. The origin of the basic fault is to be found in the considerable discrepancy between the needs of the individual in his early formative years or months and the care and nursing available at the relevant times. This creates a state of deficiency the consequences of which are only partly reversible. If the basic fault is not too severe or subsequent stress too great the individual will make a tolerable adjustment to life. However, if this is not the case and the individual is faced with a problem too difficult for him to cope with his organization will break down and he will consult his doctor com- plaining of some illness. This goes some way, perhaps, to explaining why we seem to be able to develop new illnesses as the traditional ones come under control or become more fully understood. Balint sees ill- ness as a 'form of life' and he uses psychoanalytic concepts in his analy- sis of the gratifications provided by the condition.

While these transactional influences may play an important part in the definition of the complaint, the 'organized illness' is still likely to reflect important aspects of a person's personality. In psychiatry, for example, there is still a great deal of controversy as to the relationship between manifest patterns of neurotic symptoms and underlying personality traits. Caine (1965a) has identified three major positions in relation to this question. The first is represented by the ideas of Pierre Janet (1901), who postulated that an underlying weakness of psychological synthesis produces the symptoms and the traits. As such they are both considered to be indicative of psychopathology. He classified symptoms into hysteria and psychasthenia and personality traits into obsessoid and hysteroid. The second position represents those who consider symptoms to be directly dependent on the underlying traits. Jung (1920) considered symptoms to be continuous with the trait structure, and quotes Binet as saying that 'the neurotic only accentuates and shows in relief the characteristic traits of his personality'. Such ideas are consistent with the more orthodox psychoanalytic position, where symptom formation is seen as a result of infantile experiences, which are also considered to have a definitive effect on the adult personality, e.g. the anal character and obsessional symptoms. The third position is represented by those who maintain that symptoms and personality traits are not necessarily connected. Foulds (1965) has marshalled strong evidence and produced cogent arguments to show that patients exhibiting obsessional or hysterical symptoms do not necessarily have corresponding personality traits.

While in the main symptom complexes and personality traits can be distinguished conceptually and clinically, there is no general agreement as to the exact mechanism by which symptoms are generated in a particular personality type. Our position on the organization of complaints is, on the one hand, that a narrow conceptualization of personality in trait terms has limited explanatory value and, on the other, that dynamic factors such as the transactions between patient and clinician occur within a broadly differentiated personal schema. Such a schema, we argue, relates to the patient's characteristic adjustment strategies, expectancies, values and assumptions.

Klineberg (1940) has provided strong evidence to show that what is considered to be abnormal behaviour varies from culture to culture, and that even within a culture there are fads and fashions in the way disorder may be expressed. Frank (1973), too, has focused on the way in which distressing experiences are organized in line with the commonly held beliefs and assumptions of a culture. According to Frank, many pre-industrialized societies assume that illness is a condition which involves the entire person, having direct consequences on his relationships with the spirit world and with other members of his tribe. Their classifications often bear no relationships with those of western medicine, in that they do not distinguish sharply between mental and bodily illness nor between natural and supernatural causation. Illness is seen as a condition resulting from conflicts between the individual and his group or due to the displeasure he has caused the guiding spirits of the society. The healing process or treatment is essentially an extension of the patient's concept of the universe.

The increase in social and intellectual complexity in industrialized societies has resulted in more diversified sets of assumptions and beliefs, particularly with regard to 'psychiatric illness'. Thus, the presentation of psychological distress, and expectations as to what might be the most appropriate course of action, have become differentiated in our Western culture. An example of such a differentiation is seen from the studies on the relationship between social class and psychiatric disorder. Hollingshead and Redlich (1958), in their investigations on the New Haven Community of Connecticut, found significant relationships between social class and different types of neurotic complaints. The character neuroses were found to be concentrated in Classes I and II and the patients were prepared to accept a psychogenic explanation for their difficulties. Very few such patients were found in Classes IV and V. The depressive reactions were scattered throughout the classes, but there were 50 per cent more depressives in Classes I and II than in Class V. Phobic reactions were predominantly found amongst Class IV patients. The majority of Class V patients somatized their complaints and also showed resistance to a psychogenic explanation of their symptoms. Other American studies carried out since then have confirmed the relationship between the somatic–psychological symptom dimension and social class status (Kadushin, 1964; Crandell and Dohrenwend, 1967; Derogatis, Covi, Lipman, Davis and Rickels, 1971).

On the basis of results such as these, it is possible to argue that the presentation of psychological disorder reflects internalized past social experiences which relate to a person's characteristic adjustment strategies. In an initial study carried out within this framework, Smail (1970) investigated the relationship between the direction of interest dimension and psychic–somatic symptoms in a small sample of neurotic patients. He hypothesized that patients complaining primarily of somatic symptoms would be outwardly directed in interest, while those whose primary complaints were psychological would be more inwardly directed in interest. Using the psychic vs. somatic scale of the Sympton Sign Inventory (Foulds and Hope, 1968), he found a significant correlation ($r = 0.57$, $p < 0.01$) between the symptom scores and the Direction of Interest Questionnaire in the predicted direction.

In his study, however, age can be seen to contribute to this correlation.

We have since carried out a more comprehensive study on the relationship between personal adjustment strategies, treatment expectancies and symptoms/complaints of neurotic patients. Our sample involved 253 out-patients referred for treatment to a psychotherapy clinic. All patients were considered to be suffering from a neurotic disorder on clinical grounds, and to be free from any organic, psychotic or severe personality disorder. The characteristics of the sample are shown in Table 7.1.

Table 7.1 Demographic and test score characteristics of sample

		Mean	*sd*	*Range*
Age		30.15	9.73	16–59
Mill Hill Vocabulary		53.01	21.79	13–95
DIQ		12.70	6.42	0–28
TEQ		34.52	7.53	18–55
C		41.70	11.49	7–79
Sex				
Female	139	54.9%		
Male	114	45.1%		
Marital Status				
Single	101	39.9%		
Married	128	50.6%		
Divorced/Separated	23	9.1%		
Widowed	1	0.4%		

Subjects were seen individually on their initial visit to the clinic and the following test battery was administered: the Mill Hill Vocabulary Scale Form 1 Senior, the Middlesex Hospital Questionnaire (MHQ) (Crown and Crisp, 1966), the Conservatism Scale (C), the Direction of Interest Questionnaire (DIQ) and the Treatment Expectancies Questionnaire (TEQ). Each subject was also asked to outline the problems for which help was being sought and to rate them in order of severity. These were subsequently post-coded into the following complaint categories, using the following guidelines:

(a) *Interpersonal* Difficulties which are primarily related to interpersonal relationships. These could be related to expressing feelings; controlling feelings; being over-critical of others; easily hurt by others; difficulty in understanding or being understood by others;

feeling inadequate and inferior in relation to others.

(b) *Free-floating Anxiety* Feeling tense, nervous, irritable or restless for no apparent reason. The experienced distress could range from sudden panic attacks to feeling vaguely uncomfortable and keyed-up most of the time.

(c) *Depressive* Feeling depressed and pessimistic with a loss of interest in life. Associated with these feelings could be low energy, poor appetite, crying easily, self-blame for problems and suicidal attempts.

(d) *Obsessive–Compulsive* Compelled to think and engage in actions against inner resistance. The difficulties could be characterized by compulsive checking, being compelled to do things in a certain order or a certain number of times, distressed by silly pointless thoughts.

(e) *Phobic* Excessively fearful of particular objects or events, resulting in a tendency to avoid situations. The fears could relate to animals, external objects, going into open spaces, illness or death.

(f) *Somatic* Main complaints to do with bodily pain or discomfort. These could include feeling faint and dizzy, excessive sweating, muscular trouble, difficulty in keeping balance, numbness, lump in the throat, pains over heart, head, chest or back.

The complaints rated as the most severe (i.e. the primary complaints) were related to the three dependent variables of DIQ, C, and TEQ and the results are shown in Table 7.2. The scores on each of these dependent variables were subjected to one-way analyses of variance with the complaint categories as independent variables. These revealed significant main effects for primary complaint categories on DIQ ($F = 9.10$, $P < 0.001$), C ($F = 3.77, P < 0.003$) and TEQ ($F = 10.13, P < 0.001$). The Scheffe procedure (Winer, 1971) was used to compare all possible group means at the 5 per cent level of significance, for each of the dependent variables. This showed that for the DIQ, patients with interpersonal primary complaints were significantly more inwardly directed than were all other groups, with the exception of patients with depressive primary complaints. With regard to the C scale, patients with interpersonal primary complaints were significantly more 'radical' in outlook than all other groups with no other significant differences emerging For the TEQ, patients with interpersonal and depressive primary complaints had a more marked 'psychological' treatment orientation to treatment than had those with obsessive-compulsive, phobic or somatic complaints. None of the other groups differed significantly.

Table 7.2 Mean scores on the DIQ, C, and TEQ in relation to the Primary Complaint Categories

Primary Complaint Category	DIQ	C	TEQ
Interpersonal (n = 44)	17.89	35.16	29.44
Free-floating Anxiety (n = 20)	10.50	42.40	33.05
Depressive (n = 37)	13.16	43.52	31.97
Obsessive-Compulsive (n = 47)	11.73	42.11	37.59
Phobic (n = 90)	11.05	43.37	37.05
Somatic (n = 13)	10.77	43.77	37.59

The Pearson correlations between the MHQ scales and the DIQ, C and TEQ are shown in Table 7.3. These show that the DIQ is significantly correlated with the scores on the Free-floating Anxiety and Hysteria scales. The C Scale shows a significant positive correlation with the Phobic Anxiety and Obsessional scale scores and a significant negative correlation with the Hysteria scale. The TEQ shows significant positive correlations with Phobic Anxiety and Obsessional scale scores.

Although the presentation of psychological distress may be subject to many transactional influences, our evidence suggests that in our referral system, by the time patients reach a specialized treatment unit a tendency towards what Balint (1964) calls the 'organized illness' is evident. It is our contention that, in a broad sense, this complaint organization is consistently related to certain aspects of the patients' personal adjustment strategies and treatment expectancies.

These results show that patients who emphasize interpersonal difficulties when presenting their distress are also distinct in terms of their adjustment strategies. The relationship between primary complaints and treatment expectancies suggests a broad differentiation into primary complaints presented in diffused, interpersonal terms with 'psychological' expectancies, and those with a circumscribed external locus with 'medical/physical' expectancies.

There are noteworthy points of similarity and difference between the relationships of the adjustment strategies and expectancies with the primary complaint categories on the one hand, and with the MHQ symptom scales on the other. The Phobic Anxiety and Obsessional scale scores of the MHQ are significantly correlated with the TEQ and C – a relationship which is similar to that between the latter scales and the primary complaint categories. The positive correlation between the DIQ and Free-floating Anxiety on the MHQ is, however, not matched by the DIQ correlation with this complaint category. The significant relationships between the Hysteria scale and the DIQ and C do not lend

Table 7.3 Intercorrelations between the Middlesex Hospital Questionnaire and the DIQ, TEQ and C

	Free-floating anxiety	Phobic anxiety	Obsessionality	Somatic concomitants	Depression	Hysteria	Total score
DIQ	0.17*	−0.08	−0.01	−0.05	0.12	0.32***	0.12
TEQ	0.07	0.29**	0.21**	0.10	0.09	−0.04	0.16*
C	0.02	0.17*	0.14*	0.09	−0.04	−0.17*	0.05

*   p < 0.05.
**   p < 0.01.
*** p < 0.001.

themselves to clear interpretation. In part, this may be due to the non-specific nature of the Hysteria scale (Crisp, Gaynor Jones and Slater, 1978), and in part to the conceptual confusion associated with the diagnostic term of hysteria itself (Chodoff and Lyons, 1958).

The findings in this study confirm the relationship observed by Smail (1970) between the direction of interest dimension and psychic-somatic symptoms. They are also in agreement with the relationship between somatic-psychic symptoms and treatment expectancies (Overall and Aronson, 1963; Aronson and Overall, 1966). The results we have obtained point to the patient's active influence on the presentation of neurotic disorder through the relationship between personal adjustment strategies and the complaints of psychological distress. The complaint categories — 'interpersonal', 'free-floating anxiety', 'depressive', 'obsessive', 'phobic' and 'somatic', although they correspond to traditional diagnostic labels, are not regarded here as distinct types of illness, but rather as broad descriptions of behaviour. These behaviours are also considered to reflect characteristic patterns of personal organization, with which are associated distinctive attitudes, beliefs and expectations. As Smail (1978) points out:

> the patient may, so to speak, choose his 'symptoms' in accordance with his personal stance towards the world. In this respect a number of studies suggest that whether or not a patient experiences his problems as primarily psychological distress on the one hand or somatic discomfort on the other may depend upon a more generally 'psychological' or 'objective' personal orientation to the world.

By identifying coping strategies that are common to both normals and neurotics, the close relationship between health and personal styles has been brought into focus. The relationships between complaint categories, treatment expectancies and adjustment strategies have provided a means of grouping neurotic patients in a manner which is consistent with their personal assumptions. Such groupings have the advantage over traditional classificatory systems in that they take account of personal meaning and also show continuous relationships with normal patterns of behaviour.

Summary

The objective, diagnostic approach to personal distress has been shown to have many drawbacks. While transactional factors are considered to play a part in the organization of complaints, these complaints may also reflect aspects of personality, conceptualized in terms of personal adjustment strategies.

Our data suggest a broad differentiation, between patients who emphasize interpersonal difficulties and those who present complaints with an external locus (e.g. phobic or somatic). The former are inwardly directed in interest, have 'liberal' social attitudes and 'psychological' treatment expectancies; the latter are more outwardly directed in interest, have 'conservative' social attitudes and traditional 'medical-physical' treatment expectancies.

Chapter 8
Personal construing

Our position rests to a large extent on the assumption that an individual attaches meaning to his experiences in a self-consistent manner, and that his actions in a particular situation are determined by the personal meaning of that situation to him. In this respect we share common ground with Kelly (1955), whose *Psychology of Personal Constructs* is based on the notion that each individual sees the world through the 'goggles' provided by a unique, hierarchically organized system of personal constructs. Kelly regarded the building blocks of an individual's personal construct system (i.e. constructs) as 'transparent patterns or templets which he creates and then attempts to fit over the realities of which the world is composed'. They are essentially bipolar, the two poles of a construct defining a way in which some elements in the person's world are similar to each other and thereby different from others. Each construct can only appropriately distinguish between certain elements, the area of a construct's potential applicability being termed its range of convenience, while those events to which it is maximally applicable constitute its focus of convenience. When the individual finds that events cannot be fully understood because they are largely outside the range of convenience of his construct system, he experiences anxiety.

A construct, in effect, provides the individual with an avenue along which to move and, being bipolar, presents him with a choice in terms of direction of movement. Kelly's view was that the particular choice which a person makes in construing a situation is that which he feels will provide the greatest possibilities for elaboration of his construct system, with consequent enhancement of his understanding of his experience and his ability to predict events. The essentially predictive nature of personal constructs means that construing may be either validated or invalidated by events, provided these fall within the range

111

of convenience of the constructs employed. The construct system is therefore normally in a state of flux, being subject to continuous revision in response to its changing validational circumstances as the individual constantly strives to make sense of his experience. Psychological disorder represents a block in this process, being defined by Kelly as 'any personal construction which is used repeatedly in spite of consistent invalidation'. From the personal construct theory viewpoint, psychological therapy must therefore aim to set construing in motion again by opening up pathways for the elaboration of the construct system and for reconstruction.

Kelly saw the process of reconstruction as basically cyclical, and described it in terms of Circumspection — Pre-emption — Control and Creativity Cycles. In the former, there is first circumspection of the field, followed by pre-emption, in which the relevant issue is selected, and finally control, leading to choice. The Creativity Cycle 'is one which starts with loosened construction and terminates with tightened and validated construction'. For Kelly then, as for Hudson and Coan (see Chapters 5 and 6), creative psychological functioning involves phases of both openness to experience and control, both divergent and convergent thinking, both 'loose' and 'tight' construing.

As a practical application of his theory, Kelly devised the Role Construct Repertory Test (Rep Test) — a uniquely flexible method of assessing personal construing. He claimed that this test is 'more objective because it is more projective', measuring the subject's own yardsticks rather than using the experimenter's yardsticks to measure the subject. The grid form of the Rep Test allows the investigator to explore the interrelationships between an individual's personal constructs.

Many variations of the original form of grid test have been employed and many methods of analysis used (Bannister and Mair, 1968; Ryle, 1975; Slater, 1976, 1977; Fransella and Bannister, 1977). The grid has been found to be useful in elucidating the construing of individuals in a very wide range of situations, but it is its use in the field of psychological disorder and its treatment which will concern us here.

Personal construing in psychological distress

The particular manner in which a person makes sense of his experience in psychological distress, no less than in any other area of his life, would be expected to reflect his characteristic ways of construing himself and others. Thus, predominant features of his construct system would be thought to determine those aspects of his distress which he focuses upon and presents as his symptoms. Support for this argument has been provided by studies showing that patients who tend to use 'psychological', as opposed to 'objective', constructs in describing others also tend to report psychic, as opposed to somatic, symptoms (Smail, 1970; McPherson, 1972; McPherson and Gray, 1976). McPherson and Gray interpret their results as indicating that individuals who tend to construe psychologically also tend to label their bodily sensations of anxiety as psychological. These results hold for both neurotic and schizophrenic patients. In the latter group McPherson, Buckley and Draffan (1971) have shown that the patient whose 'psychological' construing is relatively structured presents symptoms with interpersonal content, while lack of structure in this construct subsystem is associated with symptoms which reflect the meaninglessness of the patient's social and emotional world. Suicide may also be interpreted as an attempt to escape from a meaningless world, and Landfield (1971, 1976) has found that suicidal attempts were made by patients whose construing of other people is unstructured and constricted. If we consider that considerable differences have been observed between individuals from different cultures in the extent to which they structure 'psychological' constructs (Leff, 1973), a possible framework is provided for the understanding of cross-cultural differences in symptomatology.

Kelly's explanation of choice behaviour would suggest that a patient chooses to construe himself as suffering from a particular symptom because this offers greater possibilities for the elaboration of his construct system, having more implications and making life more meaningful to him, than to place himself at the opposite pole of the symptom construct. Further, as Hinkle (1965) has shown that superordinate constructs (which carry the most implications in terms of other constructs) are those on which a person is most resistant to make a change in his self-concept, it follows that the patient's condition is unlikely to improve unless the number of implications of the symptom is reduced. Repertory grid studies of obese people (Mair and Crisp, 1968), stutterers (Fransella, 1970, 1972), poorly adjusted mothers (Breen, 1975), and depressives (Silverman, 1977) have supported these views. Thus, Fransella (1972) feels that for the obese woman life is meaningful as long as she is construed as fat by herself and others, whereas loss of weight might lead to such situations as sexual advances, with which her construct system is ill-equipped to deal. 'No permanent weight loss will be achieved until the meaning of being a woman of normal weight is at least as meaningful to her as being a fat woman.' Similarly, she explains stuttering as being the most meaningful way of life for the stutterer: 'a person stutters because it is in this way that he can anticipate the greatest number of events'. She has also suggested that the obsessional behaves as he does because the only tightly structured section of his construct system is that which relates to his obsessional concerns (Fransella, 1974).

A patient's choice of symptom may be further understood if the particular implications of the symptom in terms of other constructs are examined. For example, the work of Rowe (1971, 1978) with depressives suggests that in many cases their despression allows them to construe themselves as martyrs. In the grids of patients in our samples, we have also found evidence of the 'payoffs' of a patient's symptoms (Greenwald, 1973), or what Hinkle (1965) and Tschudi (1977) would term his implicative dilemmas, and we feel that it is in such aspects of construing that the essence of the patient's predicament may be revealed. For example, the 'payoffs' for the patient who was referred for treatment of his deviant sexual behaviour may have been demonstrated in his construing of 'people who are likely to commit an indecent assault' as 'people I am proud of' and who are 'confident in themselves'.

The research findings which we have discussed are consistent with the view that, rather than the patient being a passive victim of a disease process, his construing actively determines the symptoms with which he presents. While in much research the interpretation of grids has been largely on an *ad hoc* basis, a somewhat more systematic method of grid interpretation is necessary if the grid is to be regarded as a reliable and valid measure in this area. An attempt has been made by Ryle (1975) to provide a rationale in terms of object relations theory for the interpretation of features of the grids of his patients, of which he presents many examples and which he feels can provide access to unconscious mental processes. By ranking grids presented blind to him in terms of the probability that the subject was receiving psychiatric treatment, Ryle provided impressive evidence of his ability to use this framework to identify grids revealing psychopathology (Ryle and Breen, 1971). In a further study, Ryle and Breen (1972) confirmed the majority of a series of predictions of relationships between grid measures and psychological disorder, as indicated by patient status and scores on the Middlesex Hospital Questionnaire. Summarizing their picture of neurotic construing, they state that the neurotic is

> someone who sees himself as unlike others in general and unlike his
> parents in particular, who is dissatisfied with himself, who tends to

extreme judgements and operates with a less complex construct system than do normals, and who tends to construe others in ways which depart from consensual values in respect of certain attributes.

Our concern with the validity and usefulness of repertory grid technique in the investigation of psychological disorder and its treatment has also led us to examine the relationships between responses to questionnaire measures and those to a repertory grid. The sample (which we shall refer to as Sample A) consisted of thirty male and thirty-four female neurotic out-patients referred for group psychotherapy, or individual or group behaviour therapy, to clinics at Claybury and Chase Farm Hospitals. Their ages ranged from eighteen to fifty-eight years, with a mean age of thirty-two years. None were considered to be intellectually subnormal or to be showing evidence of an organic or psychotic disorder. Prior to treatment all the patients completed the Mill Hill Vocabulary Scale, the Direction of Interest Questionnaire (DIQ), the Conservatism Scale (C), the Treatment Expectancies Questionnaire (TEQ), a short form of the Symptom-Sign Inventory (SSI) (Foulds and Hope, 1968), the Hostility and Direction of Hostility Questionnaire (HDHQ) (Caine, Foulds and Hope, 1967), the Hysteroid-Obsessoid Questionnaire (HOQ) (Caine and Hope, 1967), the Neuroticism Scale (N) of the Eysenck Personality Inventory (Eysenck and Eysenck, 1964), and ratings of the intensity of their three major symptoms. They also completed a repertory grid with fifteen elements and fifteen constructs. The elements were: self as I am now; self as I would like to be; how others see me; mother; father; man I like; man I dislike; woman I like; woman I dislike; spouse or boy/girlfriend; general practitioner; therapist; person in a position of authority; person I admire; and close relative. Nine constructs were elicited from each subject using Kelly's (1955) Self-Identification Form, and asking for differences in personality between the elements. The three problems which they had specified as their major symptoms were also used as 'symptom constructs'. In addition, three constructs were supplied: 'like me in character – unlike me in character'; 'like a psychiatric patient – unlike a psychiatric patient'; and 'ill – well'. All the subjects rated each of their elements on a seven point scale with regard to each construct.

All the grids were analysed by Slater's (1972) INGRID 72 computer programme, which carries out a principal component analysis. Drawing largely on the work of Ryle and his colleagues, we selected certain aspects of the INGRID output which we considered might be indicative of psychological disorder, viz.:

Table 8.1   Correlations between repertory grid and questionnaire measures

Repertory grid measures	S–M	S–F	Sex. id.	M–F	I–P	NS	NI	Cpt I	Cpt II	SCI
Self–ideal self distance (S–1)	0.18	0.16	−0.21	0.05	−0.09	***0.59	−0.01	0.08	0.05	***0.60
Self–mother distance (S–M)		**0.33	−0.09	0.09	−0.21	**0.37	0.00	0.01	0.19	**0.30
Self–father distance (S–F)			−0.21	−0.14	(**)−0.34	***0.48	(**)−0.36	−0.13	0.20	*0.27
Sexual identification score (sex. id.)				−0.03	0.14	−0.11	0.23	−0.09	0.12	*−0.29
Mother–father distance (M–F)					*0.28	−0.08	0.07	−0.08	−0.05	−0.03
Average ideal self–parent distance (I–P)						(**)−0.34	***0.45	0.09	−0.19	−0.09
No. of elements at distance > 1 from self (NS)							−0.21	−0.01	0.01	***0.47
No. of elements at distance > 1 from ideal self (NI)								0.03	−0.06	−0.13
Size of component I (Cpt I)									***−0.42	*0.28
Size of component II (Cpt II)										−0.14
Loading of self on component I (SCI)										
Loading of self on component II (SCII)										
'Like me' – 'ill' distance (III)										
Average 'like me' – 'symptom' distance (Symp.)										

*   p = 0.05.

**   p = 0.01.

***   p = 0.001.

( )   2-tailed.

	HDHQ						SSI								
Eysenck Neuroticism scale (EPI:N)	Hysteroid-Obsessoid Questionnaire (HOQ)	Guilt (G)	Self-criticism (SC)	Projected delusional hostility (PH)	Criticism of others (CO)	Acting out hostility (AH)	Psychotic symptoms (SSI:P)	Hysterical symptoms (SSI:H)	Obsessional symptoms (SSI:O)	Neurotic depression symptoms (SSI:D)	Anxiety state symptoms (SSI:A)	Neurotic symptoms (SSI:N)	Symp.	III	SCII
0.11	−0.25**	0.05	0.18	−0.12	−0.09	−0.12	−0.12	0.01	0.24	0.10	0.13	−0.17	−0.16	−0.26•	0.12
−0.05	−0.10	−0.11	0.10	−0.12	−0.06	−0.06	−0.08	−0.11	−0.03	−0.19	0.04	−0.16	−0.10	−0.12	0.20
−0.06	−0.23	−0.09	0.13	−0.04	−0.09	0.01	−0.08	−0.13	−0.10	0.07	−0.01	0.06	0.05	−0.15	0.27*
0.00	0.03	−0.07	−0.18	−0.01	−0.14	−0.02	0.15	0.08	0.08	0.09	0.07(*)	−0.02	0.04	−0.05	0.22
0.12	0.17	0.00	−0.07	−0.09	−0.03	−0.08	−0.14	0.07	−0.03	−0.20	−0.33	−0.04	0.02	−0.07	−0.12(*)
−0.07	0.08	0.08	−0.26(*)	−0.05	−0.07	−0.05	−0.10	0.10	0.13	0.14	0.13	−0.04	0.16	0.06	−0.31(*)
0.13	−0.20(*)	−0.05	0.19	−0.17	−0.21	−0.16	0.00	0.14	0.08	−0.10	0.25	0.15	0.01	−0.29(**)	0.38***
0.03	0.31	0.07	−0.17	−0.06	−0.04	0.12	0.05	−0.20	0.00	−0.09	−0.05	−0.15	0.01	0.33	−0.05
0.21•	−0.26	0.09	0.07	0.14	−0.02	−0.14	0.24*	0.10	0.31*	0.15	0.08	0.18	−0.14	−0.09	−0.12
−0.06	0.08***	−0.07	0.07***	−0.11	0.02	−0.03	−0.08	0.18	−0.18	0.05	0.02	0.01	0.00	−0.03	0.40***
0.19	−0.43	0.12	0.33	−0.06	−0.01	−0.10	0.04	0.03	0.42***	0.03	0.24*	0.23	−0.18	−0.37**	−0.39***
−0.03	0.06	−0.16	−0.17	−0.04	−0.11	−0.13	−0.09	0.12	−0.21	−0.10	−0.10	−0.05	0.06	0.06	
−0.05	0.12	−0.13	−0.06	−0.04	−0.02	0.03	0.02	−0.15	−0.45***	−0.34	−0.25	−0.36**	0.02		
−0.21	0.17	0.03	−0.17	0.07	0.08	0.07	0.02	0.22	−0.28	0.01	−0.24	−0.23			

—   a large distance between the self and ideal self elements, reflecting low self-esteem
—   a large distance between the self and father elements, reflecting lack of identification with the father
—   a large distance between the self and mother elements, reflecting lack of identification with the mother
—   a low sexual identification score (obtained by subtracting the distance between the self and same-sex parent elements from the distance between the self and opposite-sex parent elements), reflecting cross-sex parental identification
—   a large average distance between the ideal self and parent elements, reflecting negative evaluation of the parents
—   a large distance between the mother and father elements, suggesting the operation of splitting mechanisms in construing of the parents
—   a large number of elements at a distance of one or more from the self element, reflecting construing of the self as isolated from and dissimilar to others
—   a large number of elements at a distance of one or more from the ideal self element, suggesting construing of the ideal self as isolated and unattainable
—   a low angular distance (high correlation) between constructs 'like me in character — unlike me in character' and 'ill — well', reflecting construing of the self as ill
—   a low average angular distance between the construct 'like me in character — unlike me in character' and the symptom constructs, reflecting construing of the self as highly characterized by the symptoms
—   high loading of the self element on the first and second principal components, suggesting the operation of splitting mechanisms
—   high percentage of the variance accounted for by the first and second principal components, suggesting a construct system of low complexity and the likelihood of splitting and polarization in construing of others

The correlations obtained between the grid and questionnaire measures pertaining to psychological disorder are presented in Table 8.1, while Table 8.2 indicates those variables with loadings more extreme than ± 0.3 on each of the first three factors from a factor analysis with VARIMAX rotation (Kim, 1975). Correlations were also calculated for the group psychotherapy and behaviour therapy samples separately, and these are given in Table 8.3. One of the main features

Table 8.2 Factor analysis of pre-treatment data: high loading of variables on the factors

Variables	Factor		
	I	II	III
Social class			0.35
Verbal IQ			—0.71
DIQ			—0.39
TEQ			0.76
C			0.58
SSI:N	0.85		
SSI:P	0.54		
PH	0.41		
SC	0.75		
G	0.75		
EPI:N	0.78		
S–I		0.84	
S–M		0.31	
S–F		0.34	
Sex. Id.		—0.32	
NS		0.65	
SCI		0.66	
Therapist–GP distance (T–GP)		—0.41	
Percentage of variance	20.6	19.0	14.5

which is evident on inspection of these tables is the separation obtained between the repertory grid measures and the questionnaire measures. This could be interpreted as being in keeping with the common finding in multivariate studies of the importance of method factors, as opposed to factors associated with the hypothetical constructs tapped by the measures concerned (Campbell and Fiske, 1959; Mischel, 1968). Alternatively, it could be argued that the grid is tapping areas of psychological functioning at a different level of abstraction, and one more in tune with unconscious processes, than the much more direct questionnaire methods. Only moderate relationships would then be expected between the two types of measures.

However, a number of significant, meaningful relationships do obtain between grid and questionnaire indices of maladjustment. The grid indices concerned are: construing of the self as ill and as highly characterized by the symptoms, a large distance between the self and ideal self and between the self and father elements, isolation of the self element, large first and second components, and a high loading of the self element on the first component and on the second component.

Table 8.3 Significant correlations between repertory grid and questionnaire measures in samples of group psychotherapy (GT) and behaviour therapy (BT) patients

	SSI:N		SSI:P		AH		CO		PH		SC		G		HOQ		EPI:N	
	GT	BT	GT	BT	GT	BT	GT	BT	GT	BT	GT	BT	GT	BT	GT	BT	GT	BT
S-I		0.35												0.37*		-0.36*		
S-M										(*)-0.44								
S-F											0.52**					-0.39*	0.32*	
Sex id.																	0.36*	
M-F			-0.56***													(*)0.46		
I-P												(*)-0.43				(*)0.40		
NS	0.33*										0.44					-0.36	0.47**	
Cpt I			0.35*					0.38*										
Cpt II																-0.35*		
SCI											0.40*					-0.54** / -0.35*		
SCII																	0.43**	
Ill	-0.42*				-0.50**													
Symp.											-0.42*							-0.51**

* p = 0.05.   ** p = 0.01.   *** p = 0.001.   ( ) two-tailed.

The questionnaire indices are: large numbers of neurotic and psychotic symptoms on the SSI, a high level of neuroticism, high levels of self-criticism and criticism of others on the HDHQ, and obsessoid responding on the HOQ. Contrary to expectations, construing of the ideal self as similar to the parents and to other people in general is associated with maladjusted responding on some of the questionnaire measures. This may reflect the patients' idealization of their parents and others, leading them to construe themselves in very negative terms by contrast. Another unexpected result, contrary to the findings of Teichman (1970), is the relationship of less maladjusted scoring on questionnaire measures with construing of the parents as dissimilar to each other.

Interrelationships between the grid measures also reveal that several of those features regarded as indicative of maladjustment cluster together as expected. Thus, there are two related clusters concerning construing of the self: construing of the self as dissimilar to the ideal self and as ill, and a high loading of the self element on the first component, are significantly interrelated, as are construing of the self as dissimilar to the father and mother, and isolated from the other elements in general. However, no support is provided for the finding by Ryle and Lunghi (1972) of a relationship between construing of the self as dissimilar to the parents and of the parents as dissimilar to each other. The relationships obtained with two other measures are contrary to expectations: isolation of the ideal self element and construing of the parents as dissimilar to the ideal self tend to be related to 'adjusted' scores on the other grid measures.

The total picture of construing of the self and others in the neurotic which emerges from our findings is in substantial agreement with that provided by Ryle and Breen (1972), and suggests the validity of certain general grid indices of maladjustment. However, we do not feel that a diagnostic cookbook of grid indices is desirable, as this would only serve to perpetuate the myths of nosological psychiatry. Rather, the attempt should be made to arrive at some understanding of an individual's personal construct system, with the total configuration provided by a grid being the main concern. Nevertheless, we do consider it desirable to maximize the degree to which the grid can provide a reliable and valid picture of the individual's personal construct system while minimizing the extent to which this picture is influenced by the personal construct system of the investigator. To this end, we have used the present findings as a basis for devising general guidelines for the prediction of the changes in a particular patient's construing which would be expected to be associated with therapeutic improvement. This development of the repertory grid as a measure of therapeutic outcome is described in Chapter 10.

Personal construing, personal adjustment strategies, and treatment allocation

From the personal construct theory viewpoint, the form of therapy which a patient or therapist is likely to find most meaningful, and in which his participation is most likely to be effective, would be expected to be that which is closest to the focus of convenience of his personal construct system. Similarly, the ability of patient and therapist to construe each other's construction processes might be regarded as crucial to the success of the therapeutic venture. To quote Kelly (1955), 'Rather than deplore the client's inadequate conceptualisation of psychotherapy, we need to understand his own personal construction of change if we are to help him bring about a change'.

Repertory grid studies of the interaction in psychotherapy between the personal construct systems of patient and therapist have supported this argument. Thus, evidence has been provided that a positive therapeutic outcome is more likely if the therapist understands the patient's construct system, if patient and therapist find each other's constructs meaningful, and if their construct systems are similar in content (Cartwright and Lerner, 1963; Landfield and Nawas, 1964; Landfield, 1971). By categorizing constructs in terms of their content, Landfield found that patients who used more constructs in his 'high structure' content category showed the least improvement, while lack of change during psychotherapy was associated with the use of concrete and 'high dogmatism' constructs. He also demonstrated that therapeutic improvement was accompanied by convergence of the construct systems of patient and therapist. Studies of group psychotherapy suggest that such convergence reflects a tendency for patients to 'learn the language' of the therapist (Watson, 1972; Winter and Trippett, 1977).

Such findings support the view that psychological treatment should not be regarded as a set of techniques whose application and efficacy are completely unaffected by the ways in which patient and therapist construe the therapeutic situation. It might be reasonable to assume that the constructs which the patient or therapist applies to the patient's problem and its treatment cannot be separated from those which he uses to make sense of other areas of his personal world. Representative studies of patients' construing have been considered above, but substantive research evidence on therapists is meagre. One area of research concerns the attempts which have been made (see Chapter 7) to develop objective, specialist languages of diagnostic constructs for the functional psychiatric disorders. Such constructs have indeed been found to be no more meaningful to clinicians, and to be used no more consistently by them, than lay descriptive constructs, with which they are as highly related as with each other (Agnew and Bannister, 1973; Sperber, 1977). In another study, designed to identify the relationships between psychiatrists' attitudes to treatment and other aspects of their construing, only one of the six social attitudes being measured by a repertory grid was found to relate significantly to the measure of attitudes to treatment used (Caine and Smail, 1969). In the researchers' view, more significant relationships might have been found had the grid constructs been elicited from the subjects rather than supplied to them.

In addition to treatment attitudes and expectancies, we would expect to find meaningful relationships between personal construing and the adjustment strategies which we have described in Chapters 1 and 2. Previous research has, in fact, demonstrated such relationships in that an inward direction of interest has been found to correlate significantly with construct diversity in neurotic subjects (Smail, 1970), and with empathy as defined as the ability to construe the construction processes of another person (Smail, 1972; Wood, 1977). Empathy has also been related to cognitive complexity (Adams-Webber, 1969), which Bieri (1955) has defined as 'the tendency to construe social behaviour in a multidimensional way, such that a more cognitively complex individual has available a more versatile system for perceiving the behaviour of others than does a less cognitively complex person'. An association is therefore suggested between a unidimensional construct system and external direction of interest, although an empirical study by Bieri and Messerley (1957) seems to contra-indicate this.

If the inwardly directed person is regarded as a tender-minded, radical idealist, his repertory grid would be expected to reveal dissatisfaction with the self and an isolation of the ideal self from other elements. Our previous research findings suggest that, in addition, the inwardly directed radical would be more likely to construe psychological distress in terms favourable to an interpersonal, less structured, less symptom-oriented treatment approach. As we have seen, a number of studies relating symptomatology to the content of the construct system have classified the latter in terms of the 'psychological-objective' dimension. However, we considered that a more sensitive

Table 8.4 Correlations between scores on repertory grid measures and those on the DIQ, TEQ, and Conservatism Scale in Samples A and B

Grid measures	DIQ		TEQ		C	
	A	B	A	B	A	B
S–I	0.15	−0.02	−0.05	−0.04	0.18	−0.04
S–M	0.01	0.10	−0.09	−0.07	0.01	−0.11
S–F	−0.15	−0.27(*)	−0.12	0.04	0.03	0.09
Self–opposite sex parent distance (S–OP)	−0.03	—	0.02	—	−0.01	—
Self–same sex parent distance (S–SP)	−0.10	—	−0.22	—	0.05	—
Sex. id.	—	−0.01	—	0.01	—	−0.36(**)
M–F	—	0.07	—	−0.09	—	−0.07
I–M	0.28*	—	−0.07	—	−0.11	—
I–F	0.17	—	−0.01	—	−0.01	—
I–P	—	0.08	—	−0.20	—	−0.27*
NS	0.00	−0.08	−0.18	0.02	0.12	0.08
NI	0.25*	0.24*	−0.02	−0.18	−0.21	−0.23

					*	
Cpt I	0.17	(*)0.26	0.18	−0.07	0.27	0.14
Cpt II	*−0.27	(*)−0.26	0.03	0.23	0.06	0.06
SCI	*0.27	0.09	**−0.33	0.09	−0.01	0.01
SCII	0.07	*−0.27	−0.01	0.05	0.19	0.20
III	—	0.06	—	−0.10	—	−0.04
Symp.	—	−0.12	—	−0.05	—	0.13
T-GP	—	0.12	—	−0.05	—	0.04

* $p < 0.05$.

** $p < 0.01$.

() two-tailed test.

assessment of construct content would be provided by the use of the more differentiated classification system developed by Landfield (1971).

With reference to Landfield's construct content categories, the inwardly directed patient might be more likely to describe his difficulties in terms of inactive social interaction and low tenderness — the combination of construct poles which Landfield designates as 'low social orientation', but which might more appropriately be termed deficient social interaction in such patients. His symptoms would also be less likely to be central to his self-concept. The outwardly directed patient, on the other hand, might be more likely to describe himself and his difficulties with constructs favourable to a more structured, more directive, more symptom-oriented treatment approach, involving greater dependence on the therapist. In particular, he might be more likely to see himself in terms of high organization and high involvement — Landfield's 'high structure' construct poles — and in more concrete terms, using construct poles in Landfield's Factual Description, External Appearance, and Low Imagination categories. He might also apply to himself more construct poles in the Low Self-Sufficiency category and, finally, might see his symptoms as more central to his self-concept.

We have examined these relationships in two samples of neurotic out-patients. One sample (Sample A) has been described earlier in the chapter. The other (Sample B) was similarly selected and consisted of twenty-eight males and twenty-seven females, with a mean age of thirty-one years and an age range from seventeen to fifty-eight. Prior to treatment all patients in both samples completed the DIQ, the C Scale, the TEQ, and a repertory grid consisting of fifteen elements and fifteen constructs. Every grid was analysed by Slater's (1972) INGRID 72 programme. In addition, each elicited construct was categorized on the basis of Landfield's (1971) classification system with the following modifications: the construct dimension was categorized as a whole, rather than the two construct poles separately; each construct was forced into a category; and multiple coding of a construct was not permitted, only the most pertinent category being used in each case. In Sample A the construct poles which correlated at a statistically significant level with the symptom poles were also classified, as were those which correlated significantly with the poles 'like me in character' and 'ill'. To maximize reliability with this sample, an index was kept of all the elicited construct poles, showing the categories to which they had been assigned, and this was referred to in categorizing each construct pole elicited subsequently.

The correlations in the two samples between the scores on the DIQ, TEQ, and C Scale and those on measures derived from the INGRID analysis are presented in Table 8.4, while Table 8.5 gives similar correlations for the Sample A group psychotherapy and individual behaviour therapy patients calculated separately. The somewhat inconsistent results reflect, in our opinion, the difficulties involved in using the grid for nomothetic purposes. However, our prediction of an isolation of the ideal self from the other elements in the grid in more inwardly directed patients has been confirmed in both samples. More puzzling is the

Table 8.5 Correlations between scores on repertory grid measures and those on the DIQ, TEQ, and Conservatism Scale in the group psychotherapy (GT) and behaviour therapy (BT) patients in Sample A

Grid measures	DIQ		TEQ		C	
	GT	BT	GT	BT	GT	BT
S–I	0.23	−0.07	**−0.50	0.27	*−0.38	0.22
S–M	0.17	0.15	−0.04	−0.13	−0.22	−0.14
S–F	−0.24	−0.28	0.02	0.05	−0.09	0.26
Sex. id.	−0.06	0.06	−0.06	0.14	−0.27	(**)−0.58
M–F	0.22	0.04	−0.25	0.10	0.03	−0.36
I–P	0.00	0.25	**−0.48	0.13	−0.31	−0.26
NS	0.15	−0.20	−0.21	−0.04	−0.07	0.15
NI	0.19	*0.43	−0.30	−0.17	−0.27	−0.31
Cpt I	0.04	(**)0.56	0.02	0.13	0.23	0.07
Cpt II	−0.05	(*)−0.48	0.24	0.19	−0.13	0.14
SCI	0.14	0.26	−0.22	0.32	−0.11	0.04
SCII	−0.12	−0.39	0.11	−0.12	0.14	0.18
Ill	−0.25	0.25	0.07	−0.33	0.06	−0.11
Symp.	−0.18	−0.33	0.06	0.15	0.12	0.26
T–GP	−0.01	−0.14	0.23	0.18	0.14	0.20

* p < 0.05.

** p < 0.01.

() two-tailed test.

association of an inward direction of interest with a large first component, and a small second component, from the INGRID analysis. This may, however, indicate a heightened self awareness in our inwardly directed patients as the first component of the grid tended to be concerned with construing of the self, particularly as a self-identification form of grid was used. A similar interpretation may be placed on the significant relationships concerning the loading of the self element on the components.

The results obtained on categorizing the elicited constructs in terms of Landfield's content categories are rather more impressive. The categories used are indicated in Table 8.6, which presents the percentage of constructs allocated to each category in our samples and also corresponding percentages from the studies by Landfield (1971), Fransella (1972), and Sperlinger (1976). The relative preponderance of Self-Sufficiency constructs elicited from our samples may be due to the subjects being more disturbed, and preoccupied with their need for help, than Landfield's college students, Fransella's stutterers with 'no demonstrable psychiatric disorder or psychiatric history', and Sperlinger's non-psychiatric patients, whom he found to use fewer Self-Sufficiency constructs than his 'improved depressed subjects'. Tables 8.7 and 8.8 show the relationships in Sample B between scores on the DIQ and C Scale and the numbers of elicited constructs in the categories with which we were particularly concerned, together with all those with which significant results were obtained. The only relationship which conforms with expectations is that between outward direction of interest and the use of more Factual Description constructs. One which is contrary to expectations is the use of more High Forcefulness constructs by those with more radical social attitudes. It is possible, however, that a more sensitive assessment of the content of the construct system might be obtained by only considering those construct poles which correlate significantly with the symptom poles, and with the construct poles 'like me in character' and 'ill'. The significant associations in Sample A between the numbers of such construct poles in selected content categories and scores on the DIQ, C Scale, and TEQ are therefore presented in Table 8.9. Inner direction of interest is now found to relate, as expected, to tendencies to construe illness in terms of inactive social interaction and not to construe the symptoms in terms of low self-sufficiency. Conservative social attitudes are related to construing of the symptoms and illness in terms of low self-sufficiency. A medical/physical treatment set, as measured by the TEQ, is associated with construing of the self, the symptoms, and illness in terms of low self-sufficiency, and construing of the symptoms

Table 8.6 Percentages of elicited constructs in Landfield's Content Categories in present and previous samples

Category	Landfield sample (n = 30) %	Rank	Fransella sample (n = 19) %	Rank	Sperlinger sample (n = 25) %	Rank	Winter sample (Sample A) Group therapy (n1 = 32) %	Rank	Behaviour therapy (n2 = 26) %	Rank	n1 + n2 (n = 58) %	Rank	Wijesinghe sample (Sample B)(n = 55) %	Rank
Social interaction	12	2	39.2	1	12.7	3	9.6	4	6.7	5	8.3	4	14.8	2
Forcefulness	20	1	14.6	2	14	2	15.4	1	19.3	1	16.7	1	10.4	5
Organization	6	6	2.7	11.5	5.3	7.5	7.8	5	4.7	7	6.9	5	4.7	7
Self-sufficiency	5	9.5	3.4	10	3	11	10.4	3	18.3	2	13.9	3	11.4	3
Status	5	9.5	8.4	3	7	5.5	3.1	11	1.7	12	2.5	12	1.6	13
Factual description	1	16.5	0.7	17.5	7	5.5	4.2	10	1.3	13	2.9	10	6.7	6
Intellective	5	9.5	7.8	4	2.7	12	1.8	14	4.0	8	2.8	11	3.5	10
Self-reference	0	19.5	0.0	21.5	0.3	19.5	5.5	8	3.3	10	4.5	8	4.7	8
Imagination	1	16.5	0.5	19	2	14	1.3	16	2.3	11	1.8	14	0.6	19
Alternatives	5	9.5	0.9	15	2	14	2.8	12	0.3	17	1.8	14	1.5	14
Sexual	0	19.5	0.8	16	0	21	1.3	16	0.3	17	0.9	16.5	1.3	15
Morality	6	6	3.8	9	4	10	6.3	7	6.7	5	6.4	7	4.5	9
External appearance	1	16.5	0.7	17.5	0.3	19.5	0.8	18.5	0.7	14.5	0.7	18.5	0.3	20
Emotional arousal	7	4	7.3	5	14.3	1	6.5	6	6.7	5	6.6	6	17.1	1
Diffuse generalization	–	–	2.6	13	2	14	–	–	0.3	17	1.8	14	2.0	11
Egoism	3	12.5	4.6	6.5	1.7	16	2.3	13	17.3	3	14.6	2	10.5	4
Tenderness	9	3	4.6	6.5	9.3	4	12.5	2	0.7	14.5	0.7	18.5	0.8	17.5
Time orientation	1	16.5	2.7	11.5	5.3	7.5	0.8	18.5	3.7	9	4.2	9	1.9	12
Involvement	6	6	4.5	8	0.7	18	4.7	9	–	–				
Comparatives	–	–	0.4	20	–	–	0.0	20	0.0	19.5	0.0	20	–	–
Extreme qualifiers	3	12.5	0.0	21.5	1.3	17	1.3	16	0.0	19.5	0.9	16.5	0.8	17.5
Humour	2	14	1.4	14	5	9	–	–	–	–			1.1	16
Non-classifiable	–	–	–	–	–	–	–	–	–	–			–	–

Table 8.7 Cross-tabulation of Conservatism Scale (high, medium and low values)* by construct categories for sample B (n = 55)

Construct categories	Conservatism Scale			χ^2	p
	Low (n = 17)	Medium (n = 22)	High (n = 16)		
Social interaction (active)	38 (11.95%)	17 (7.17%)	21 (8.86%)	3.75	n.s.
Forcefulness (high)	24 (7.55%)	14 (5.90%)	9 (3.80%)	6.16	< 0.05
Organization (high)	5 (1.57%)	11 (4.64%)	4 (1.69%)	6.16	< 0.05
Factual description	25 (7.86%)	10 (4.22%)	18 (7.59%)	3.32	n.s.
Tenderness (high)	23 (7.23%)	29 (12.24%)	19 (8.02%)	4.53	n.s.
Involvement (high)	5 (1.57%)	5 (2.11%)	2 (0.84%)	1.25	n.s.
Imagination (low)	4 (1.26%)	0 (0)	1 (0.42%)	3.66	n.s.

*The scores on C were recoded into high (above the 66th percentile), medium (between the 34th and 66th percentiles) and low (below the 34th pecentile).

in terms of high structure. By contrast, a psychological treatment set is associated with construing of the self, the symptoms, and illness in terms of inactive social interaction.

With regard to within grid relationships, the most relevant for our purposes are those which involve the aspects of construing most closely correlated with the DIQ, the C Scale, and the TEQ *vis-à-vis* those which have to do with the patient's view of his problems and their treatment. In the latter category, we are particularly concerned with the extent to which the patient construes himself as ill, and as highly characterized by his symptoms, and the extent to which he construes his therapist as likely to be similar to his general practitioner (and therefore, presumably, likely to employ a directive, structured, 'medical' approach). The relevant correlations, from Sample A, are presented in Table 8.10. It can be seen that, as expected, construing of the self as highly characterized by the symptoms, construing of the therapist as likely to be similar to the general practitioner, and the use of a large number of Self-Sufficiency constructs are highly interrelated. Patients who construe the therapist as dissimilar to the general practitioner also show a high level of dissatisfaction with themselves. Those who construe themselves

Table 8.8 Cross-tabulation of Direction of Interest Questionnaire (high, medium and low values)* by construct categories for Sample B ($n = 55$)

	Direction of Interest Questionnaire				
Construct categories	High ($n = 17$)	Medium ($n = 21$)	Low ($n = 17$)	x^2	p
Social interaction (active)	28 (11.38%)	33 (10.58%)	17 (7.26%)	2.42	n.s.
Organization (high)	10 (4.06%)	4 (1.28%)	6 (2.56%)	4.35	n.s.
Factual description	5 (2.03%)	18 (5.77%)	30 (12.82%)	23.05	<0.0001
Emotional arousal	43 (17.48%)	63 (20.19%)	29 (12.39%)	6.21	<0.05
Tenderness (high)	14 (5.69%)	34 (10.90%)	23 (7.37%)	6.81	<0.05
Involvement (high)	3 ((1.2%)	4 (1.28%)	5 (1.60%)	0.64	n.s.
Imagination (low)	1 (0.41%)	2 (0.64%)	2 (0.85%)	0.37	n.s.

*The scores on the DIQ were recoded into high (above the 66th percentile), medium (between the 34th and 66th percentiles) and low (below the 34th percentile)

as ill, and who use a large number of Self-Sufficiency constructs are more likely to see their ideal selves as attainable, although construing of the self as ill tends to be associated with construing of the actual and ideal selves as dissimilar. The only measure with which relationships are generally contrary to expectations is the loading of the self element on Component One, high values of which are associated with construing of the self as ill and the use of a large number of Self-Sufficiency constructs.

We have therefore identified certain features of construing which appear to differentiate personal adjustment strategies reflecting 'inner' and 'outer' orientations and to influence the way in which patients construe their distress and its treatment. These same features of the patient's construing, partly by virtue of their effect on the manner in which he presents his distress, can also be expected to influence the clinician's decisions regarding the patient's treatment allocation. It has been possible to test this hypothesis by examining the differences in construing in Sample A between the patients clinically assigned to group psychotherapy and those assigned to individual behaviour

Table 8.9 Significant χ^2 values for associations in Sample A between DIQ, TEQ, and C scores and the content of construct poles applied to Self, Symptoms, and Illness

Content Category		DIQ	TEQ	C
Inactive social interaction	Self		*** 10.86	
	Symptoms		*** 32.70	
	Illness	* 3.18	* 4.94	
Low self-sufficiency	Self		* 4.02	
	Symptoms	** 3.44	*** 19.32	*** 19.30
	Illness		* 4.68	* 3.41
High structure	Self			
	Symptoms		* 3.25	
	Illness			

* p < 0.05.
** p < 0.01.
*** p < 0.001 (all one-tailed tests).
———— = inverse association.

therapy. Table 8.11 indicates the differences in pre-treatment scores on the INGRID measures and it can be seen that, as expected, the group psychotherapy patients identify themselves less strongly with their symptoms, and see their therapist as less likely to be similar to their general practitioner, than do the behaviour therapy patients. In addition, they see themselves as more similar to other people, and therefore perhaps more suited to an interpersonally oriented treatment approach, although this difference falls just short of significance (p = 0.08) on allowing for the difference in verbal ability between the two groups.

Table 8.12 presents the significant associations between treatment allocation and the content of the constructs elicited from the patients. The major differences between the two treatment groups are, indeed, on those content categories which we have related to adjustment strategies and treatment expectancies. Thus, as expected, the behaviour therapy patients produce more Self-Sufficiency constructs and are more likely to construe themselves and their symptoms in such terms. The

Table 8.10 Correlations between selected repertory grid meaures in sample A

Grid Measure	NI	S–I	Symp.	III	SCI	SS	Soc.	T-G.P.
No. of elements at distance > 1 from ideal self (NI)		−0.01	0.01	0.33**	−0.13	−0.28*	−0.08	0.01
Self-ideal self distance (S–I)			−0.16	−0.26 (*)	0.60***	0.15	−0.04	−0.41***
Average 'like me' – 'symptom' distance (symp.)				0.02	−0.18 (**)	−0.28*	−0.04	0.29*
'Like me' – 'ill' distance (ill)					−0.37	−0.17	0.21	−0.04
Loading of self on Component I (SCI)						0.36 (**)	0.01	−0.22
No. of self-sufficiency constructs (SS)							−0.17	−0.29*
No. of social interaction constructs (Soc.)								0.10
Therapist – GP distance (T–GP)								

* $p < 0.05$.

** $p < 0.01$.

*** $p < 0.001$.

() two-tailed test.

Table 8.11 Differences between pre-treatment scores of group psychotherapy and behaviour therapy patients on the repertory grid in sample A

		S-I	Sex.id.	S-M	S-F	M-F	I-P	NS	NI	T-GP	Cpt I	Cpt II	SCI	SCII	III	Symp.
Small group therapy	Mean	1.26	1.00	1.06	1.06	0.87	1.07	8.97	5.38	0.69	47.20	21.13	0.83	0.54	78.83	68.44
	sd	0.32	0.29	0.32	0.24	0.35	0.29	3.36	1.88	0.28	10.62	5.75	0.47	0.38	18.95	16.76
Behaviour therapy	Mean	1.39	1.08	1.10	1.12	0.84	1.03	10.68	5.28	0.46	44.26	22.76	0.91	0.73	76.20	59.13
	sd	0.25	0.37	0.27	0.26	0.34	0.26	2.48	2.01	0.21	7.73	4.61	0.51	0.48	31.94	18.70
	t	1.59	0.92	0.44	0.86	0.27	0.54	2.13	0.18	3.45	1.16	1.16	0.68	1.63	0.36	1.89
	df	55	54	54	54	53	54	55	55	55	55	55	55	55	49	50
	p	0.12	0.36	0.66	0.39	0.79	0.59	0.037	0.86	0.001	0.25	0.25	0.50	0.11	0.36	0.032
		2-tail	2-tail	2-tail	2-tail	2-tail	2-tail	2-tail	2-tail	1-tail	2-tail	2-tail	2-tail	2-tail	1-tail	1-tail

Table 8.12 Significant χ^2 values for associations in Sample A between treatment allocation and the content of total constructs elicited and those applied to self, symptoms, and illness

Content category	Group psychotherapy				Behaviour therapy			
	Total	Self	Symptoms	Illness	Total	Self	Symptoms	Illness
Low self-sufficiency					*** 14.88	** 6.08	* 3.27	
High involvement						** 7.52	** 8.71	
Low organization			* 10.29	* 4.80				
Inactive social interaction			** 5.64	* 3.78				
Low tenderness			*** 11.58				** 7.06	
High tenderness								
Self-reference			*** 9.25					
Low humour			* 4.91					
Alternatives	(*) 5.11							
Factual description	(*) 4.09							

* p < 0.05;   ** p < 0.01.   *** p < 0.001.   ( ) two-tailed test.

expected findings are also obtained with the construct poles concerning high and low structure as the behaviour therapy patients see themselves and their symptoms more in terms of high involvement, and their symptoms and illness less in terms of low organization, than the group psychotherapy patients. In addition, the results with the construct poles concerning 'deficient social interaction' are as predicted, for the group psychotherapy patients see their symptoms and illness more in terms of inactive social interaction, and their symptoms more in terms of low tenderness, than the behaviour therapy patients. They also associate more Self-Reference constructs with their symptoms, possibly reflecting their heightened self-awareness, and see their symptoms more in terms of low humour. The finding that the group therapy patients use more constructs in the Factual Description category is contrary to expectations but is based on a very small number of constructs, the elicitation procedure for this sample not encouraging the production of such constructs.

The patients in this sample were therefore being allocated to the treatments which, in terms of the content of their construct systems, they might have been expected to find most meaningful. These relationships between patients' construing and their treatment allocation may have been in large part mediated by the clinician's perception of their presenting symptoms, for the latter did appear to reflect the predominant content of their construct systems. Thus, the behaviour therapy patients tended to present with more clear-cut, circumscribed symptoms, perhaps revealing their preoccupation with 'high structure' constructs, together with symptoms involving dependence on others. By contrast, the group psychotherapy patients tended to present with much more diffuse symptoms, and particularly with difficulties in social interaction.

Summary

Evidence has been presented that neurotic disorder is reflected in certain characteristics of the individual's construing of himself and others, as measured by a repertory grid. Further, we have found that the patient's use of distinctive constructions of his distress and therapy is associated with his allocation to a particular form of psychological treatment. Our findings suggest that these constructions have a basis in more general patterns of construing, which reflect the individual's typical adjustment strategies.

The patient with an inward direction of interest, radical social attitudes, and 'psychological' treatment expectancies (who in our situation tends to be allocated to group psychotherapy) is characterized by the following features of construing:

1   he construes his situation in terms of deficient social interaction;
2   his ideal self is isolated and unattainable;
3   he does not identify strongly with his presenting symptoms;
4   he expects his therapist to be different from his general practitioner.

The patient with an outward direction of interest, conservative social attitudes, and 'medical/physical' treatment expectancies (who in our situation tends to be allocated to behaviour therapy) exhibits the following pattern:

1   he construes his situation as implying:
    (a) dependency;
    (b) a high degree of structure;
2   his ideal self is relatively less isolated;
3   his presenting symptoms are central to his self-concept;
4   he anticipates a 'medical' treatment approach in that he expects his therapist to be like his general practitioner.

Chapter 9
Small group psychotherapy and behaviour therapy: therapeutic assumptions

In the foregoing chapters, we have largely focused on characteristics of patients and staff which we have found to be relevant to treatment ventures. These characteristics are also reflected in the assumptions that underlie therapeutic systems, thus providing a basis for matching patient, therapist and treatment. Therefore, before we can discuss our results on treatment outcome, we need to make explicit the distinctions we make between therapeutic assumptions, more particularly those between small group psychotherapy and behaviour therapy.

The conceptual shift in phenomena previously subsumed under the rubrics of religion and witchcraft to that of mental illness is generally regarded as a matter of scientific progress. An advertent attempt has been made to portray psychiatry as a medical speciality, linked to a concept of science as objective and morally neutral. Within this framework socially unacceptable behaviour has been labelled 'abnormal' and then categorized into the 'signs' and 'symptoms' of supposedly pathological processes or disease entities. For about two centuries now, psychiatrists have struggled to identify these pathological processes, their nature and origin. The results so far are inconclusive, and there is very little agreement either within the medical profession or among social scientists on any of the issues concerning the causes and treatment of functional 'mental illness'.

It is therefore gratifying to note that some soul searching has begun within psychiatry, especially in the last two decades. One of the most prominent critics of the concept of mental illness and institutional psychiatry has been Thomas Szasz (1967) who argues:

> It is customary to define psychiatry as a medical speciality concerned with the study, diagnosis and treatment of mental illnesses. This is a worthless and misleading definition. Mental illness is a

myth. Psychiatrists are concerned with mental illnesses and their treatments. In actual practice they deal with personal, social and ethical problems in living.

Szasz says that using the concept of mental illness for 'problems in living' is both scientifically and politically unacceptable:

the notion of a person 'having mental illness' is scientifically crippling. It provides professional assent to a popular rationalisation, namely that problems in human living experienced and expressed in terms of bodily feelings or signs (or in terms of other 'psychiatric symptoms') are significantly similar to diseases of the body. It also undermines the principle of responsibility, upon which a democratic political system is necessarily based, by assigning to an external source (i.e. the 'illness') the blame for anti-social behaviour. We know that for the individual patient this precludes an enquiring, psychoanalytic approach to problems which 'symptoms' at once hide and express. Codifying every type of occurrence that takes place in a medical setting as, ipso facto, a medical problem makes about as much sense as suggesting that when physicists quarrel their arguments constitute a problem in physics.

As the cracks are beginning to appear in the scientific facade it is becoming increasingly clear that psychiatric practice is as much a matter of social and moral judgments as of scientific. Initially the primarily moral nature of treatment was recognized, and early psychiatric institutions such as the Bicêtre and the Salpétrière in France were known both as hospitals and prisons. Pinel (1801), for example, emphasized that the fundamental principle in treatment was in fact moral:

The extreme importance which I attach to the maintenance of order and moderation in lunatic institutions, and consequently to the physical and moral qualities requisite to be possessed by their governors, is by no means to be wondered at, since it is a fundamental principle in the treatment of mania to watch over the impetuosities of passion, and to order such arrangements of police and moral treatment as are favourable to that degree of excitement which experience approves as conducive to recovery.

Today this moral principle has been cloaked with the dignity of scientific truth, while the principles of treatment have not changed since Pinel. The ethics of long-term incarceration in mental hospitals, the 'flattening' of recalcitrant thoughts and emotions with tranquillizers, electroshocks and leucotomy and the gentle persuasion to conform to the modal instructions of the representatives of established society are never questioned, as these are supposed to be 'medical' problems. With the strait-jackets, padded cells, anti-spasmodics and locked wards becoming crude symbols of the past, there is an air of benign humanitarianism about the psychiatric hospital. In fact the psychiatrist armed with shock-box and major tranquillizer is even feeling safe enough to take the madman to the community at large. In this ostensibly meliorative trend within psychiatry there is a very subtle message. It can be argued that modern techniques under the guise of 'advances in treatment' are actually becoming increasingly effective in serving the basic homeostatic function of maintaining dominant cultural values and thus in keeping political order. As Szasz (1971) points out, 'the concept of mental illness serves the same social function in the modern world as did the concept of witchcraft in the late Middle Ages', which, he suggests, 'enables the "sane" members of society to deal as they think fit with those of their fellows whom they can categorize as "insane"'.

Therefore it seems mock-heroic that Western psychiatrists should be concerned because their colleagues in the Soviet Union label political dissidents as paranoids with 'reformist delusions' and incarcerate them in mental hospitals, when they themselves are frequently engaged in social regulation and institutional control. In saying this we are not attempting to condone the practices in the Soviet Union, but to highlight the moral dilemma in this respect of those working in the psychiatric field. This point has been made forcibly by Hallick (1971), and Clare (1976) has discussed Szasz's ideas in relation to general psychiatry, leaving aside, however, their implications for the more specific problems of psychotherapy and behaviour therapy.

Apart from psychiatry, the discipline that has had the most influence on the treatment of psychiatric patients is psychology. Just as psychiatry has used the 'medical model', psychology has modelled itself on the natural sciences. In the search for scientific prestige, it can be argued, the values and assumptions of a now outmoded concept of science as the repository of ultimate truth are still accepted uncritically by certain influential schools of psychology. The moral implications of this particular stance have been expressed by Bannister (1973):

psychologists have mimicked the natural sciences, or more particularly the intellectual and physical paraphernalia of the natural sciences. They have developed a premature technical jargon, over-valued electronic apparatus, contracted counting fever and, as objects of study, have often favoured the neurone, the wood louse or the computer, over man. There has been a monstrous study of trivia because trivia allows for a point by point imitation of the concrete procedures of the natural science experiment.

Many of the major issues which should concern us have been neglected because they do not readily yield to the mechanical application of such a format. Above all, the vision of psychology as an 'objective' science has blinded psychologists to the fact that their discipline is inevitably awash with moral and political issues. To take the most obvious and central: if we say the object of science is prediction and control and we note that the subject matter of psychology is human beings, then we are in effect saying that we wish to engage in the prediction and control of people. This statement can hardly be regarded as 'objective' or devoid of moral and political implications.

The inescapable truth that psychiatrists and psychologists have to face is that their disciplines form an integral part of cultural and political processes, and are very largely fashioned and shaped by prevailing social attitudes. This, though it may seem to be a radical point of view, is one which even medical orthodoxy, as represented by the editors of the *British Medical Journal* (29 September 1973), has accepted:

> psychiatrists should be aware of associations between their social attitudes and the treatments they use. Disagreements too between psychiatrists about efficacy of various forms of treatment are not based on reason alone. They stem in part at least from deeper roots.

The principal argument we present here is that the treatment of the 'mentally ill', rather than having a 'scientific' basis, is largely dependent on the assumptions and value judgments of the theorists, and the social, cultural and political forces which were operative at the time of their formulation. Rychlak (1968) has stated that psychiatric and psychological schools are either extraspective or introspective. The former disregards personal meaning and explains a person's distress with reference to an external framework. The latter attempts to deal with such distress with the subject's own frame of reference. Wijesinghe (1978) has elaborated this distinction by reference to the assumptions relating to (a) the nature of disorder; (b) the nature of the treatment process; and (c) the patient–therapist relationship. On this basis he has suggested that the major orientations to treatment could be ordered along a broad spectrum. At one end of this spectrum are those approaches to treatment which make generalizations about behaviour and deal with it in an objective, mechanistic manner with regard to the patient–therapist relationship, and in which the therapist's approach to the patient is authoritative and impersonal, while the patient views the therapist as a skilled expert to be treated with deference. At the other end of the spectrum are those approaches to treatment which attempt to understand and explain a person's distress within his own frame of reference. The major emphasis in treatment is placed on the therapeutic relationship, where the individuality and autonomy of the patient is emphasized, and the patient and therapist relate to each other on mutual terms.

We suggest that such a treatment spectrum reflects to a considerable extent the essential underlying 'social/political' nature of the therapeutic alliance. As we have discussed in Chapters 3, 4 and 6, the attitudes and personalities of health care professionals, members of the general public, and psychiatric patients tend to show a polarization into those who are 'outer directed' in interest with 'conservative' social attitudes on the one hand and those who are 'inner directed' with 'radical' social attitudes on the other. Our research evidence has indicated that the former favour organic or behavioural forms of psychiatric treatment, and the latter psychotherapeutic or sociotherapeutic forms.

Our concern here is with small group psychotherapy which, in general, we class as introspective, and behaviour therapy, which we identify as extraspective. However, as we shall see, the former may show a wide range of underlying relationship assumptions some of which appear to lie closer to the extraspective end of Rychlak's treatment spectrum.

Small group psychotherapy

A wide variety of group techniques have currently gained acceptance in the psychiatric setting, and as such can all be termed therapeutic groups. The common features of these techniques are that they involve multi-person interaction situations, guidance from a leader, and the objectives of symptom relief with relevant attitude and personality change.

The First World War provided a great impetus to the development of group psychology and similarly, since the end of the Second World War, there has been a growing involvement with group psychotherapy. Anthony (1972) points out that the relationship between these group movements and war is not entirely accidental:

> In war, individual man is forced into groups of all sizes and structures for reasons of survival. In war, he loses much of his identity and becomes better known for fighting, rationing and security purposes as a number. The understanding and maintenance of group morale becomes a critical factor in the country's struggle for existence.

It is therefore significant that in Britain, some of the more important ideas in the development of small group psychotherapy came from the Northfield Army Neurosis Centre in Birmingham, during the war. These led to Bion's (1961) leaderless selection group and Foulkes's (1964) group-analytic method.

A further reason for the rise of group ideologies is based on the growing consensus of opinion that 'mental illness' is a reflection of social and political disorder and, as Frank (1948) has argued, society itself may be regarded as the patient with treatment directed towards the group and not the individual.

Caine (1965b) has outlined a number of factors which may have contributed towards the shift from the traditional doctor–patient relationship on a one-to-one basis to that of the multi-person group situation:

1   Growing dissatisfaction with individual psychotherapy, both in terms of substantiated results and in terms of failure to cope with the sheer mass of the problem,

2   The emphasis of such neo-Freudian writers as Fromm (1943), Horney (1951) and Sullivan (1953) on interpersonal relations and cultural factors in neurotic breakdown,

3   The recognition of the deleterious effects on mentally ill patients and on staff of authoritarian institutional regimes (Martin, 1955, 1962; Barton, 1959),

4   The application of social scientific theory to psychotherapy (Foulkes and Anthony, 1957),

5   The increasing recognition of the importance of social experience in learning and communication processes in psychiatry, education and other fields (Jacques, 1951; Johnson, 1953; Anthony, 1953; Martin, 1962).

The term group therapy covers a very wide range of techniques, each having its own assumptive system, so that it is clearly impossible to consider it as a uniform approach to treatment. The defining features of group psychotherapy have been identified by Foulkes and Anthony (1957) as (a) that the group relies on verbal communication; (b) that the individual member is the object of treatment; (c) that the group forms the main therapeutic agency.

Our concern here is with psychotherapy conducted in small groups (i.e. seven to ten members), which is the most commonly practised form of group psychotherapy in Britain. While a number of attempts have been made to classify small group psychotherapy, no generally accepted system exists. This is in part due to the rapid rise and decline of different group practices and in part due to the large number of variables that are encompassed by the group situation. However, taking the more important approaches to small group psychotherapy, it is possible to classify groups broadly into those based on psychoanalytic principles and those which are non-psychoanalytic in nature.

1 Psychoanalytic approaches

For the most part such group therapy approaches are based on concepts derived from individual psychoanalysis. Clearly Freud's theories have had a revolutionary effect not only on psychology and psychiatry, but on the whole fabric of human thought. Nevertheless, as Brown (1961) notes, it was Freud's method of approaching psychological problems, rather than any really new discoveries, that brought about this transformation. Freud's theories were formulated in an era in which the dominant values of Western society were determined by scientific materialism. Nineteenth century science had taken a great leap forward: the laws of conservation and transformation of energy in physics and Darwin's theory of natural selection in biology were notable advances. The concept of the unconscious, which, according to psychoanalytic theory, plays a predominant part in mental activity, had featured in the writings of Herbart, and the philosophies of Schopenhauer, Spinoza and von Hartmann. These influences of nineteenth-century philosophy and science, and Freud's own medical training, led to his fervent belief in rationalism and his emphasis on the scientific nature of his theories.

Freud attached enormous importance to the manner in which sexual and aggressive instincts were expressed during the early years of life. The oral and anal stages, the oedipal situation and the later phallic stage were considered to be all crucial milestones in the development of the individual personality. Neurotic symptoms were seen as a function of unconscious attempts to deal with instinctual conflicts arising in the early years of life. A central feature of the psychoanalytic treatment method is the uncovering of connections between repressed drives and symptoms. As the contents of the unconscious cannot of necessity be consciously reported by patients, Freud felt he had found an access to this material through the involuntary drift of the free associations of the patient as well as through the contents of his dreams. A basic assumption in the psychoanalytic treatment process is that a patient's current perceptions, particularly those developed in relation to the therapist (the transference), are projections of unresolved feelings in relation to 'significant others' in his early life.

In later years Freud (1959) began to move away from a purely individually based psychology, placing a greater emphasis on the psychology of the group. In the subsequent application of basic psychoanalytic principles to group treatment, however, many variations and themes have been developed. A major divergence has arisen between those who see the multi-person situation as a convenient way of individually psychoanalysing a number of patients at the same time and those who argue that all psychoanalytic principles must be modified when applied to the group situation. In following this line it is possible to distinguish psychoanalytic small group methods from the group-analytic method of treatment.

(a) Psychoanalytic small group methods
Wolf (1975) has maintained that bringing several individuals together should in no way alter the treatment of the individual patient. He undertakes 'psychoanalysis in groups' based on the four basic treatment principles of dream interpretation, free association, analysis of resistance and transference. Wolf and Schwartz (1962) have argued that the group situation permits a much deeper level of exploration than individual analysis, and that resistance is dealt with more quickly in the group situation. The therapist is seen as a responsible authority figure who sets the tone of the group meeting, leads the patients in the pursuit of unconscious material, helps them to overcome resistance and interpret transference feelings. Slavson (1964), who refers to his method as analytic group psychotherapy, places emphasis on the individual patient, and considers synergy or group cohesion to be a destructive force in the treatment of the individual patient. He identifies the therapeutic process as 'a conditioned reality, planned and structured by the

therapist'. In Britain, a further variation in psychoanalytic group methods follows the work of Bion (1961), who draws a parallel between the development of the group and stages of infantile development. The group is accordingly considered to pass through three phases, namely, (1) dependency — attempts to make the leader behave omnipotently; (2) fight-flight — finding solutions by escape or conflict; (3) pairing — pairing between group members, all of which are influenced by unconscious wishes of the members and organized in relation to the leader. These psychoanalytic group methods of treatment attempt to maintain the traditional two person pattern of individual analysis. The therapist adopts an impersonal, unobtrusive role which, it is maintained, stimulates projection of feelings derived from infantile relationships. The transference relationship remains the primary focus in therapy, and the therapeutic effects are largely considered to hinge upon the interpretation of these feelings and their subsequent resolution.

(b) The group-analytic method

The group-analytic method developed by Foulkes (1964) from the work in the Northfield Experiment, has common ground with psychoanalysis in its general clinical and theoretical orientation. However, we suggest, there appears to be a definite shift in emphasis from the dynamics of the individual patient and therapist to the dynamics of the group. Two levels of interaction in the therapeutic process may be identified: at an unconscious level, transference phenomena can be manifested and utilized therapeutically; at a more superficial level, difficulties in the process of communication itself and the relationships developed between the patient members of the group may become the focus of therapy, with an emphasis on 'here and now' transactions. The therapist's function is seen by this school as both supportive and analytic. In these activities the therapist does not assume active leadership, but follows the lead of the group as its instrument. It would appear from this that in the group-analytic attempt to integrate the dynamics of the individual with those of the group, the therapeutic alliance has undergone considerable modification. The therapist-centred structure inherent in traditional psychoanalysis would appear to have been replaced by a more autonomous role as far as the patient is concerned.

2 Non-psychoanalytic approaches

By non-psychoanalytic approaches to group psychotherapy we mean treatment based on one of several different theoretical systems, all of which have moved away from the intra-psychic focus of Freudian theory. A common assumption in such therapies is that mental disorder stems from distortions in perception, improper social learning and inadequate social development. A major emphasis in the treatment process is on reality confrontation, so that the group work is primarily with the manifest content. The therapist's role is to act as a 'real person', while the patient is given full autonomy in the therapeutic transactions.

Two major influences may be discerned in the shift from intra-psychic factors to outer, social and environmental ones. First, the socio-political doctrine of Karl Marx pointed to the essential dialectic between the individual and his society. Marx argued that the individual's consciousness is conditioned by society, just as society is influenced by the individual. Second, the impact of cybernetics, based on the idea of information exchange, has led to conceptualizing the individual organism as an 'open' system in dynamic interaction with the environment. The initial impact of these influences was seen in the writings of the neo-Freudians, Horney (1951) and Fromm (1943). They rejected some of the principal tenets of Freudian theory, such as the oedipus complex, the anatomical basis of the psychological differences between the sexes and the inevitability of the stages of libido development. Instead, they stressed the importance of interpersonal relationships and socio-cultural factors.

A radical change in traditional attitudes and a redefinition of the patient's role is seen in some of the theoretical systems that have made a complete break with Freudian theory. In such therapies the patient is seen not as a carrier of disease, but as a source of positive value to himself and others, including the therapist, with whom he is involved in the treatment venture. The two non-psychoanalytic systems that we will be concerned with here, are the client-centered group psychotherapy of Carl Rogers and the existential approach to group psychotherapy. While the theories concerned were not exclusively designed for group psychotherapy, their emphasis on social learning make them particularly adaptable for this purpose.

(a) Client-centered group psychotherapy

Rogers (1961) has argued that man is essentially a trustworthy and constructive being, whose psychological disorder or incongruence (i.e. a person being vulnerable or anxious) is caused by inadequate or improper social learning. While he accepts the possibility of past experiences modifying current perceptions, he contends that all motivations and emotions that are effective are in the 'here and now'. He considers that the full potential for change resides within the client, so that he is of positive value to himself, his fellow patients and even to the therapist. The group situation is expected to provide a safe climate where members can begin to explore their incongruencies and the urgings of their inner feelings and experiences. Thus, the therapeutic process is basically experiencing new and more accurate perceptions and the recognition of significant relationships between perceptions. Through this process the client becomes increasingly aware of his true feelings and also 'congruent' in the relationship with the therapist. In client-centered groups each member is responsible for himself, determining what he will talk about and setting his own pace. Rogers (1961) has identified empathy, warmth and genuineness as the most important personal attributes for the therapist. Meador (1975) has recognized three similar attitudes which help to establish a group climate in which the growth potential of the members will be released, namely, the experiencing and expression of one's own reality; the caring for persons in the group, with a respect for their uniqueness; and a 'deeply sensitive non-judgemental understanding'.

(b) Existential group psychotherapy

In existential psychotherapy patients are considered to be suffering from disturbed modes of being in the world, resulting in isolation, alienation and an inability to communicate meaningfully. In patients with psychological disorder, the capacities of openness, receptivity and responsiveness are considered to be distorted or blocked to varying degrees (Hora, 1975). The main therapeutic aims are for the patient to accept his anxieties and discover 'authentic' modes of existence. This, he says, is best achieved by a free expression of thoughts and feelings, leading to an unburdening of defensive strivings. The group process is considered to consist of a phase of self-discovery followed by increasing self-understanding, which then leads to a phase of experimentation in learning to let go of defensive strivings. The therapist's role in existential group psychotherapy is not to evaluate, judge or interpret, but to meet his patients in an existential encounter. Thus, Hora (1975) says, 'The existential psychotherapist does not try to "do" psychotherapy, he lives it.'

In the main the therapeutic alliances in the non-psychoanalytic approaches to small group psychotherapy would appear to be on a mutual, non-hierarchical basis. The personal qualities of both the patient and the therapist are considered to be more important than technical skills, procedural arrangements, or 'expert' knowledge. The proliferation of various forms of small group psychotherapy is an indication of the highly contentious nature of the assumptions underlying this method of treatment. Thus, there are major differences in opinion on both theoretical and practical issues, between the psychoanalytic and non-pscychoanalytic group therapists, just as there are differences within these groups.

As we have seen from previous chapters, there is no general agreement on issues such as the selection of patients for a group or the number and composition of a group. Most practitioners have based their selection on factors such as age, intelligence, social class, diagnosis, etc., without taking into account the patient's own expectations and assumptions. The failure to acknowledge and utilize constructively these beliefs and assumptions may well underlie some of the traditional problems associated with group therapy, such as high rates of premature termination and the non-realization of group goals.

The transference is still held by psychoanalytic group therapists to be the most central feature in the treatment process. Nevertheless, as Mischel (1973) points out, clinicians have not been able to demonstrate the 'very high degree of underlying cross situational generality' which is assumed by the transference. There is also very little agreement as to what constitutes an effective therapeutic approach, opinion varying from that which favours a neutral, detached attitude (Mowbray and Roger, 1963) to that favouring a spontaneous, self-revealing approach (Jourard, 1964).

As small group psychotherapy is frequently a long drawn out procedure, it is often difficult to establish that any changes taking place in patients undergoing therapy are in fact due to the treatment rather than to extra-group influences, spontaneous remission, or simply to the passage of time. These difficulties, together with the limited results suggested by published outcome studies of small group psychotherapy (Malan, Balfour, Hood and Shooter, 1976), pose a serious challenge to the assumptions underlying this form of treatment.

Our principal concern here is on the extent to which assumptions underlying a given method of group therapy match the personal assumptions of the patient, particularly with regard to the therapeutic alliance. In this respect, within small group psychotherapy, we can identify a range of assumptions which can be related to the personal adjustment strategies and expectancies that we have discussed in this book. The psychoanalytic small group methods, due to Freud's particular view of science, have retained a reductionist, mechanistic infra-structure in which the patient–therapist relationship is non-mutual and impersonal. The group-analytic method shows a definite shift toward a more flexible, 'democratic' approach with an attempt to incorporate the therapeutic properties of the group itself, which include social learning, mutual support, and sharing. However, it is in the non-psychoanalytic approaches that we have discussed that a truly open and equal therapeutic alliance is seen, which best characterizes the introspective treatment model.

Behaviour therapy

Behaviour therapy, as a designation, covers a heterogeneous collection of techniques which have evolved from learning theory and behaviourism in psychology. Although behaviourism has been a force from the early part of this century, its systematic application to psychiatric problems dates from approximately the 1950s. Brown (1961), commenting on the birth of behaviourism, points out that the extreme environmentalism which it embodies is characteristic of new or post-revolutionary societies. These societies, he argues, are committed to the belief:

> that men are naturally good, are born free and equal with almost infinite potentialities, and that therefore whatever troubles they suffer must be due to social and environmental factors rather than to individual ones. Stemming from John Locke and Rousseau, this belief passed to the United States by way of Jeffersonian democracy and to the Soviet Union by way of Marx, whose dictatorship of the proletariat was, of course, to be succeeded by a Rousseauesque classless society; it is therefore not surprising to find that both these countries shared in the birth of Behaviourism (which rejects 'original sin' in the form of innate ideas).

Seaborn Jones (1968) maintains that the scientific ideology to which behaviourism is so dedicated may have been a result of the success enjoyed by nineteenth-century physics and the relative lack of development of academic psychology during this period. In keeping with the belief that scientific procedures such as quantitative measurement and controlled experiments were the key to success, the physiological studies of Pavlov were subsequently used as a basis for developing a treatment model.

Watson's behaviourist framework was based largely on mechanical laws of learning, with the exclusion of heredity, instinct and unconscious factors. Watson's ideas have proliferated and Breger and McGaugh (1965) now identify three different theoretical positions, namely: (1) those ideas of Dollard and Miller which hinge on Hullian learning theory; (2) those based on the classical conditioning theories of Watson and Pavlov as represented by Wolpe and Eysenck; and (3) those ideas based on Skinner's instrumental conditioning theory.

While the first position has stimulated a great deal of experimental work on animals, it has failed to generate any distinctive techniques of clinical relevance. The Wolpe–Eysenck position has led to the development of a number of techniques such as systematic densitization, aversion therapy, and covert sensitization which have been mainly applied to neurotic disorders. The Skinnerian ideas have led to the development of operant conditioning schedules and token economy programmes, which have had particular clinical relevance to the problems of chronic psychotic and mentally handicapped patients.

In the aetiology of neurotic behaviour, Wolpe (1958) has argued, symptoms result from the conditioning of anxiety responses to otherwise neutral stimuli. For example, phobic disorders (with which the behaviour therapists have had notable success) are explained on the basis of an association between a phobic object and anxiety, giving rise to the phobic avoidance pattern. Thus the neurosis is equated wholly with the symptoms and no place is given to unconscious factors in its genesis or maintenance. In a broader formulation Skinner (1953) says that all psychiatric symptoms could be considered as operant responses arising from inappropriate reinforcement, which has prevented satisfactory adjustment.

Following from the assumption that the disorder is confined to observable symptoms, the treatment process is concerned exclusively with the removal of symptoms. Wolpe (1958) put forward the principle of 'reciprocal inhibition', which involves producing a response antagonistic to anxiety in the presence of an anxiety evoking stimulus, and so extinguishing the maladaptive pattern. Thus, in systematic desensitization, a widely practised behaviour therapy procedure, the patient is taught to relax and then helped to tolerate a hierarchy of graded fear situations. The relaxed response is considered to inhibit the anxiety associated with the phobic stimulus, by counter-conditioning.

Skinner (1953) has developed operant conditioning programmes as a basis for modifying maladaptive behaviour. Such programmes are based on the assumption that maladaptive patterns can be erased and acceptable patterns reinstated by systematic reinforcement. Cigarettes, sweets or any other rewards which the patient appreciates are made contingent upon 'acceptable' target behaviours, with these rewards being denied if 'unacceptable' behaviours occur.

In emphasizing the scientific nature of the techniques, the importance of the patient-therapist relationship has been largely ignored. Wolpe (1954) argued that the patient-therapist relationship played no part in the treatment. Similarly, in operant conditioning, the therapist is seen as a manipulator of behaviour by using rewards and punishments (Krasner, 1961), but not in any way personally involved in the treatment process. The therapist has been referred to as a 'reinforcement machine', and attempts have been made to replace him with an automated machine in the treatment proceedings.

Although there is evidence to show that behaviour therapy techniques can be relatively quick and effective in dealing with a variety of psychiatric disorders, there is little support for the argument that the success of these techniques is related to the theoretical and experimental background on which they are purportedly based. Smail (1978) has drawn attention to the weakness of the behaviour therapist's theoretical position:

> Where there is no consciousness, no purpose, there can be no meaning, no values. How can the behaviour therapist decide what to do when he is, on his own theory, no more than the helpless result of his reinforcement history — how, indeed, can he account for his own behaviour as subject-scientist when only objectivity is possible? He can only do so, of course, because he shuts his eyes to those aspects of his activity which fail to fit in with his scientific philosophy; he ignores his own experience, distorts that of others, and ends up as a kind of psychological fraud.

Taking the principle of reciprocal inhibition where, according to Wolpe (1954), the response of muscular relaxation is considered to inhibit the anxiety eliciting stimulus, Breger and McGaugh (1965) point out that the use of terms stimulus and response in this context

> are only remotely allegorical to the traditional use of these terms in psychology. The 'imagination of a scene' is hardly an objectively defined stimulus, nor is something as general as 'relaxation' a specifiable or clearly observable response . . . counter-conditioning is no more objective, no more controlled and no more scientific than

classical psychoanalysis, hypnotherapy or treatment with tranquilizers.

Breger and McGaugh further observe that many of the published cases of Wolpe and other proponents of the behaviourist viewpoint are described in terms of interpersonal conflicts and complex cognitive strategies rather than in terms of stimuli and responses, an inconsistent departure from their theoretical position.

There is a growing body of evidence which raises the possibility of conceptualizing the main treatment effects in terms of the subject's attitudes and expectancies, rather than on the basis of conditioning principles. Marcia, Rubin and Efran (1969) have produced evidence to show that the expectancies of patients are related to symptom change by systematic densitization. Leitenberg, Agras, Barlow and Oliveau (1969) have demonstrated the combined effectiveness of 'instructions' and 'praise' in increasing the efficacy in the desensitization of snake phobics. However, Oliveau, Agras, Leitenberg, Moore and Wright (1969) were able to show that while the 'instructions' had a significant effect on the improvement of snake phobics, 'praise' given after successful imagination of hierarchy items did not have a similar effect.

Although many behaviour therapists have considered the therapeutic relationship to be unimportant to the treatment process, we argue that it plays a very central role in treatment. The expertise and skill, both for the formulation and execution of a behavioural programme resides with the therapist, the patient being directed and guided to an explicitly stated goal. In this alliance, the therapist very clearly has control over the situation and the patient depends on his authoritative direction. It is this aspect which makes behaviour therapy a distinctively extraspective approach to treatment.

Summary

We have argued in this chapter that psychiatric and psychological approaches to treatment are based on the assumptions and value judgments of theorists and clinicians which, in turn, are related to the social and political influences of the time. Following Rychlak (1968), we have distinguished between introspective and extraspective approaches to treatment. We have argued that small group psychotherapy, with its emphasis on emotional and personal issues, may be classed generally as introspective. Nevertheless, within this treatment approach, there exists a wide range of underlying assumptions, some closer to the extraspective end. By contrast, the assumptions underlying behaviour therapy show typical extraspective features, where the treatment is based on reductionist, mechanistic principles and conducted in an objective, impersonal manner. The ultimate value of these assumptions for therapeutic transactions, we maintain, depends on the extent to which they are congruent with the personal adjustment strategies and treatment expectancies of the individual patient.

Chapter 10
Treatment outcome

Over a quarter of a century has now passed since Eysenck (1952) arrived at his much quoted conclusion that the available studies of the outcome of psychotherapy

> fail to prove that psychotherapy, Freudian or otherwise, facilitates the recovery of neurotic patients. They show that roughly two-thirds of a group of neurotic patients will recover or improve to a marked extent within about two years of the onset of their illness, whether they are treated by means of psychotherapy or not.

While it could be argued that Eysenck was faced with a dearth of acceptable, well-controlled studies at the time of his review, subsequent research has not caused him to alter his position (Eysenck, 1965) or Rachman (1972) to arrive at any fundamentally different conclusions in a book which Eysenck (1978) regards as 'a classic in the literature'. Similarly, despite an orientation more sympathetic to psychotherapy than those of Eysenck and Rachman, Truax and Carkhuff (1967) also claim that

> If all the studies on outcome were to be averaged on the basis of the number of clients involved, it is clear that the overall results would be close to zero effect beyond that observed in comparable clients not receiving counseling or psychotherapy.

However, Meltzoff and Kornreich (1970) are critical of earlier reviews and more optimistic about the weight of evidence in favour of the efficacy of psychotherapy:

> In short, reviews of the literature that have concluded that psycho-therapy has, on the average, no demonstrable effect are based upon

an incomplete survey of the existing body of research and an insufficiently stringent appraisal of the data. We have encountered no comprehensive review of controlled research on the effects of psychotherapy that has led convincingly to a conclusion in support of the null hypothesis. On the contrary, controlled research has been notably successful in demonstrating significantly more behaviour change in treated patients than in untreated controls. In general, the better the quality of the research the more positive the results obtained.

Central to Eysenck's argument is his assertion that spontaneous remission is observed in two thirds of untreated neurotic patients over a two year period, but this estimate has not gone unchallenged (e.g. Kiesler, 1966; Malan, Bacal, Heath and Balfour, 1968; Bergin, 1971). Even if the occurrence of spontaneous remission is accepted, this would not *per se* argue against the capacity of psychotherapy to provide relief from neurotic disorder, for the processes which are operative in spontaneous remission may be essentially the same as those which operate in successful therapy. There has also been criticism of Bergin's (1966) explanation of the unimpressive findings of psychotherapy outcome research as merely indicating the null 'average therapeutic effect' which would be obtained by lumping together cases which improve and those which deteriorate as a result of the same powerful therapeutic processes. May (1971) and Shapiro (1975) question Bergin's selection of the evidence and the methodological adequacy of the studies which he cites, while Yalom (1971) suggests that the results of these studies may reflect the invalidity of the assumption that positive change on the outcome measures employed is unidirectional for all patients.

The assumption of unidirectionality of positive outcome for different patients is an example of the many 'uniformity myths' that have plagued the area of research on psychotherapy (Kiesler, 1966). Only relatively recently has the trend of research been towards greater specification of patient, therapist, therapy, and outcome variables and away from assuming the homogeneity of each of these groups. For example, the samples of patients and the control groups studied have often been heterogeneous and their composition either inadequately described or bearing little relation to the population with which the therapy concerned is used clinically. However, there is sufficient evidence to reach the hardly surprising conclusion that treatment response is not independent of the characteristics of the person being treated (Garfield, 1971). The most consistent research results are with actuarial variables, such as social class, and provide a picture of the 'good psycho-therapy patient' as someone whose background is similar to that of the typical therapist.

There has also been a rather cavalier approach in outcome research to the selection of the therapists who carry out the treatments under study, and Bergin and Strupp (1972) point out that many of these are 'neophytes who often fail to merit the appellation "therapist"'. Although doubts have been cast on the methodological adequacy of the studies which attempt to identify the characteristics of the 'good therapist' in terms of such dimensions as the rather obscure A–B categorization or the Rogerian triad of accurate empathy, non-possessive warmth, and genuineness (Bednar and Mobley, 1971; Shapiro, 1976), such studies do at least suggest that the qualities of the therapist are not irrelevant to the determination of treatment outcome. One major shortcoming of much research is a tendency to ignore the fact that therapy is an interactive process whose components can only artificially be con-sidered in isolation. For example, it would be a unique therapist who could be genuinely warm with all his patients.

Another set of variables which needs to be specified in an investiga-tion of treatment outcome consists of those defining the nature of the treatment under study, for psychotherapy in its generic sense subsumes a very wide variety of therapeutic techniques. However, despite the claims of proponents of these various techniques, large-scale reviews of comparative studies have found little difference in improvement rates between different therapies (Meltzoff and Kornreich, 1970; Robach, 1971; Luborsky, Singer and Luborsky, 1975). Luborsky *et al.* do suggest some differences between particular techniques. In their evaluation of research reports they arrive at the following conclusions: pharmacological agents appeared to be more effective than psycho-therapy, but a combination of both approaches was superior to either taken separately; psychotherapy combined with an appropriate medical treatment was indicated for psychosomatic conditions; and behaviour therapy was regarded as the treatment of choice for phobic states. Chesser (1976) feels that research findings also support the effective-ness of behaviour therapy methods in the treatment of sexual devia-tions, compulsive disorders, and 'undesirable behaviour' in chronic schizophrenics, and it appears that the common feature of the com-plaints which are most appropriately treated by behaviour therapy is their circumscribed nature. The Luborsky *et al.* review indicates that group and individual psychotherapy are generally found to be equally effective. However, the common observation that about one third of patients offered group psychotherapy drop out of treatment within the first twelve sessions (Yalom, 1966) makes the refinement of selection criteria for this form of treatment a matter of prime importance. The importance of treatment expectancies in this regard is indicated by studies which associate positive outcome in group therapy with preparation for therapy or previous experience of individual psychotherapy (Bednar and Lawlis, 1971; Malan, Balfour, Hood, and Shooter, 1976).

Lewis and McCants (1973) feel that 'disappointing results are inevitable from research in group psychotherapy which defines patient problems, the process of individual change, and the outcome of treatment in disparate units of measurement and ignores the necessity for idiographic diagnostic and outcome measures'. This is a criticism which is pertinent not only to most studies of group psychotherapy — a notable exception being that by Malan and his colleagues — but to outcome research generally. Many studies have employed multiple outcome criteria, but consistency is lacking in the results obtained on the basis of different criteria, and predictors of change on one measure have not been found to predict change on another. Similarly, factor analysis of the results tends to yield factors associated more with the methods of measurement used than with any higher-order conceptual variables (Cartwright, Kirtner, and Fiske, 1963). Bergin (1971) concludes from his review that 'divergent processes are occurring in therapeutic change, that people themselves embody divergent dimensions or phenomena, and that divergent methods of criterion measurement must be used to match the divergency in human beings and in the change processes that occur within them'. In particular, he recommends the inclusion in outcome studies of measures tapping both the domain of external behaviour and that of subjective experience, for it has been suggested that conflicting research findings may be due to an invalid assumption of the equivalence of these two types of measures (Truax and Carkhuff, 1967; Malan, 1973). That different levels of change may be associated with different therapies is suggested by Caine and Smail's (1969) finding that while patients treated in a therapeutic community setting showed changes in symptoms, attitudes, and personality, patients subjected to a predominantly physical treatment regime were found to have changed only at the symptom level at follow-up. Nevertheless, in many studies choice of outcome measures does not seem to be indicated by their relevance to the focus of therapeutic attack. Our concern with the development of an appropriate outcome measure for our studies of group psychotherapy and behaviour therapy has led us to examine these issues further.

An individualized measure of treatment outcome

In his review, Bergin advocates the tailoring of outcome criteria to the individual patient rather than, as in many studies, assuming that change on a particular dimension is necessarily an indication of positive outcome for every patient. As well as therapeutic change not being unidimensional for all patients, it is also not unidirectional, and several authors have made the point that the direction of desirable therapeutic change on an outcome dimension is dependent on the patient's initial position on that dimension (Yalom, 1971). An appropriate instrument for the assessment of therapeutic outcome is therefore one which combines objectivity in scoring with an approach which is sufficiently idiographic and flexible to allow individualized outcome measures to be derived from it. It should also be sensitive to those aspects of psychological disorder which the therapies under study aim to modify. We consider that the repertory grid fulfils these requirements. Being derived from a theory which emphasizes the uniqueness of the individual, it allows the measurement of dimensions of therapeutic change which are of personal relevance to the patient and, as we have seen in Chapter 8, it is able to reveal aspects of construing, at different levels of awareness, which are indicative of psychological disorder. At its most straightforward, it can be used as a symptom measure, by providing indices of the relationships between a self element or construct and constructs describing the patient's symptoms, while it has been claimed that, in much less direct fashion, it can also tap aspects of construing at the level of unconscious processes.

The repertory grid literature contains many single case studies of changes in construing during individual psychotherapy, and some of these suggest that the nature of such changes is predictable and that a pre-treatment grid assessment could indicate the optimal focus of therapeutic attack (Crisp, 1964; Mair and Crisp, 1968). Ryle has adopted this approach with a series of patients. On the basis of clinical impressions and an initial grid assessment he has defined the aims of treatment for each individual in terms of changes in grid scores and in ratings of the 'dilemmas, traps, and snags' which limit their construing of themselves and others (Ryle and Lunghi, 1969; Ryle 1975, 1979). The extent of such changes during therapy, he maintains, reflects the degree of clinical improvement. Ryle also examined the degree of change in his patients in those features which (as discussed in Chapter 8) he had found to characterize the grids of neurotics and, while the results were not entirely consistent, more positive changes on these variables occurred in the grids of the most clinically improved patients than in the remainder.

A number of studies have also demonstrated the sensitivity of the repertory grid to aspects of the therapeutic process in group psychotherapy, suggesting its usefulness as an outcome measure for this form of treatment (Watson, 1970, 1972; Fransella and Joyston-Bechal, 1971; Caplan, Rohde, Shapiro, and Watson, 1975; Ryle and Lipshitz, 1976; Wijesinghe and Wood, 1976). Changes in grid scores have been examined in relation to treatment outcome in encounter groups and therapy groups for alcoholics (Lieberman, Yalom, and Miles, 1973; Heather, Edwards, and Hore, 1975; Hoy, 1977). While feeling that 'the presence of intelligible consistent patterns between grids' and the relationships between grid data and other variables in their research provides an indication of the validity of the grid in this area, Caplan *et al.* provide the cautionary reminder that their analyses are of an essentially *post hoc* nature and that 'the method of *post hoc* interpretation which has sometimes been used to infer "dynamic" changes from grids . . . is notoriously untrustworthy'. The necessity of predictive grid studies of therapy is therefore highlighted and, as in the work on individual therapy, attempts have been made to devise individualized predictions of the changes in construing which will occur during successful group psychotherapy. Thus, desirable changes in construing have been indicated by the patients themselves (Fielding, 1975) and by the therapists on the basis of the patients' initial grid and interview (Dresser, 1969; Morris, 1977). In their study of an out-patient psychotherapy group, Winter and Trippett (1977) also made individualized predictions of successful outcome in grid terms on the basis of inspection of the first grid completed by each patient. These were compared with general predictions applied to each patient, which were largely based on Ryle and Breen's (1972) description of characteristics of 'neurotic construing' (see Chapter 8). Significantly more individualized than general predictions were confirmed at post-treatment assessment so that support was provided for the position that outcome criteria should be tailored to the individual patient.

One of the major deficiencies in the Winter and Trippett study was the lack of an independent measure of change other than therapist ratings, so that no general conclusions could be drawn as to the validity of the grid as a measure of the changes which actually occurred during therapy. The authors also suggest that a clear rationale for making the individualized predictions would have been desirable, and that it might have been possible to devise a more appropriate set of general predictions. Our development of the repertory grid as an outcome measure has led us to attempt to correct these deficiencies. To this end, from Sample A (described in Chapter 8) the first ten men and ten women accepted for group psychotherapy, and similarly for behaviour therapy, were selected for follow-up. They were serially reassessed on a repertory grid (consisting of the same elements and constructs as at the pre-treatment assessment together with any new elicited constructs which the patient felt to be important), the Symptom-Sign Inventory (SSI), the Hostility and Direction of Hostility Questionnaire (HDHQ), the Hysteroid–Obsessoid Questionnaire (HOQ), the Eysenck Neuroticism Scale (N), and symptom ratings three months after commencement of treatment and at six month intervals therafter for as long as they were willing to participate in the research. At termination of treatment, their therapists rated their degree of change in each of the areas of presenting symptoms, general social functioning, and intrapersonal functioning.

Individualized predictions were made of changes in each patient's grid which might be conducive to less disturbed intra- and inter-personal functioning. In addition, a set of general predictions was made of breakdown in those aspects of construing which we have listed in Chapter 8 as possibly indicative of maladjustment (excluding the size of the first two principal components and including the correlation between constructs 'like me in character – unlike me in character' and 'like a psychiatric patient – unlike a psychiatric patient'). A further set of predictions of change in construing, referred to as the extremity control predictions, was made on the basis of the hypothesis that for each patient there would be a decrease in the extremity of all construct correlations or element distances whose extremity was initially high. The criteria of extremity were arbitrarily chosen as (1) construct correlations at or below the 5 per cent level of significance, and (2) element distances of an extremity representing an occurrence of 5 per cent or less in a sample of grids analysed by the M.R.C. service (Slater, 1972).

The percentage of each set of predictions confirmed for each patient at the assessment following the termination of their therapy was computed. Use of the Wilcoxon test to compare these sets of percentages provides support for the hypothesis that significantly more individualized than general predictions are confirmed ($z = 6.14$; $p = < 0.001$; one-tail), while the hypothesis that significantly more individualized than extremity control predictions are confirmed is rejected ($z = 0.57$; not significant; one-tail). Thus, although the findings of Winter and

Trippett in support of individualized outcome measures have been replicated, there remains the possibility that the success of the individualized predictions may merely have been a reflection of the fact that the great majority of these predictions were of a decrease in the extremity of some grid measure, and that the content of the particular measure concerned may therefore be irrelevant. Such a reduction in the 'extremity' of a person's construing could, of course, in itself be indicative of positive therapeutic outcome (Hamilton, 1968; Chetwynd, 1977).

This issue is clarified when the relationships between the success of the three sets of grid predictions and the degree of change in other measures is considered. While confirmation of both the individualized and the general grid predictions tend to be highly associated with changes considered to be positive on other measures, this is not the case with the extremity control predictions. Similarly, on dividing the patients into 'improvers' and 'non-improvers' on the basis of their degree of change on those measures which defined the major dimensions of therapeutic change (see Table 10.1), it is found that in the former group significantly more individualized than extremity control predictions are confirmed ($t = 41$; $n = 18$; $p = < 0.05$; one-tail), while in the latter this is not the case ($t = 40$; $n = 13$; not significant). It would appear, therefore, that while there is a tendency for regression to the mean in serial grids administered during therapy, such changes bear little or no relationship to increase in the psychological adjustment of the person completing the grids and are therefore of no value as outcome criteria. In order to make grid predictions which do have some bearing on therapeutic outcome, it is necessary to take into account the content of the grid measures concerned. The process of making individualized grid predictions in effect consists of an integration of the processes of making general and of making extremity control predictions. From the set of measures which the predictor feels to be relevant to psychological maladjustment, those measures on which scores exceed a certain criterion of extremity in a particular individual's grid are selected and a decrease in their extremity predicted.

The individualized predictions in the present study, as in that by Winter and Trippett, were made on an *ad hoc* basis and are therefore subject to the criticism that, based as they are on the interaction between the construct systems of predictor and patient, they are not amenable to replication. An attempt was therefore made to categorize retrospectively all the individualized predictions used in the present study as a preliminary to developing general guidelines for making

Table 10.1 Criteria for improvement ratings

Improvement rating*		+3	+2	+1	0	-1	-2	-3
Self-ideal self distance	Change	<-0.4	-0.21 to -0.4	-0.01 to -0.2	0.00	+0.01 to +0.2	+0.21 to +0.4	>+0.4
Self-mother distance		<-0.4	-0.21 to -0.4	-0.01 to -0.2	0.00	+0.01 to +0.2	+0.21 to +0.4	>+0.4
Average ideal-parent distance		>+0.4	+0.21 to +0.4	+0.01 to +0.2	0.00	-0.01 to -0.2	-0.21 to -0.4	<-0.4
% age of individualized grid predictions confirmed		90.1 to 100	70.1 to 90	50.1 to 70	50.0	30.1 to 49.9	10.1 to 30	0 to 10
SSI : total symptoms	Change	<-10	-6 to -10	-1 to -5	0	+1 to +5	+6 to +10	>+10
EPI : neuroticism		<-10	-6 to -10	-1 to -5	0	+1 to +5	+6 to +10	>+10
HDHQ : hostility		<-10	-6 to -10	-1 to -5	0	+1 to +5	+6 to +10	>+10
Therapist's rating of change		14 to 15	12 to 13	10 to 11	9	7 to 8	5 to 6	3 to 4

*Patients receiving a total, composite improvement rating of 6 or above on these measures were designated as 'improvers'; the remainder were designated as 'non-improvers'.

Table 10.2 The individualized grid predictions: percentages confirmed

Type of prediction	Number	Percentage confirmed		
		Total	Improvers	Non-improvers
(a) Element distances:				
(i) decrease in distance between self and ideal self	38	74.2	95.0	36.4
(ii) decrease in distance between self and father	18	64.3	75.0	50.0
(iii) decrease in distance between self and mother	21	64.7	81.8	33.3
(iv) decrease in distance between ideal self and father	22	58.8	37.5	75.0
(v) decrease in distance between ideal self and mother	16	50.0	50.0	50.0
(vi) decrease in distance between mother and father	20	43.8	55.6	37.5
(vii) decrease in distance between self and spouse	1	N	N	N
(viii) decrease in distance between ideal self and therapist	1	100.0	–	100.0
(b) Increase in Sexual identification score	19	61.5	66.7	50.0
(c) Relationships between elements and constructs:				
(i) increase in angular distance between self element and symptom pole of symptom construct	87	71.6	82.7	56.0
(ii) increase in angular distance between self element and 'low desirability' construct pole	85	88.6	97.9	73.1
(iii) decrease in angular distance between self element and 'low desirability' construct pole	2	N	N	N
(iv) increase in angular distance between father element and 'low desirability' construct pole	2	100.0	100.0	100.0
(v) increase in angular distance between mother element and "low desirability' construct pole	4	25.0	–	25.0
(vi) increase in angular distance between therapist element and 'low desirability' construct pole	1	100.0	–	100.0

(d) Sum of squares accounted for by self element:				
(i) decrease	16	90.9	100.0	80.0
(ii) increase	1	100.0	—	100.0
(e) Increase in variation about mean of self construct	4	75.0	66.7	100.0
(f) Construct correlations:				
(i) increase in angular distance between construct pole 'like me' and symptom pole of symptom construct	41	80.6	91.3	64.3
(ii) decrease in angular distance between construct pole 'like me' and symptom pole of symptom construct	2	50.0	—	50.0
(iii) increase in angular distance between construct pole 'like me' and 'low desirability' construct pole	44	89.5	96.4	80.0
(iv) decrease in angular distance between construct pole 'like me' and 'low desirability' construct pole	3	N	N	N
(v) increase in angular distance between symptom pole and 'high desirability' construct pole	22	85.7	77.8	100.0
(vi) increase in angular distance between 'low desirability' and 'high desirability' construct poles	11	81.8	100.0	50.0
(vii) increase in angular distance between symptom pole and 'low desirability' construct pole	24	73.7	76.9	66.7
(viii) change towards social consensus in a relationship between construct poles	21	87.5	92.3	66.7
(g) Decrease in variation about mean of construct associated with pathology	1	100.0	100.0	—
(h) Increase in construct mean of symptom construct	3	N	N	N
(i) Average 'z' score from conversion of construct correlations to 'z' scores:				
(i) decrease	9	50.0	66.7	33.3
(ii) increase	2	0.0	0.0	0.0

N = No follow-up data available.

such predictions. The classification presented in Table 10.2 indicates the number of predictions falling into each category, as well as the frequency of confirmation of each type of prediction, both in the total sample and in the 'improvers' and 'non-improvers' separately. Lack of confirmation of a prediction could be due to one of three reasons: faulty choice of the measure, change in the predicted direction on the measure not being associated with increased psychological adjustment; the use of too lenient a criterion of a pathological score on the measure; or the fact that the patient concerned has not improved. The predictions which received least confirmation, those of a decrease in the distance between ideal self and parent elements, and between mother and father elements, appear to fall into the first category, as they are also those for which the relationships between pre-treatment position on the measure and that on other measures are contrary to expectations (see Chapter 8), and whose confirmation tended to be associated with deterioration on other measures (see Table 10.3). The predictions concerning change in our measure of rigidity of construing (arrived at by converting the first fifteen constructs in a patient's grid to a 'z' score and averaging all the 'z' scores thus obtained) also lack strong confirmation, but this may be due to methodological factors. In the case of the predictions, also relatively unsuccessful, of an increase in initially low sexual identification scores, it would appear that it was not the choice of measure, but rather the choice of the criterion of pathologically low scoring, that was inappropriate. If the cut-off point for classification of a sexual identification score as pathological is somewhat reduced, the ratio of confirmed to disconfirmed predictions using this measure is much improved. While precise guidelines can be provided for predictions of change in some measures, such as element distances, the predictions concerning changes in relationships between constructs and elements or other constructs contain a greater subjective element on the part of the predictor. Thus, some of these predictions involve a judgment of the desirability of the characteristics described by a construct or of the degree of social consensus of a relationship between constructs. Nevertheless, such predictions do receive a high level of confirmation in our study, and we feel that they concern fundamental aspects of the patient's improvement. Their nature is more fully described by Winter (1979).

We are now in a position to amend the classification of individualized grid predictions presented in Table 10.2 in order to produce a set of guidelines for the making of those predictions whose validity as outcome criteria has been supported in the research described. It is suggested that the researcher wishing to derive outcome predictions from inspection of a patient's pre-treatment grid should scan the grid in the areas indicated in the list below, which is not considered exhaustive. He should then select those features which exceed his criterion of extremity, which will depend on the confidence with which a particular prediction is made. The measures are as described in Chapter 8.

(a) Element distances:
(i) if the distance between the self and ideal self elements is initially high, this distance will decrease;
(ii) if the distance between the self and ideal self elements is initially low, this distance will increase;
(iii) if the distance between the self and father elements is initially high, this distance will decrease;
(iv) if the distance between the self and mother elements is initially high, this distance will decrease.

(b) Sexual identification score: if this score is equal to or less than −0.20, it will increase.

(c) Relationships between elements and constructs:
(i) if there is a low angular distance (i.e. high relationship) between the self element and the symptom pole of a symptom construct, this distance will increase;
(ii) if there is a high angular distance between the self element and the symptom pole of a symptom construct, this distance will decrease;
(iii) if there is a low angular distance between the self element and a 'low desirability' construct pole, this distance will increase;
(iv) if there is a very high angular distance between the self element and a 'low desirability' construct pole considered to be descriptive of psychological distress, this distance will decrease;
(v) if there is a very low angular distance between the father element and a 'low desirability' construct pole, this distance will increase;
(vi) if there is a very low angular distance between the mother element and a 'low desirability' construct pole, this distance will increase.

(d) Sum of squares accounted for by the self element: when this sum of squares is initially very high, it will decrease.

(e) Variation about the mean of the self construct: when this score is initially very low, it will increase.

Table 10.3 Correlations between Change Scores

	Gen. pred.	Con. pred.	S-IC	S-MC	S-FC	Sex. id. C	M-FC	I-PC	NSC
% age of individualized grid predictions confirmed (Ind. pred.)	*☆ 0.50	0.05	*** 0.70	* 0.38	* 0.36	0.08	−0.17	(*) −0.34	** 0.43
% age of general grid predictions confirmed (Gen. pred.)		−0.19	*** 0.63	** 0.46	0.27	0.20	0.19	−0.22	☆* 0.47
% age of extremity control grid predictions confirmed (Con. pred.)			−0.25	0.17	0.01	0.08	−0.03	−0.08	−0.32
Change in self-ideal self distance (S-IC)				*** 0.58	0.26	0.10	−0.16	(*) −0.35	*** 0.65
Change in self-mother distance (S-MC)					0.16	0.12	(*) −0.31	(***) −0.58	* 0.35
Change in self-father distance (S-FC)						−0.02	−0.17	−0.24	0.27
Change in sexual identification score (Sex. id. C)							−0.08	(**) −0.46	0.16
Change in mother-father distance (M-FC)								* 0.34	−0.20
Change in average ideal-parent distance (I-PC)									(**) −0.48
Change in no. of elements at distance >1 from self (NSC)									
Change in no. of elements at distance >1 from ideal self (NIC)									
Change in no. of symptoms (SSIC)									
Change in symptom ratings (SRC)									
Change in hostility (HC)									
Change in direction of hostility (DHC)									
Change in acting out hostility (AHC)									
Change in criticism of others (COC)									
Change in projected delusional hostility (PHC)									
Change in self-criticism (SCC)									
Change in guilt (GC)									
% age of individualized HDHQ predictions confirmed (H. pred.)									
Change in neuroticism (EPI: NC)									
Therapist rating (TR)									
Duration of therapy (Dur.)									

* $p = 0.05$
** $p = 0.01$
*** $p = 0.001$
()   two-tailed.

NIC	SSIC	SRC	HC	DHC	AHC	COC	PHC	SCC	GC	H. pred.	EPI:NC	TR	Dur.
-0.06	0.33*	0.47**	0.30	-0.18	0.21	0.33*	-0.07	0.13	0.18	0.15	0.39*	0.37*	0.20
0.10	0.36*	0.47**	0.23	0.07	0.15	0.07	0.12	0.30	0.14	0.05	0.30	0.26	0.04
-0.19	0.00	0.27	0.05	-0.34	0.13	0.21	-0.18	-0.34	0.08	0.19	0.04	0.01	0.05
0.25	0.42**	0.48**	0.37*	0.14	0.40*	0.05	-0.05	0.34☆	0.20	0.19	0.47**	0.34*	0.07
-0.01	0.16	0.41	0.00	-0.26	0.29	-0.01	-0.23	-0.11	0.07	-0.04	0.14	0.34☆	0.00
-0.39(*)	0.05	0.28	0.36*	0.21	-0.04	0.21	0.16	0.31	0.19	0.00	0.17	0.35☆	0.24
0.01	-0.16	0.02	0.33*	0.02	0.18	0.25	-0.10	0.20	0.06	0.27	-0.09	-0.25	-0.13
0.11	0.03	-0.25	-0.01	0.20	-0.19	-0.06	-0.14	0.12	0.26	-0.08	-0.09	-0.05	-0.06
0.29	-0.09	-0.32	-0.41(*)	0.05	-0.44(*)	-0.20	0.14	-0.20	-0.15	-0.27	-0.28	0.00	0.31*
-0.06	0.33*	0.19	0.58***	0.32*	0.49**	0.17	-0.18	0.57***	0.19	0.10	0.47**	0.09	-0.07
	-0.11	-0.26	-0.13	-0.12	-0.04	-0.15	0.40*	-0.09	-0.26	0.03	-0.13	-0.23	-0.01
		0.52***	0.31*	0.16	0.20	-0.11	0.02	0.27	0.50*	0.22	0.60***	0.33**	-0.04
			0.22	0.22	0.08	0.11	-0.11	0.25	0.22	0.28	0.47**	0.36*	0.02
				0.40*	0.33*	0.46**	-0.10	0.73***	0.55***	0.62***	0.62***	0.03	-0.13
					-0.03	-0.19	0.16	0.80***	0.45**	0.47**	0.31*	-0.07	-0.02
						-0.08	-0.22	0.04	0.18	0.18	0.29	0.04	-0.33
							-0.21	0.10	-0.12	0.28	0.08	-0.11	-0.03
								-0.13	-0.19	-0.09	-0.02	-0.33	-0.04
									0.46**	0.50**	0.59***	-0.03	-0.05
										0.44**	0.48**	0.35*	-0.01
											0.43*☆	-0.22	-0.18
												0.22	-0.21
													0.41**

(f) Construct correlations:
   (i) if there is a low angular distance between the symptom pole of a symptom construct and the construct pole 'like me in character', this distance will increase;
   (ii) if there is a high angular distance between the symptom pole of a symptom construct and the construct pole 'like me in character', this distance will decrease;
   (iii) if there is a low angular distance between a 'low desirability' construct pole and the construct pole 'like me in character', this distance will increase;
   (iv) if there is a very high angular distance between a 'low desirability' construct pole and the construct pole 'like me in character', this distance will decrease;
   (v) if there is a low angular distance between the symptom pole of a symptom construct and a 'high desirability' construct pole, this distance will increase;
   (vi) if there is a low angular distance between a 'low desirability' and a 'high desirability' construct pole, this distance will increase;
   (vii) if there is a low angular distance between the symptom pole of a symptom construct and a 'low desirability' construct pole, and if the relationship between these constructs is considered inappropriate, the distance will increase;
   (viii) any other relationship between constructs which is considered non-consensual will change in the direction of social consensus.

In our study, no attempt was made to tailor predictions of change in scores on the questionnaire measures to the individual patient, except in the case of the HDHQ. Degree of confirmation of the individualized predictions on this measure did not differ significantly from that of general predictions, applied to each patient, of decrease in hostility and intropunitiveness ($z = 1.27$; not significant; one-tail). This would appear to be due to the homogeneity of the sample with respect to hostility, as to all the global aspects of felt distress tapped by the questionnaire measures and, on the grid, construing of the self as dissimilar to the ideal self. So, while the questionnaire measures used can provide gross criteria of therapeutic outcome of some general relevance, these measures may be insufficiently sensitive or pertinent to the focus of psychotherapy to monitor adequately the therapeutic process. For this purpose measures at the level of abstraction of the individualized indices of aspects of construing would appear to be necessary, and individualized measures should also be used with heterogeneous or small samples.

A change score was calculated for each measure with each subject on the basis of the difference in scores between the initial and post-treatment assessment, assigning a positive value to a score representing movement in the direction expected to be associated for that measure with improvement in the sample as a whole, and eliminating negative values from the final score by adding a constant to the change scores on some measures. The change scores on different measures are generally positively intercorrelated (see Table 10.3) and a factor analysis of the

Table 10.4 Factor analysis of change data: loadings of variables on the factors

Factor	I	II	III
Ind. pred.	0.31	0.28	0.60
S–IC	0.58	0.34	0.41
S–M C	0.80	0.09	0.17
S–F C	0.26	−0.03	0.49
Sex. id. C	0.21	−0.05	−0.06
M–F C	−0.40	0.03	−0.09
I–P C	−0.80	−0.12	0.13
NSC	0.48	0.27	0.09
NIC	−0.09	−0.08	−0.11
SSIC	0.04	0.89	0.17
SRC	0.29	0.40	0.44
HC	−0.15	0.52	−0.23
DHC	−0.24	0.11	−0.02
EPI:NC	0.22	0.66	0.01
TR	0.18	0.19	0.55
Dur.	−0.14	−0.18	0.59
% age variance	40.0	16.9	16.0

change data is comparable to that of the pre-treatment data in that factors appear to be largely determined by the methods of measurement used (see Table 10.4). Examination of the degree of change on different measures in those patients who had remained in therapy for at least nine months provides support for the arguments of Foulds (1959, 1965) and Caine (1965b) that therapeutic change is most easily achieved at the symptom level, less so at the level of attitudes, and still less likely on personality variables. Thus, as can be seen from Table 10.5, much the most significant decreases are in the number of neurotic symptoms to which patients admit and in Neuroticism, which we would regard as a symptom measure in view of its high correlation with other such measures. On the grid, significant decreases are found in the distance between self and ideal self elements and in isolation of the self element (cf. Fielding, 1975), both of which appear from the pre-treatment correlation matrix to be associated with felt distress and symptom variables. At the level of attitudinal variables, there are significant decreases in self-criticism, guilt, and criticism of others, but there is no significant change on the personality measure employed (HOQ). It had been expected that change would be less, and of a more superficial nature, in those patients who dropped out of group psychotherapy within the first three months than in the patients who remained in group therapy for a longer period. However, it can be seen from Table 10.6 that there is no appreciable difference in degree of improvement between these two groups. This provides some confirmation of previous research findings (Garfield, 1963; Malan, Balfour, Hood and Shooter, 1976) and support for the common practice in psychotherapy research of excluding drop-outs from the analysis rather than classing them as treatment failures. Similarly, it was expected that the changes observed in the group psychotherapy patients would be more fundamental than those in the behaviour therapy patients, but no significant differences were found between the change scores of these two groups. This was possibly due to the fact that the behaviour therapists in the treatment settings considered could not by any means be construed as 'behaviourists' in that they were often all too eager, at least as far as purity of the research design is concerned, to combine more intensive psychotherapeutic work with the use of behavioural techniques. However, other explanations can also be advanced. Removal of symptoms by behaviour therapy may instigate what Yalom (1971) has termed an 'adaptive spiral' of changes in construing of the patient by himself and others comparable to those induced by psychotherapy. Alternatively, it may be that the most important factor in facilitating major therapeutic change is not the 'depth' of the intervention but the extent of the match between characteristics of the patient and those of the treatment.

Treatment selection

Recognition of the absurdity of the uniformity myths in psychotherapy research leads inexorably to the conclusion that there are no panaceas

Table 10.5 Differences between pre-treatment and post-treatment test scores of patients remaining in therapy for nine months (n = 19–20)

		SSI:N*	SSI:P	AH	CO	PH	SC	G	HOQ	EPI:N	S-I	Sex.id
Pre-treatment	Mean	14.81	5.43	5.30	5.60	1.45	7.40	3.00	21.70	16.50	1.47	1.11
	sd	7.02	3.54	2.11	2.74	1.28	2.16	1.26	5.23	4.47	0.26	0.40
Post-treatment	Mean	11.14	4.81	4.95	4.45	1.15	6.35	2.45	22.40	14.55	1.31	1.05
	sd	7.74	3.74	2.54	3.24	1.04	2.46	1.85	4.72	6.14	0.26	0.34
	t	4.20	0.98	0.94	1.88	1.37	2.54	2.34	0.55	3.02	2.08	0.72
	df	20	20	19	19	19	19	19	19	19	18	18
	p	<0.001	0.17	0.18	0.038	0.093	0.010	0.015	0.59	0.004	0.026	0.48
		1-tail	1-tail	1-tail	1-tail	1-tail	1-tail	1-tail	2-tail	1-tail	1-tail	2-tail

		S-M	S-F	M-F	I-P	NS	NI	T-GP	SCI	SCII	III	Symp.
Pre-treatment	Mean	1.11	1.00	0.92	1.16	10.94	5.68	0.60	1.02	0.61	72.62	64.15
	sd	0.34	0.25	0.26	0.25	2.77	2.16	0.25	0.51	0.45	17.59	18.39
Post-treatment	Mean	1.06	0.97	0.99	1.13	8.16	6.26	0.57	0.89	0.60	71.79	64.54
	sd	0.30	0.26	0.34	0.23	2.75	1.79	0.23	0.58	0.24	20.08	14.78
	t	0.73	0.62	1.45	0.52	2.46	1.06	0.46	0.97	0.12	0.16	0.09
	df	18	18	18	18	18	18	18	18	18	18	17
	p	0.24	0.27	0.17	0.30	0.012	0.31	0.65	0.12	0.45	0.88	0.46
		1-tail	1-tail	2-tail	1-tail	1-tail	2-tail	2-tail	1-tail	1-tail	2-tail	1-tail

*For abbreviations see Table 8.1, pp. 116–17

Table 10.6 Differences between change scores of group psychotherapy drop-outs and stayers

		Ind. pred.	S-IC	Sex. id. C	S-MC	S-FC	I-PC	M-FC	NSC	NIC	SSIC
Stayers (n = 8-9)	Mean	75.60	1.05	0.86	0.98	1.00	1.06	0.87	10.38	9.13	14.33
	sd	16.88	0.31	0.38	0.33	0.26	0.23	0.19	4.27	2.70	5.20
Drop-outs (n = 7-8)	Mean	76.95	1.08	1.02	0.93	0.92	0.98	1.06	12.00	9.63	18.13
	sd	15.05	0.24	0.21	0.11	0.20	0.12	0.20	3.25	1.30	8.58
	t	0.17	0.20	1.05	0.40	0.63	0.94	1.98	0.86	0.47	1.12
	df	14	14	14	14	14	14	14	14	14	15
	p	0.87	0.84	0.31	0.70	0.54	0.36	0.068	0.41	0.64	0.28
		2-tail	2-tail	2-tail	2-tail	2-tail	2-tail	2-tail	2-tail	2-tail	2-tail

		SRC	EPI:NC	HC	DHC	AHC	COC	PHC	SCC	GC	TR
Stayers	Mean	12.78	11.78	11.44	11.89	9.78	10.44	10.22	10.89	10.33	11.67
	sd	2.73	3.07	5.25	5.09	1.79	3.54	1.20	2.09	1.32	2.35
Drop-outs	Mean	11.43	13.29	14.71	12.57	11.71	11.71	10.14	11.29	11.00	9.75
	sd	2.23	6.21	5.12	6.66	1.60	3.45	0.69	3.55	1.83	1.16
	t	1.06	0.64	1.25	0.23	2.25	0.72	0.16	0.28	0.85	2.09
	df	14	14	14	14	14	14	14	14	14	15
	p	0.31	0.53	0.23	0.82	0.041	0.48	0.88	0.78	0.41	0.054
		2-tail	2-tail	2-tail	2-tail	2-tail	2-tail	2-tail	2-tail	2-tail	2-tail

amongst the psychological therapies and that treatment selection is of paramount importance. The question 'Is this treatment effective?', and research based on it, can be considered to reflect an inappropriate application of the medical model and of outdated scientific models to psychological disorders and their treatment. We would agree with Bergin (1971) that it should be replaced by much more specific questions of the type 'What treatment, given by whom, is most effective for this individual with that specific problem, and under which set of circumstances?' To this we would add 'using this particular criterion of outcome'. We would not claim that our research on treatment selection and outcome is entirely free of the criticisms which have been levelled at previous studies, constrained as it is by being largely carried out in an active National Health Service psychotherapy clinic with an attempt at minimal interference with the normal running of the clinic. Nevertheless, while we have not attempted the 'radical change' in research methodology which Smail (1978) favours, a concern with the 'non-radical objections' to previous research permeates our work.

We have argued that the most effective treatment for a particular patient is likely to be that which is consonant with his expectancies and more general assumptions and beliefs, as reflected in the constellation of personal adjustment strategies with which we have been concerned. As discussed in previous chapters, support for our general framework has been provided by research demonstrating the influence of expectancies on treatment outcome in therapies as diverse as drug treatment (Frank, Nash, Stone, and Imber, 1963), behaviour therapy (Marcia, Rubin, and Efran, 1969) and psychotherapy (see Frank, 1968; Garfield, 1971). In addition, positive response to group psychotherapy has been related to 'psychological-mindedness' (Abramowitz and Abramowitz, 1974), while a large body of research has provided evidence that successful therapeutic outcome is facilitated by congruence between patient expectations, conceptualized in terms of the internal-external locus of control dimension, and the degree of structure and directiveness in therapeutic conditions (see Strickland, 1978). Positive response to ECT has been associated by Fink (1974) with authoritarian attitudes as measured by the California F-Scale, scores on which have been found to correlate with those on the C Scale. Finally, as we have seen in Chapter 8, response to psychotherapy has been related by Landfield (1971) to the content of the patient's construct system.

In terms of the framework which we have adopted, we would expect patients with an 'inner' orientation on the measures which we have employed to be more likely to respond positively to group psychotherapy and those with an 'outer' orientation to be more likely to respond to a more structured approach such as behaviour therapy. We have examined these relationships in various samples of neurotic out-patients referred to the Psychotherapy Clinic at Claybury Hospital. Response to therapy was evaluated in a number of ways. In a sample of one hundred group psychotherapy patients, described in Chapter 1, commitment to treatment was defined by designating those who had remained in therapy for at least nine months as long stayers (Caine and Wijesinghe, 1976). As expected, such patients show a more psychological treatment set at pre-treatment TEQ assessment than the drop-outs (see Table 10.7). There are no significant differences between the groups on the DIQ and C Scale but, as we have argued above, the validity of regarding drop-outs as treatment failures can be questioned. Nevertheless, the relationship between TEQ scores and length of stay in group psychotherapy has been replicated in a recent study carried out at the Paddington Centre for Psychotherapy on a sample of twenty-six patients (Elkan, Kreeger, Ferguson, Green, Epstein, Vermount, and Stokes, personal communication). It can be seen from Table 10.8 that the use of a cut-off point of twenty-seven on the TEQ predicts attendance in group psychotherapy with 73 per cent accuracy. Employment of this criterion for treatment selection would have rejected two of the ten good attenders. The finding that patients who had received prior individual psychotherapy obtain lower TEQ scores ($u = 27$; $p < 0.025$; one-tail) suggests the role of modification of expectancies in mediating the relationship found by Malan, Balfour, Hood and Shooter (1976) between prior individual psychotherapy and outcome in group psychotherapy.

An additional evaluation of treatment response in our sample of group psychotherapy patients was made by obtaining ratings of progress by the therapist on twenty-six of the long stayers. It can be seen from Table 10.7 that those rated as responding to therapy have a more psychological treatment set and a more inward direction of interest, although there is no significant difference between the groups on the C Scale. A postal follow-up was also carried out on all the patients two years after discharge, although only a quarter of those contacted provided feedback on their treatment response. On the basis of self-report these were divided into a successful and an unsuccessful group, and the expected difference between the groups is now obtained on the C Scale as well as on the TEQ and DIQ (see Table 10.7). The successful group also obtained higher scores on the SSI Personal Disturbance Scale suggesting a greater willingness to admit to symptoms.

Table 10.7 Differences between pre-treatment scores of group psychotherapy patients divided on the basis of three measures of treatment response

(a) *Long stayers versus drop-outs*

		TEQ	*DIQ*	*C*
Long stayers	Mean	32.30	15.09	38.75
(n = 32-3)	sd	4.82	7.68	13.64
Drop-outs	Mean	35.75	14.67	39.15
(n = 52)	sd	6.75	7.04	12.13
	t	2.72	0.36	0.29
	df	83	82	82
	p	<0.001 1-tail	n.s.	n.s.

(b) *Patients seen by their therapists as progressing versus those seen as not progressing*

		TEQ	*DIQ*	*C*
Progressing	Mean	30.22	17.89	34.44
(n = 18)	sd	4.50	7.53	15.56
Not progressing	Mean	35.00	10.62	43.12
(n = 8)	sd	5.00	6.75	11.50
	t	2.19	2.31	1.50
	df	24	24	24
	p	<0.01 1-tail	<0.01 1-tail	n.s.

(c) *Patients rating themselves as successfully treated versus those rating themselves as unsuccessfully treated*

		TEQ	*DIQ*	*C*
Successful	Mean	28.16	17.33	32.08
(n = 12)	sd	6.62	8.29	9.04
Unsuccessful	Mean	34.25	11.75	45.66
(n = 12)	sd	6.78	5.23	10.73
	t	2.22	1.97	3.35
	df	22	22	22
	p	<0.01 1-tail	<0.05 1-tail	<0.001 1-tail

Table 10.8 Relationships between TEQ scores and length of attendance in group psychotherapy

		Never attended or below group's median	Exceeding group's median or 9 months + in therapy
TEQ score	27 and below	5	8
	28 and above	11	2

Fisher Test: $p < 0.025$ (one-tailed).

Treatment response was also evaluated by the therapists and the patients in a further study of patients allocated to psychotherapy and behaviour therapy at the Psychotherapy Clinic (Wijesinghe, 1978). No significant interactions were found between response to a particular form of treatment and pre-treatment scores on the DIQ and C Scale, but this may have been due to failure to control for other variables with a bearing on outcome. For example, the inclusion in both samples of patients who had been treated individually together with those who had been treated in groups may have obscured differences between the two broad treatment conditions in terms of the introspective–extraspective dimension (see Chapter 9). Finally, in a preliminary study of response to ECT in endogenous depressives, Anyaegbuna (1979) has found that patients rated as successfully treated by psychiatrists show more medical-physical expectancies on the TEQ than those not so rated.

The outcome measures employed in the studies which we have described cannot be regarded as entirely acceptable, and so we took the opportunity to examine the differences in pre-treatment scores between the 'improvers' and 'non-improvers' in the samples of group psychotherapy and behaviour therapy patients which we used in developing our repertory grid outcome criteria. The differences on the DIQ, TEQ, and C Scale, together with all other significant differences in the group psychotherapy sample are presented in Table 10.9. As expected, the patient who improves in group psychotherapy shows a more psychological treatment set on the TEQ and more radical social attitudes on the C Scale than the 'non-improver'. Although the difference in TEQ scores between the groups falls short of statistical significance ($p = 0.12$) on allowing for the higher verbal ability of the 'improvers', we feel that it may be inappropriate to control for verbal ability in this area as preference for activities in the verbal, rather than the practical, sphere may be an integral feature of an inner orientation and the development of

Table 10.9 Differences between pre-treatment scores of small group psychotherapy improvers and non-improvers

		Verbal IQ	DIQ	TEQ	C	PH	S-I	NS	SCI
Improvers (n = 7-9)	Mean	113.57	18.25	24.63	22.75	1.00	1.49	10.22	0.96
	sd	9.71	5.70	3.11	9.88	0.71	0.16	2.54	0.35
Non-improvers (n = 7-9)	Mean	101.29	17.25	33.50	47.38	2.22	1.13	7.56	0.57
	sd	8.94	6.76	6.63	8.80	1.79	0.16	3.71	0.46
	t	2.46	0.32	3.43	5.26	1.91	4.75	1.78	2.02
	df	12	14	14	14	16	16	16	16
	p	0.015	0.380	0.002	<0.001	0.038	<0.001	0.047	0.030
		1-tail	1-tail	1-tail	1-tail	1-tail	1-tail	1-tail	1-tail

a psychological treatment set (cf. Hudson, 1966). The group psychotherapy 'improver' also exhibits little projected delusional hostility on the HDHQ. On his repertory grid, the self element loads highly on the first component, indicating a heightened self-awareness, and there is a low level of self-esteem, suggesting greater motivation to change (cf. Sperlinger, 1976). Specific features of the content of the constructs which he applies to his problems are obscured by the fact that his symptom constructs carry considerably fewer implications in terms of other constructs than do those of the 'non-improver' ($\chi^2 = 12.30$; $p = < 0.0005$; one-tail). In addition, the group psychotherapy 'improver' in this sample tends to be male ($\chi^2 = 8$; $p = < 0.01$; two-tail), possibly due to the fact that the therapist in one of the groups studied was male, while in the other an experienced male therapist worked successively with three less experienced female co-therapists.

For the behaviour therapy patients, only two significant differences emerge between the 'improvers' and the 'non-improvers'. As can be seen from Table 10.10 the patient who improves in behaviour therapy has conservative social attitudes. His symptoms also carry many more implications in terms of other constructs than do those of the 'non-improver' ($\chi^2 = 18.92$; $p = < 0.0005$; one-tail). That centrality of the symptoms to the self-concept is particularly important in predicting improvement in behaviour therapy is also suggested by inspection of the correlations between pre-treatment and change scores.

Table 10.10 Differences between pre-treatment scores of behaviour therapy improvers and non-improvers

		DIQ	*TEQ*	*C*
Improvers	Mean	11.19	39.73	45.82
(n = 11)	sd	7.91	3.29	11.04
Non-improvers	Mean	12.00	38.20	33.40
(n = 5)	sd	3.81	10.26	12.01
	t	0.22	0.46	2.03
	df	14	14	14
	p	0.42	0.33	0.03
		1-tail	1-tail	1-tail

Our general position would lead us to expect that the most distinct groups of patients in our samples would consist of those who show improvement in group psychotherapy and those who improve with behaviour therapy. Comparison of the 'improvers' in these two forms of

Table 10.11 Significant differences between pre-treatment scores of improvers in small group psychotherapy and behaviour therapy

		Verbal IQ	DIQ	TEQ	C	SSI:P	AH	T-GP	III
Small group psychotherapy	Mean	113.57	18.25	24.63	22.75	7.11	6.11	0.65	78.45
(n = 7-9)	sd	9.71	5.70	3.11	9.88	2.37	1.45	0.25	22.36
Behaviour therapy	Mean	98.91	11.18	39.73	45.82	4.09	4.27	0.41	64.45
(n = 11)	sd	11.25	7.91	3.29	11.04	2.30	2.10	0.23	9.49
	t	2.84	2.15	10.10	4.69	2.88	2.22	2.19	1.89
	df	16	17	17	17	18	18	18	18
	p	0.006	0.023	<0.001	<0.001	0.005	0.020	0.021	0.038
		1-tail	1-tail	1-tail	1-tail	1-tail	1-tail	1-tail	1-tail

therapy does, indeed, reveal highly significant, expected differences in pre-treatment scores (see Table 10.11). The group psychotherapy 'improvers' are more inner directed, and have more 'psychological' treatment expectancies and more radical social attitudes, than the behaviour therapy 'improvers'. They are of higher verbal ability, as well as admitting to a greater urge to act out hostility and more psychotic symptoms, perhaps indicating that they are more open to the experience of psychological distress. In addition, they see themselves as less ill and expect their therapist to be less similar to their general practitioner, suggesting that their view of their difficulties is less 'medical' than that of patients who respond to behaviour therapy. This is consistent with Heine's (1962) finding of premature termination of psychotherapy in patients who do not differentiate the therapist from other medical practitioners. Finally, the symptom constructs are far less meaningful to the group psychotherapy 'improvers', in terms of their relationships to other constructs, than to the behaviour therapy 'improvers' ($\chi^2 = 43.45$; $p = < 0.0005$; one-tail).

In general, then, our findings point to certain major areas as being relevant to treatment selection. One concerns the superordinacy of the patient's symptom constructs in his construct system, and our findings help to clarify theoretical arguments regarding treatment selection. We have seen in Chapter 8 that Fransella (1972) takes the view that a person suffers from a particular complaint because that is the way he knows how to be. It might be thought, then, that a treatment, such as behaviour therapy, which focuses on the complaint could be counter-productive in that it would serve to elaborate even further the person's construing of himself as having the complaint. Alternatively, if the 'symptom may be regarded as a part of a person's experience of himself which he has singled out and circumscribed as in some ways incongruous with the rest of his experience of himself' (Wright, 1970), then a positive therapeutic outcome might be more likely if the therapist tailors his endeavours to the patient's construct system by agreeing to the patient's demands for direct attack on and removal of this alien part of himself. Our results suggest that if the symptom occupies a central, superordinate position in the patient's construct system, a therapeutic approach which does not focus upon it will not be meaningful to the patient and therefore will be unlikely to be effective. However, if such a patient's symptoms are directly attacked, and their intensity reduced, by an approach such as behaviour therapy, he may be freer to concentrate on other construct subsystems, perhaps elaborating his construing of himself as a person without symptoms. A less symptom-centred approach might then be appropriate, and such switching of therapeutic approaches was fairly common practice in the treatment settings under study. Figure 1 presents a model of the relationships between treatment outcome and personal construing which our findings might suggest.

The other areas which we have related to treatment outcome in various samples are the patient's treatment expectancies and typical adjustment strategies. Thus, the TEQ has been found to be consistently predictive of response to group psychotherapy in all the studies considered, and might be usefully incorporated into the treatment selection procedure in clinical practice. There is also evidence for the importance of the C Scale in this regard, but the findings with the DIQ are less consistent. A possible model of the relationships between the patient's treatment outcome and his treatment expectancies, direction of interest, and social attitudes is presented in Figure 2.

In addition to the findings which we have presented, preliminary discriminant function analyses have suggested the pre-eminence of the TEQ in predicting allocation to therapy, the importance of the TEQ and DIQ in predicting response to group psychotherapy, and that of the C Scale in predicting response to behaviour therapy. Further discriminant analyses with larger samples will allow the derivation of specification equations to enable the optimum use of these scales in treatment selection. At present, however, we would suggest that the clinician wishing to use the scales in this way might find it of value to arrive at a composite score by adding the score on the TEQ to that on the C Scale and subtracting the DIQ score. Thus, if we order our samples in terms of stringency of criteria of response to group psychotherapy and behaviour therapy, the progression of mean scores obtained on this composite measure is very much as expected (see Table 10.12).

The use of a cut-off point of 59 on the composite measure in our samples, with higher scores predicting drop out from group psychotherapy, would have resulted in a 67.5 per cent correct classification of patients in terms of their length of stay in groups. Allocation of patients to group psychotherapy on the basis of this measure alone would therefore have been as successful, if judged by subsequent drop-out rate, as clinical allocation is generally found to be (Yalom, 1966). A much more stringent test of the value of our composite measure as a predictor of response to therapy might be provided by considering the scores of the 'improvers' and 'non-improvers' in Sample A. The use of linear regression suggests that a cut-off point in the region of 47 would separate the group psychotherapy 'improvers' in this sample from the

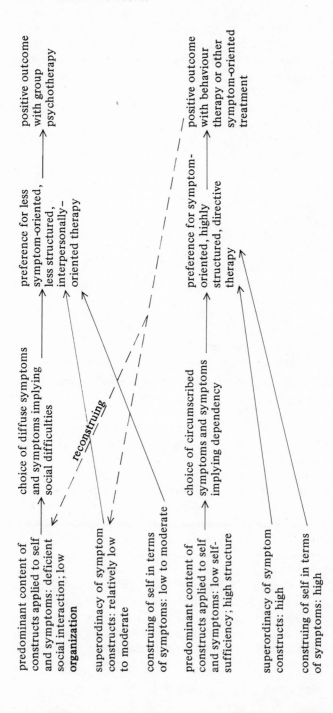

Figure 1   Postulated relationships between construing and response to therapy

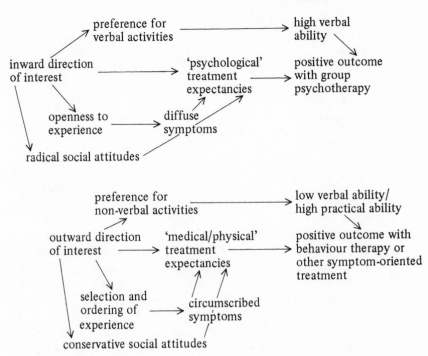

Figure 2 Postulated relationships between personal adjustment strategies treatment expectancies, and response to psychological therapies

Table 10.12 Mean scores on composite measure of expectancies/adjustment strategies in relation to treatment outcome in various samples

Group psychotherapy	n	Mean	sd
Improvers (multiple outcome measures: Sample A)	8	29.12	11.15
Improvers (self ratings)	11	43.45	16.34
Long stayers (> 9 months)	36	50.22	18.55
Patients allocated to group psychotherapy	92	58.95	18.64
Non-improvers (self ratings)	4	62.50	13.68
Non-improvers (multiple outcome measures: Sample A)	8	63.63	10.69
Patients transferred to behaviour therapy after unsuccessful group therapy	10	64.00	11.73
Drop-outs (< 9 months)	44	64.31	17.17
Patients not accepting offer of group psychotherapy	20	66.15	17.91

Table 10.12 (cont.)

Behaviour therapy	n	Mean	sd
Non-improvers (multiple outcome measures: Sample A)	5	59.60	21.42
Patients allocated to behaviour therapy	116	69.68	16.60
Improvers (self ratings)	15	69.00	16.33
Improvers (multiple outcome measures: Sample A)	12	75.17	14.31

'non-improvers' and, indeed, if a cut-off point of 49 had been used, with lower scores predicting improvement in group psychotherapy, a 100 per cent correct classification would have been achieved. With the behaviour therapy patients, use of a cut-off point of 59, with higher scores predicting improvement, would have resulted in an 82.4 per cent correct classification, and the misclassification of only one 'improver'. The cut-off points chosen in clinical practice might depend on the availability of resources for different types of treatment. With patients scoring in the intermediate range (i.e. 49 to 59), the clinician might do well to supplement the test scores by attending particularly in the clinical interview to the extent to which the patient is symptom-centred and to the constructs which he uses in describing his symptoms, himself, and his notions of therapeutic change.

Summary

Research on treatment outcome in the psychological therapies has been dominated by inappropriate assumptions of the uniformity of the variables under study. In particular, outcome measures have failed to take into account the individuality of the patient. We have provided evidence that valid individualized outcome measures can be derived from a repertory grid and that predictions of therapeutic change on such measures are more successful than general grid predictions applied to each patient. Guidelines have been presented for the derivation of individualized outcome criteria from a patient's pre-treatment grid.

We have argued that successful therapeutic outcome is facilitated by matching of patient and therapy. Evidence has been provided that positive therapeutic response is associated with congruence of therapy allocation with the patient's treatment expectancies, adjustment strategies, and personal construing. More specifically, our findings suggest that the patient who responds to group psychotherapy, as compared to the patient who does not respond, exhibits the following characteristics:

1 he has 'psychological' treatment expectancies:
2 he has radical social attitudes;
3 he has an inward direction of interest;
4 his symptoms do not carry many implications in terms of other constructs.

The patient who responds positively to behaviour therapy in our situation exhibits contrasting characteristics:

1 he has conservative social attitudes;
2 his symptoms occupy a superordinate position in his construct system.

A combination of test scores for use in the treatment selection procedure has been suggested.

Chapter 11
Conclusions

In the foregoing chapters we have discussed a number of related adjustment strategies which we have considered to be subsidiary aspects of two basic universal polarities. These basic polarities have been seen by a number of writers to be deeply embedded in the history of human thought. In ancient Eastern writings such as the I Ching they have been designated as Yin and Yang. In classical Western thought Aristotle has referred to them as the 'formal' and 'effective' causes. Their potential energy has been recognized in the evolutionary process in such diverse fields as physics, biology, psychology and sociology.

As clinical psychologists our concern has been with the relevance of these basic polarities to the problems of personal adjustment, particularly with regard to neurosis. Some aspects of our work in abnormal psychology have been anticipated in the field of normal personality functioning by Coan (1974) and we have been able to achieve something of an integration of the two areas. Thus, in the study of personality, we have argued that different authors have emphasized different aspects of the universal polarities, designating them as 'direction of interest', 'conservatism', 'convergent–divergent thinking', 'openness to experience' and 'control'. We have found that these normal adjustment strategies are indeed related and have relevance for the neuroses in terms of attitudes to psychiatric treatment, symptom patterns, the personal construing of patients, allocation to treatment, and response to treatment. The integration of adjustment strategies to give a consistent approach to environmental stimuli, life experiences and problems, we have designated as the 'personal style' of the individual. We have further argued that something of a match between the personal style of the patient and that of the therapist is essential for successful outcome in the psychological therapies of small group psychotherapy and behaviour therapy.

In our approach we have not exclusively aligned ourselves to a particular psychological school. A heavy dependence on the ideas of Jung, Coan, existential psychology and personal construct theory may nevertheless be seen in our work. In this connection we have been concerned with such factors as personal meaning, expectancies, and attitudes, which have been traditionally neglected in the selection of patients for psychiatric treatment, and in process and outcome research. In this respect we have recognized the patient as an active agent in his own treatment with that purposive, creative and exploratory potential emphasized by Koestler (1976), Bertalanffy (1966) and Collinson (1968). In this we share these authors' rejection of a concept of science which is reductionist, mechanistic, and deterministic and which treats consciousness as an epiphenomenon. However, our position is distinct from the wholly idiographic nature of existentialist enquiry. Just as we recognize the unique and distinctive nature of the individual, we have stressed that the individual personality is organized in relation to others, sharing some common ground. In this we are in basic agreement with Allport (1963), who maintains that the psychology of personality is neither exclusively nomothetic nor exclusively idiographic.

From this position the personal adjustment strategies that we have discussed in this book are important for two reasons. Firstly, they have personal relevance in that they reflect an individual's characteristic values, attitudes and expectancies. Secondly, they extend beyond the individual and tap behavioural propensities common to particular groups.

Although we recognize that genetic factors may well influence the maturation and organization of the adjustment strategies, we are also concerned with the part played by social learning in their expression or inhibition. It has not been possible within the scope of this book to examine the influence of such learning in detail but it is worth noting that preliminary work in this connection has revealed positive findings (Wijesinghe, 1978). Of particular significance is the relationship between personal adjustment strategies and social class, as the latter has been shown to be an important mediator variable both in the presentation of disorder (Hollingshead and Redlich, 1958) and the expectations concerning treatment (Aronson and Overall, 1966). Consistent with previous findings, patients with a middle class background were seen to present their distress in more 'psychological' terms and to have treatment expectancies that favoured group psychotherapy. These patients were also more likely to be inwardly directed in interest. Patients from a working class background presented with focalised phobic or somatic symptoms, had traditional, mechanistic attitudes to treatment and an outwardly directed life style. Pearlin and Kohn (1966) have noted that middle class parents value self-direction more highly than do working class parents. Working class parents place greater emphasis on conformity to external proscription and value obedience in their children. The transfer of learning from their everyday experiences to therapeutic situations might well lead middle class patients to assume leadership, to challenge the therapist, to become involved in other patients' problems — all features characteristic of small group psychotherapy. By contrast working class patients might be more likely to accept direction and guidance from authority figures and therefore be more amenable to physical treatments or behaviour therapy.

Whether such a broad generalization in terms of social class is justified or not, our contention is that two different kinds of socialization would appear to be implicated in the development of a personal style. In addition, since personal development and growth depend on both maturation and learning, it would be interesting to explore what different aspects of the learning process are required by different treatment methods. Studies of these different aspects in relation to T groups have been reported by Koll and Fry (1975). Similar studies might profitably be carried out with regard to small group psychotherapy and behaviour therapy. Future research might well focus on such important learning situations as early childhood, school, work, and traumatic life events to determine their effect on the manifestation of the adjustment strategies with their concomitant implications for the neuroses and their treatment.

Following Goldstein and Stein (1976), we have stressed the importance of matching patient, therapist and treatment variables in therapeutic ventures. However, we do not see such a match to be fixed and constant in time. Given that we largely adopt a growth and development point of view with regard to the neuroses, in some cases an initial match may lead to changes in the patient which moves him on to a further stage in development. This, we suggest, would be reflected in changes in aspects of his adjustment strategies and expectancies. Rematching in line with these changes would be necessary if the patient is to make a satisfactory further adjustment. Thus, for example, we have observed in our clinic that while some patients were successfully treated by behaviour therapy alone, others were transferred to group psychotherapy after initial symptomatic relief from behaviour therapy — and vice versa.

The present work brings into focus several important connections and cross-connections which require further investigation, both to strengthen the present findings and in extending them to form a more comprehensive framework. We have presented evidence in support of the argument that a patient's pattern of presenting complaints and his treatment expectancies are a function of his characteristic personal adjustment strategies and ways of construing himself and others. However, it should be remembered that the complaints and expectancies of the patients in our samples may not have been in their pristine condition at the initial research assessment, as this occurred after the patient had already been subject to the influence of his general practitioner and a psychiatrist. Noting Balint's (1964) ideas on the interactions between the patient and his physician in the organization of 'illness', it would be necessary to study the relationships between presenting complaints, adjustment strategies and expectancies at the time of initial contact with the general practitioner. This could be followed by a longitudinal study of subjects' expectancies and adjustment strategies over the course of their careers as patients. To this end, it would be of interest to carry out serial assessments of patients (using the expectancy and adjustment measures) during the sequential stages of assessment and treatment. Further, by using the repertory grid in a similar manner, serial changes in the content of our patients' personal construct systems could be examined, particularly in the constructs which they apply to themselves and their symptoms. Such research might throw further light on the question of why some patients may require either an extraspective or an introspective form of treatment, while others may require successive positive outcomes from both extraspective and introspective approaches to make a completely satisfactory adjustment to their situation.

While some of our findings (notably those with the Treatment Expectancies Questionnaire, Attitudes to Treatment Questionnaire, Direction of Interest Questionnaire, and Conservatism Scale) are consistent across several different samples, others must be considered to require replication. Thus, the attempt to relate patients' personal adjustment strategies, treatment expectancies and treatment allocation to the content of their personal construct systems should be repeated with larger samples, with constructs elicited from each patient without constraints. Perhaps the extraction of the patients' personal constructs from taped pre-treatment interviews might be a less artificial elicitation procedure. The findings concerning the patients' primary complaints of distress also merit further investigation. One possible area of inquiry would be to study the relevance of 'self-diagnosis' (i.e. patients rating themselves in relation to given diagnostic categories) for treatment allocation and outcome. The relationships between patients' presentation of distress, response to treatment, and openness and control should also be investigated. Similar studies could be made of 'successful' and 'unsuccessful' therapists. In addition independent replication of the comparison of individualized and general grid outcome predictions is necessary since in both reported studies the predictions were made by the same researcher.

Ultimately, the value of the framework we have presented will depend on its usefulness for the allocation of patients to treatment and for the evaluation of treatment outcome. Systematically designed studies should therefore focus on the response to treatment of groups of patients matched on their adjustment strategies and treatment expectancies. Therapists should also be matched on the same measures, while the type of treatment using both individual and group formats should be clearly defined as extraspective or introspective. Although we have focused on the implications of this framework for small group psychotherapy and behaviour therapy, some preliminary evidence suggests that patients' attitudes towards treatment and more general social attitudes influence their response to electroconvulsive therapy (Anyaegbuna, 1979) and thus indicates its wider applicability.

Finally, the consistency of the research evidence convinces us that the personal styles that we have identified in this work provide a firm basis for a better understanding of the neuroses, and a more systematic framework for the selection of both staff and patients.

Bibliography

Abbati, V. P. (1974), 'A project on psychiatric nursing – an examination of factors related to the selection, success and therapeutic orientation of psychiatric student nurses as compared with general student nurses', dissertation submitted for the BPS Diploma in Clinical Psychology. The British Psychological Society, Leicester.

Abramowitz, S. I. and Abramowitz, C. V. (1974), 'Psychological-mindedness and benefit from insight-oriented group therapy', *Archives of General Psychiatry*, 30, pp. 610–15.

Adams-Webber, J. R. (1969), 'Cognitive complexity and sociality', *British Journal of Social and Clinical Psychology*, 8, pp. 211–16.

Adorno, T. W., Frenkel-Brunswick, E., Levinson, D. J. and Sanford, R. N. (1950), *The Authoritarian Personality*, Harper and Row, New York.

Agnew, J. and Bannister, D. (1973), 'Psychiatric diagnosis as a pseudo-specialist language', *British Journal of Medical Psychology*, 46, pp. 69–73.

Albee, G. W. (1969), 'Emerging concepts of mental illness and models of treatment: the psychological point of view', *American Journal of Psychiatry*, 125, pp. 870–6.

Allen, B. V., Weins, A. N., Weitman, M. and Saslow, G. (1965), 'Effects of warm-cold set on interviewee speech', *Journal of Consulting Psychology*, 29, pp. 480–2.

Allport, G. W. (1937), *Personality*, Henry Holt, New York.

Allport, G. W. (1963), *Pattern and Growth in Personality*, Holt, Rinehart & Winston, London.

Altschul, A. T. (1972), *Patient-Nurse Interaction*, Churchill Livingstone, Edinburgh and London.

Anthony, E. J. (1953), 'Group psychotherapy', in J. Burton (ed), *Group Discussion in Educational, Social and Working Life*, Central Council for Health Education, London.

Anthony, E. J. (1972), 'The history of group psychotherapy', in H. I. Kaplan and B. Sadock (eds), *The Origins of Group Psychoanalysis*, Dutton, New York.

193

194 *Bibliography*

Anyaegbuna, B. (1979), 'Loss of short-term memory after electro-convulsive therapy; and personality factors related to response to ECT: an empirical investigation', unpublished B. A. dissertation, Middlesex Polytechnic, London.

Aronson, H. and Overall, B. (1966), 'Treatment expectations of patients in two social classes', *Social Work*, 11, pp. 35–41.

Atkinson, J. W. (1957), 'Motivational determinants of risk-taking behaviour', *Psychological Review*, 64, pp. 359–72.

Austin, M. D. (1971), 'Dream recall and the bias of intellectual ability', *Nature*, 231, p. 59.

Balint, M. (1964), *The Doctor, the Patient and his Illness,* Pitman, London.

Bannister, D. (1962), 'Personal construct theory: a summary and experimental paradigm', *Acta Psychologica*, 20, pp. 104–20.

Bannister, D. (1973), 'The shaping of things to come', *Bulletin of the British Psychological Society*, 26, pp. 293–5.

Bannister, D. and Mair, J. M. M. (1968), *The Evaluation of Personal Constructs*, Academic Press, London.

Bannister, D., Salmon, P. and Lieberman, D. M. (1964), 'Diagnosis-treatment relationships in psychiatry: a statistical analysis, *British Journal of Psychiatry*, 110, pp. 726–32.

Barron, F. X. (1958), 'The psychology of the imagination', *Scientific American*, 199, p. 151.

Barron, F. X. (1968), *Creativity and Personal Freedom*, Van Nostrand, New York.

Bartlett, F. C. (1932), *Remembering,* Cambridge University Press, Cambridge.

Barton, R. (1959), *Institutional Neurosis*, J. Wright, Bristol.

Bednar, R. L. and Lawlis, G. F. (1971), 'Empirical research in group psycho-therapy', in A. E. Bergin and S. L. Garfield (eds), *Handbook of Psychotherapy and Behavior Change*, Wiley, New York, London, Sydney, Toronto.

Bednar, R. L. and Mobley, M. J. (1971), 'A–B therapist perceptions and preferences for schizophrenic and psychoneurotic clients', *Journal of Abnormal Psychology*, 78, pp. 192–7.

Bergin, A. E. (1966), 'Some implications of psychotherapy research in therapeutic practice', *Journal of Abnormal Psychology*, 71, pp. 235–46.

Bergin, A. E. (1971), 'The evaluation of therapeutic outcomes', in A. E. Bergin and S. L. Garfield (eds), *Handbook of Psychotherapy and Behaviour Change*, Wiley, New York, London, Sydney, Toronto.

Bergin, A. E. and Strupp, H. H. (1972), *Changing Frontiers in the Science of Psychotherapy*, Aldine Atherton, Chicago, New York.

Bertalanffy, L. von (1966), 'General systems theory and psychiatry', in S. Arieti (ed.), *American Handbook of Psychiatry*, III, pp. 705–21.

Bieri, J. (1955), 'Cognitive complexity-simplicity and predictive behaviour', *Journal of Abnormal and Social Psychology*, 51, pp. 263–8.

Bieri, J. and Messerley, S. (1957), 'Differences in perceptual and cognitive behaviour as a function of experience type', *Journal of Consulting Psychology*, 21, pp. 217–21.

Bion, W. R. (1961), *Experiences in Groups*, Tavistock, London.

Boshier, R. (1973), 'Conservatism and superstitious behaviour', in G. D. Wilson (ed.), *The Psychology of Conservatism*, Academic Press, London, New York.

Brady, J. P., Reznikoff, M. and Zeller, W. W. (1960), 'The relationship of expectation of improvement to actual improvement of hospitalized psychiatric patients', *Journal of Nervous and Mental Disease*, 130, pp. 41–4.

Braginsky, B. and Braginsky, D. (1967), 'Schizophrenic patients in the psychiatric interview: an experimental study of their effectiveness at manipulation', *Journal of Consulting Psychology*, 31, pp. 453–7.

Braginsky, B. M., Braginsky, D. D. and Ring, K. (1969), *Methods of Madness*, Holt, Rinehart & Winston, New York.

Braginsky, B., Grosse, M. and Ring, K. (1966), 'Controlling outcomes through impression management: an experimental study of the manipulative tactics of mental patients', *Journal of Consulting Psychology*, 30, pp. 295–300.

Breen, D. (1975), *The Birth of a First Child, Towards an Understanding of Feminity*, Tavistock, London.

Breger, L. and McGaugh, J. L. (1965), 'Critique and reformulation of "learning theory" approaches to psychotherapy and neurosis', *Psychological Bulletin*, 63, pp. 338–58.

Bromley, D. B. (1966), *The Psychology of Human Ageing*, Penguin, Harmondsworth.

Brown, J. A. C. (1961), *Freud and the Post-Freudians*, Penguin, Harmondsworth.

Caine, T. M. (1964), 'Personality tests for nurses', *Nursing Times*, 60, pp. 973–4.

Caine, T. M. (1965a), 'Obsessoid and hysteroid components of personality', in G. A. Foulds (ed.), *Personality and Personal Illness*, Tavistock, London.

Caine, T. M. (1965b), 'Changes in symptom, attitude, and trait measures among chronic neurotics in a therapeutic community', in G. A. Foulds (ed.), *Personality and Personal Illness*, Tavistock, London.

Caine, T. M. (1966), 'Perceptual sensitization, response suppression and psychopathology', *British Journal of Psychology*, 57, pp. 301–6.

Caine, T. M. (1970), 'Appendix I' in D. Boorer (ed.), *A Question of Attitudes*, The Hospital Centre, London.

Caine, T. M. (1975), 'Attitudes to patient care and OT students', *Occupational Therapy*, 38, p. 239.

Caine, T. M., Foulds, G. A. and Hope, K. (1967), *Manual of the Hostility and Direction of Hostility Questionnaire (HDHQ)*, University of London Press, London.

Caine, T. M. and Hope, K. (1964), 'Validation of the Maudsley Personality Inventory E Scale', *British Journal of Psychiatry*, 55, pp. 447–52.

Caine, T. M. and Hope, K. (1967), *Manual of the Hysteroid-Obsessoid Questionnaire (HOQ)*, University of London Press, London.

Caine, T. M. and Leigh, R. (1972), 'Conservatism in relation to psychiatric treatment', *British Journal of Social and Clinical Psychology*, 11, pp. 52-6.

Caine, T. M. and Smail, D. J. (1969), *The Treatment of Mental Illness: Science, Faith and the Therapeutic Personality*, University of London Press, London.

Caine, T. M. and Wijesinghe, B. (1976), 'Personality, expectancies and group psychotherapy', *British Journal of Psychiatry*, 129, pp. 384-7.

Caine, T. M., Wijesinghe, B. and Wood, R. R. (1973), 'Personality and psychiatric treatment expectancies', *British Journal of Psychiatry*, 122, pp. 87-8.

Campbell, D. and Fiske, D. (1959), 'Convergent and discriminant validation by the multitrait-multimethod matrix', *Psychological Bulletin*, 56, pp. 81-105.

Caplan, H. L., Rohde, P. D., Shapiro, D. A. and Watson, J. P. (1975), 'Some correlates of repertory grid measures used to study a psychotherapeutic group', *British Journal of Medical Psychology*, 48, pp. 217-26.

Carrigan, P. M. (1960), 'Extraversion–introversion as a dimension of personality: a re-appraisal', *Psychological Bulletin*, 57, pp. 329-60.

Cartwright, D. S. and Cartwright, R. D. (1958), 'Faith and improvement in psychotherapy', *Journal of Counselling Psychology*, 5, pp. 174-7.

Cartwright, D. S., Kirtner, W. L. and Fiske, D. W. (1963), 'Method factors in changes associated with psychotherapy', *Journal of Abnormal and Social Psychology*, 66, pp. 164-75.

Cartwright, R. D. and Lerner, B. (1963), 'Empathy, need to change and improvement with psychotherapy', *Journal of Consulting and Clinical Psychology*, 27, pp. 138-44.

Cattell, R. B. and Eber, H. W. (1957), *Handbook of the Sixteen Personality Factor Questionnaire*, Institute of Personality and Ability Testing, Champaign, Illinois.

Chance, E. (1959), *Families in Treatment*, Basic Books, New York.

Chertok, L. (1966), 'An introduction to the study of tensions among psychotherapists', *British Journal of Medical Psychology*, 39, pp. 237-43.

Chesser, E. S. (1976), 'Behaviour therapy: recent trends and current practice', *British Journal of Psychiatry*, 129, pp. 289-307.

Chetwynd, J. (1977), 'The psychological meaning of structural measures derived from grids', in P. Slater (ed.), *Dimensions of Intrapersonal Space*, Wiley, London.

Chodoff, P. and Lyons, H. (1958), 'Hysteria, the hysterical personality and hysterical conversion', *American Journal of Psychiatry*, 114, p. 734.

Clare, A. (1976), *Psychiatry in Dissent*, Tavistock Publications, London.

Clark, D. (1964), *Administrative Therapy*, Tavistock Publications, London.

Clark, W. C. (1969), 'Sensory decision theory analysis of the placebo effect on the criterion for pain and thermal sensitivity (d')', *Journal of Abnormal Psychology*, 74, pp. 363–71.

Coan, R. W. (1972), 'Measurable components of openness to experience', *Journal of Consulting and Clinical Psychology*, 39, p. 346.

Coan, R. W. (1974), *The Optimal Personality*, Routledge & Kegan Paul, London.

Coan, R. W., Fairchild, M. T. and Dobyns, Z. P. (1973), 'Dimensions of experienced control', *Journal of Social Psychology*, 91, pp. 53–60.

Coghill, G. E. (1929), *Anatomy and the Problem of Behaviour*, Cambridge University Press, Cambridge.

Collinson, J. B. (1968), 'Ill-defined procedures in learning and growth', *Archives of General Psychiatry*, 19, pp. 290–9.

Comfort, A. (1961), *Darwin and the Naked Lady*, Routledge & Kegan Paul, London.

Comrey, A L., Backer, T. E. and Glaser, M. (1973), *A Sourcebook for Mental Health Measures*, Human Interaction Research Institute, Los Angeles.

Crandell, D. L. and Dohrenwend, B. P. (1967), 'Some relations among psychiatric symptoms, organic illness, and social class', *American Journal of Psychiatry*, 123, pp. 1527–38.

Crisp, A. H. (1964), 'An attempt to measure an aspect of "transference"', *British Journal of Medical Psychology*, 37, pp. 17–30.

Crisp, A. H., Gaynor Jones, M. and Slater, P. (1978), 'The Middlesex Hospital Questionnaire: a validity study', *British Journal of Medical Psychology*, 51, pp. 269–80·

Crown, S. and Crisp, A. H. (1966), 'A short clinical diagnostic self-rating scale for psychoneurotic patients', *British Journal of Psychiatry*, 112, pp. 917–23.

Darwin, C. (1928), *The Origin of Species*, Everyman's Library, Dent, London.

De Charms, R. (1968), *Personal Causation: The Internal Affective Determinants of Behaviour*, Academic Press, London.

Dent, J. K. (1978), *Exploring the Psycho-social Therapies through the Personalities of Effective Therapists*, U.S. Department of Health, Education and Welfare, Rockville, Maryland.

Derogatis, L. R., Covi, L., Lipman, R. S., Davis, D. M. and Rickels, K. (1971), 'Social class and race as mediator variables in neurotic symptomatology', *Archives of General Psychiatry*, 25, pp. 31–40.

Draguns, J. G. and Phillips, L. (1971), *Psychiatric Classification and Diagnosis: An Overview and Critique*, General Learning Press, Morristown, New Jersey.

Dresser, I. G. (1969), 'Repertory grid technique in the assessment of psychotherapy', unpublished M. Phil. thesis, University of London.

Drever, J. (1952), *A Dictionary of Psychology*, Penguin, Harmondsworth.

Dyer, A. R. (1974), 'R. D. Laing: post-critical perspective', *British Journal of Psychiatry*, 124, pp. 252–9.

Eysenck, H. J. (1952), 'The effects of psychotherapy: an evaluation', *Journal of Consulting Psychology*, 16, pp. 319–24.

Eysenck, H. J. (1953), *The Structure of Human Personality*, Methuen, London.

Eysenck, H. J. (1954), *The Psychology of Politics*, Routledge & Kegan Paul, London.

Eysenck, H. J. (1965), 'The effects of psychotherapy', *International Journal of Psychiatry*, 1, pp. 99–142.

Eysenck, H. J. (1978), 'Double standards and single standards', *Bulletin of the British Psychological Society*, 31, p. 56.

Eysenck, H. J. and Eysenck, S. B. G. (1964), *Manual of the Eysenck Personality Inventory*, University of London Press, London.

Eysenck, H. J. and Eysenck, S. B. G. (1969), *Personality Structure and Measurement*, Routledge & Kegan Paul, London.

Fielding, J. M. (1975), 'A technique for measuring outcome in group psychotherapy', *British Journal of Medical Psychology*, 48, pp. 189–98.

Fink, M. (1974), 'Induced seizures and human behaviour', in M. Fink, S. Kety, J. McGough, and T. A. Williams (eds), *Psychobiology of Convulsive Therapy*, Wiley, New York.

Fischer, E. H. and Turner, J. L. (1970), 'Orientation to seeking professional help: development and research utility of an attitude scale', *Journal of Consulting and Clinical Psychology*, 35, pp. 79–90.

Fitzgerald, E. T. (1966a), 'Measurement of openness to experience: a study of regression in the service of the ego', *Journal of Personality and Social Psychology*, 4, pp. 655–63.

Fitzgerald, E. T. (1966b), 'The Measurement of Openness to Experience: a Study of Regression in the Service of the Ego', unpublished doctoral dissertation, University of California.

Fleishman, E. A. (1969), *Manual for Leadership Opinion Questionnaire*, Science Research Associates Ltd., Chicago, Henley-on-Thames.

Foulds, G. A. (1959), 'The relative stability of personality measures compared with diagnostic measures', *Journal of Mental Science*, 105, pp. 783–87.

Foulds, G. A. (1965), *Personality and Personal Illness*, Tavistock, London.

Foulds, G. A. and Hope, K. (1968), *Manual of the Symptom Sign Inventory*, University of London Press, London.

Foulkes, S. H. (1964), *Therapeutic Group Analysis*, George Allen & Unwin, London.

Foulkes, S. H. and Anthony, E. J. (1957), *Group Psychotherapy*, Penguin, Harmondsworth.

Frank, J. D. (1959), 'The dynamics of the psychotherapeutic relationship', *Psychiatry*, 22, pp. 17–39.

Frank, J. D. (1968), 'The influence of patients' and therapists' expectations of the outcome of psychotherapy', *British Journal of Medical Psychology*, 41, pp. 349–56.

Frank, J. D. (1973), *Persuasion and Healing*, Johns Hopkins Press, Baltimore.

Frank, J. D., Nash, E. H., Stone, A. R. and Imber, S. D. (1963), 'Immediate and long-term symptomatic course of psychiatric outpatients', *American Journal of Psychiatry*, 120, pp. 429-39.

Frank, L. K. (1948), *Society as the Patient*, Rutgers University Press, New Jersey.

Fransella, F. (1970), 'Stuttering: not a symptom but a way of life', *British Journal of Communication Disorder*, 5, pp. 22-9.

Fransella, F. (1972), *Personal Change and Reconstruction*, Academic Press, London.

Fransella, F. (1974), 'Thinking in the obsessional', in H. R. Beech (ed.), *Obsessional States*, Methuen, London.

Fransella, F. and Bannister, D. (1977), *A Manual for Repertory Grid Technique*, Academic Press, London, New York, San Francisco.

Fransella, F. and Joyston-Bechal, M. P. (1971), 'An investigation of conceptual process and pattern change in a psychotherapy group over one year', *British Journal of Psychiatry*, 119, pp. 199-206.

Freud, S. (1922), *Introductory Lectures on Psychoanalysis*, Hogarth Press Ltd., London.

Freud, S. (1958), 'Case of Schreber', *Collected Works Vol. XII, Paper on techniques and other works*, Hogarth Press, London.

Freud, S. (1959), *Group Psychology and the Analysis of the Ego*, Hogarth Press, London.

Friedman, H. J. (1963), 'Patient-expectancy and symptom reduction', *Archives of General Psychiatry*, 8, pp. 61-7.

Fromm, E. (1943), *The Fear of Freedom*, Allen & Unwin, London.

Garfield, S. L. (1963), 'A note on patients' reasons for terminating therapy', *Psychological Reports*, 13, p. 38.

Garfield, S. L. (1971), 'Research on client variables in psychotherapy', in A. E. Bergin and S. L. Garfield (eds), *Handbook of Psychotherapy and Behavior Change*, Wiley, New York, London, Sydney, Toronto.

Gazzaniga, M. S. (1967), 'The split brain in man', *Scientific American*, August, pp. 24-9.

George, F. H. and Handley, J. H. (1957), 'A language for perceptual analysis', *Psychological Review*, 64, pp. 14-25.

Getzels, J. W. and Jackson, P. W. (1962), *Creativity and Intelligence*, Wiley, New York.

Gleidman, L. H., Stone, A. R., Frank, J. D., Nash, E. H. Jr., and Imber, S. D. (1957), 'Incentives for treatment related to remaining or improving in psychotherapy', *American Journal of Psychotherapy*, 11, pp. 589-98.

Goffman, E. (1971), *Asylums: Essays on the Social Situation of Mental Patients and other Inmates*, Penguin, Harmondsworth.

Goldstein, A. P. (1960), 'Therapist and client expectation of personality change in psychotherapy', *Journal of Counselling Psychology*, 7, pp. 180-4.

Goldstein, A. P. (1962), *Therapist-patient Expectancies in Psychotherapy*, Pergamon Press, New York.

Goldstein, A. P. and Shipman, W. G. (1961), 'Patients' expectancies, symptom reduction and aspects of the initial psychotherapeutic interview', *Journal of Clinical Psychology*, 17, pp. 129–33.

Goldstein, A. P. and Stein, N. (1976), *Prescriptive Psychotherapies*, Pergamon Press, New York.

Greenwald, H. (1973), *Decision Therapy*, Wyden, New York.

Griffiths, R. D. (1970), 'Personality assessment', in P. Mittler (ed.), *The Psychological Assessment of Mental and Physical Handicap*, Methuen, London.

Guilford, J. P. (1956), 'The structure of intellect', *Psychological Bulletin*, 53, pp. 267–93.

Guilford, J. P.and Braly, K. W. (1930), 'Extraversion and introversion', *Psychological Bulletin*, 27, pp. 96–107.

Hall, J. N. (1974), 'Nurse attitudes and specialized treatment settings: an exploratory study', *British Journal of Social and Clinical Psychology*, 13, pp. 333–4.

Hallick, S. L. (1971), *The Politics of Therapy*, Science House, New York.

Hamilton, D. L. (1968), 'Personality attributes associated with extreme response style', *Psychological Bulletin*, 69, pp. 192–203.

Hartshorne, H. and May, M. A. (1928), *Studies in the Nature of Character; Vol. I, Studies in Deceit*, Macmillan, New York.

Heather, N., Edwards, S., and Hore, B. D. (1975), 'Changes in construing and outcome of group therapy for alcoholism', *Journal of Studies on Alcohol*, 36, pp. 1238–53.

Heine, R. W. (ed.), (1962), *The Student Physician as Psychotherapist*, University of Chicago Press, Chicago.

Helson, H. (1964), *Adaption Level Theory: an Experimental and Systematic Approach to Behaviour*, Harper & Row, New York.

Hinkle, D. (1965), 'The change of personal constructs from the viewpoint of a theory of construct implications', unpublished Ph.D. thesis, Ohio State University, Columbus, Ohio.

Hollingshead, A. B. and Redlich, F. C. (1958), *Social Class and Mental Illness*, Wiley, New York.

Hora, T. (1975), 'Existential psychiatry and group psychotherapy', in G. M. Gazda (ed.), *Basic Approaches to Group Psychotherapy*, Thomas, Illinois.

Horney, K. (1951), *Neurosis and Human Growth*, Routledge & Kegan Paul, London.

Hoy, R. M. (1977), 'Some findings concerning beliefs about alcoholism', *British Journal of Medical Psychology*, 50, pp. 227–35.

Hudson, L. (1966), *Contrary Imaginations*, Penguin, Harmondsworth.

Hudson, L. (1968), *Frames of Mind*, Penguin, Harmondsworth.

Jackson, P. W. and Messick, S. (1965), 'The person, the product and the response: conceptual problems in the assessment of creativity', *Journal of Personality*, 33, p. 1.

Jacques, E. (1951), *The Changing Culture of a Factory*, Tavistock, London.

Jaensch, E. R. (1930), *Eidetic Imagery*, Routledge & Kegan Paul, London.

James, W. (1907), *Pragmatism*, Longmans, Green, London.

Janet, P. (1901), *The Mental State of Hystericals*, Pitman, New York and London.

Johnson, M. L. (1953), 'The ABC of group discussion: theory', in J. Burton, (ed.), *Group Discussion in Educational, Social and Working Life*, Central Council for Health Education, London.

Jones, M. S. (1952), *Social Psychiatry*, Tavistock, London.

Jourard, S. M. (1964), *The Transparent Self*, Van Nostrand, Princeton.

Jung, C. G. (1920), *Collected Papers on Analytical Psychology*, Baillière Tindall and Cox, London.

Jung, C. G. (1933), *Psychological Types*, Routledge & Kegan Paul, London.

Jung, C. G. (1954), *The Practice of Psychotherapy*, Routledge & Kegan Paul, London.

Jung, C. G. (1959), *Modern Man in Search of a Soul*, Routledge & Kegan Paul, London.

Kadushin, C. (1964), 'Social class and the experience of ill health', *Social Inquiry*, 34, pp. 67–80.

Kanfer, F. H. and Saslow, G. (1965), 'Behavioural analysis', *Archives of General Psychiatry*, 12, pp. 529–38.

Katz, D. and Shanck, R. L. (1938), *Social Psychology*, Wiley, New York.

Kelly, F. S., Farina, A. and Mosher, D. L. (1971), 'Ability of schizophrenic women to create a favourable impression on an interview', *Journal of Consulting and Clinical Psychology*, 36, pp. 404–9.

Kelly, G. A. (1955), *The Psychology of Personal Constructs*, Norton, New York.

Kennard, D. (1973), 'Measuring the atmosphere', *Association of Therapeutic Communities News Letter*, privately circulated.

Kepes, B. (1956), *The New Landscape*, Theobald, Chicago.

Kiesler, D. J. (1966), 'Some myths of psychotherapy research and the search for a paradigm', *Psychological Bulletin*, 65, pp. 110–36.

Kiesler, D. J. (1973), *The Process of Psychotherapy*, Aldine Publishing Co., Chicago.

Kim, J. (1975), 'Factor analysis', in Nie, N. H., Hull, C. H., Jenkins, J. G., Steinbrenner, K. and Bent, D. H. (eds), *Statistical Package for the Social Sciences*, McGraw-Hill, New York.

Klineberg, O. (1940), *Social Psychology*, Holt, New York.

Koestler, A. (1976), *The Act of Creation*, Hutchinson, London.

Kogan, N. and Morgan, E. T. (1969), 'Task and motivational influences on the assessment of creative and intellective ability in children', *Genetic Psychology Monographs*, 80, pp. 91–127.

Koll, D. G. and Fry, R. (1975), 'Towards an applied theory of experiential learning', in Cooper, C. (ed.), *Theories of Group Processes*, Wiley, London, pp. 33–5.

Krasner, L. (1961), 'The therapist as a social reinforcement machine', in H. H. Strupp (ed.), *Second Research Conference on Psychotherapy*, American Psychological Association, Chapel Hill, North Carolina.

Kreitman, N. (1962), 'Psychiatric orientation: a study of attitudes among psychiatrists', *Journal of Mental Science*, 108, pp. 317-28.

Kreitman, N., Sainsbury, P. P., Morrisey, J., Towers, J. and Scrivener, J. (1961), 'The reliability of psychiatric assessment: an analysis', *Journal of Mental Science*, 107, pp. 887-908.

Kris, E. (1952), *Psychoanalytic Explorations in Art*, International Universities Press, New York.

Kuder, G. F. (1952), *The Kuder Preference Record (Personal Form AH)*, Science Research Associates, Chicago.

Kuhn, T. S. (1962), *The Structure of Scientific Revolutions*, Chicago University Press, Chicago.

Külpe, O. (1904), *Bericht über der 1st Kongress fur experimentille Psychologie*.

Laing, R. D. (1960), *The Divided Self*, Tavistock Publications, London.

Laing, R. D. (1967), *The Politics of Experience, and the Bird of Paradise*, Penguin, Harmondsworth.

Landfield, A. W. (1971), *Personal Construct Systems in Psychotherapy*, Rand McNally, Chicago.

Landfield, A. W. (1975), 'The complaint: a confrontation of personal urgency and professional construction', in D. Bannister (ed.), *Issues and Approaches in the Psychological Therapies*, Wiley, London, New York.

Landfield, A. (1976), 'A personal construct approach to suicidal behaviour', in P. Slater (ed.), *The Measurement of Intrapersonal Space by Grid Technique: I Explorations of Intrapersonal Space*, Wiley, London.

Landfield, A. W. and Nawas, M. M. (1964), 'Psychotherapeutic improvement as a function of communication and adoption of therapist's values', *Journal of Counseling Psychology*, 11, pp. 336-41.

Lecky, P. (1951), *Self Consistency: A Theory of Personality*, Island, New York.

Leff, J. P. (1973), 'Culture and the differentiation of emotional states', *British Journal of Psychiatry*, 123, pp. 299-306.

Leitenberg, H., Agras, W. S., Barlow, D. H. and Oliveau, D. C. (1969), 'Contribution of selective positive reinforcement and therapeutic instructions to systematic desensitization therapy', *Journal of Abnormal Psychology*, 74, pp. 113-18.

Lennard, H. L. and Bernstein, A. (1960), *The Anatomy of Psychotherapy*, Columbia University Press, New York.

Lennard, H. L. and Bernstein, A. (1969), *Pattern in Human Interaction*, Jossey-Bass, San Francisco.

Levine, D. (1972), 'A cross-national study of attitudes toward mental illness', *Journal of Abnormal Psychology*, 80, pp. 111-14.

Lewin, K. (1936), *A Dynamic Theory of Personality*, McGraw-Hill, New York.

Lewin, K., Dembo, T., Festinger, L. and Sears, P. (1944), 'Level of aspiration', in J. McV. Hung (ed.), *Personality and the Behaviour Disorders: I,* Ronald Press, New York.

Lewis, P. and McCants, J. (1973), 'Some current issues in group psychotherapy research', *International Journal of Group Psychotherapy,* XXIII, pp. 268–78.

Libby, W. F. (1970), 'Creativity in Science', in J. D. Roslansky (ed.), *Creativity,* North Holland Publishing Company, London.

Lieberman, M. A., Yalom, I. D. and Miles, M. B. (1973), *Encounter Groups: First Facts,* Basic Books, New York.

Lillie, F. J. (1973), 'Psychiatry and mental distress', in G. D. Wilson (ed.), *The Psychology of Conservatism,* Academic Press, London.

Lipkin, S. (1954), 'Clients' feelings and attitudes in relation to the outcome of client-centred therapy', *Psychological Monographs.* 68, No. 1 (Whole no. 372).

Luborsky, L., Singer, B. and Luborsky, L. (1975), 'Comparative studies of psychotherapies: Is it true that "everybody has won and all must have prizes?"', *Archives of General Psychiatry,* 32, pp. 995–1008.

McClelland, D. C. (1962), 'On the psychodynamics of creative physical scientists', in H. E. Gruber (ed.), *Contemporary Approaches to Creative Thinking,* Atherton, London, New York.

MacKinnon, D. W. (1962), 'The nature and nurture of creative talent', *American Psychologist,* 17, 484; reprinted (1966) in B. Semeonoff (ed.), *Personality Assessment,* Penguin, Harmondsworth.

MacKinnon, D. (1970), 'Creativity: a multi-faceted phenomenon', in J. D. Roslansky (ed.), *Creativity,* North Holland Publishing Company, London, Amsterdam.

McPherson, F. M. (1972), '"Psychological" constructs and "psychological" symptoms in schizophrenia', *British Journal of Psychiatry,* 120, pp. 197–8.

McPherson, F., Buckley, F. and Draffan, J. (1971), '"Psychological" constructs and delusions of persecution and "non-integration" in schizophrenia', *British Journal of Medical Psychology,* 44, pp. 277–80.

McPherson, F. M. and Gray, A. (1976), 'Psychological construing and psychological symptoms', *British Journal of Medical Psychology,* 49, pp. 73–9.

Maddi, S. R. (1967), 'The existential neurosis', *Journal of Abnormal Psychology,* 72, pp. 311–25.

Mair, J. M. and Crisp, A. H. (1968), 'Estimating psychological organization, meaning and change in relation to clinical practice', *British Journal of Medical Psychology,* 41, pp. 15–29.

Malan, D. H. (1973), 'Therapeutic factors in analytically oriented brief psychotherapy', in R. Gosling (ed.), *Support, Innovation, and Autonomy,* Tavistock Clinic Golden Jubilee Papers, Tavistock, London.

Malan, D. H., Bacal, H. A., Heath, E. S. and Balfour, F. H. G. (1968), 'A study of psychodynamic changes in untreated neurotic patients: I Improvements that are questionable on dynamic criteria', *British Journal of Psychiatry,* 114, pp. 525–51.

Malan, D. H., Balfour, F. H. G., Hood, V. G. and Shooter, A. M. N. (1976), 'Group psychotherapy', *Archives of General Psychiatry*, 33, pp. 1303-15.

Marcia, J. E., Rubin, B. M. and Efran, J. S. (1969), 'Systematic desensitization: expectancy change or counter conditioning?' *Journal of Abnormal Psychology*, 74, pp. 382-7.

Marks, I. (1973), 'The psychiatric nurse as therapist: developments and problems', *Nursing Times*, 69, pp. 137-8.

Marshall, I. N. (1967), 'Extraversion and libido in Jung and Cattell', *Journal of Analytical Psychology*, 12, pp. 115-36.

Martin, D. V. (1955), *Institutionalisation*, *Lancet*, pp. 1188-90.

Martin, D. V. (1962), *Adventure in Psychiatry*, Cassirer, Oxford.

Maxwell, A. E. (1961), *Analysing Qualitative Data*, Chapman and Hall, London.

May, P. R. (1971), 'For better or for worse? Psychotherapy and variance change: a critical review of the literature', *Journal of Nervous and Mental Disease*, 152, pp. 184-92.

May, R. (1958), 'The origins and significance of the existential movement in psychology', in R. May, E. Angel and F. Ellerburger (eds), *Existence*, Basic Books, New York.

Mayo, P. (1966), 'Some psychological changes associated with improvement in depression', *British Journal of Social and Clinical Psychology*, 6, pp. 63-8.

Meador, B. D. (1975), 'Client-centered group therapy', in G. M. Gazda (ed.), *Basic Approaches to Group Psychotherapy*, Thomas, Illinois.

Meehl, P. E. (1960), 'The cognitive activity of the clinician', *American Psychologist*, 15, pp. 19-27.

Meltzoff, J. and Kornreich, M. (1970), *Research in Psychotherapy*, Atherton Press, New York.

Meyer, V., Liddell, A., and Lyons, M. (1977), 'Behavioural interviews', in A. R. Ciminero, H. Adams and K. Calhoun (eds), *Handbook of Behavioural Assessment*, Wiley, London.

Milgram, S. (1974), *Obedience to Authority*, Tavistock, London.

Mischel, W. (1968), *Personality and Assessment*, Wiley, New York, London, Sydney.

Mischel, W. (1973), 'On the empirical dilemmas of psychodynamic approaches, issues and alternatives', *Journal of Abnormal Psychology*, 82, pp. 335-44.

Moos, R. and Swartz, J. (1972), 'Treatment environment outcome', *Journal of Nervous and Mental Disease*, 154, pp. 254-75.

Morris, J. B. (1977), 'Appendix I: The prediction and measurement of change in a psychotherapy group using the repertory grid', in F. Fransella and D. Bannister (eds), *A Manual for Repertory Grid Technique*, Academic Press, London, New York, San Francisco.

Mowbray, R. M. and Davies, B. (1971), 'Personality factors in choice of medical speciality', *British Journal of Medical Education*, 5, pp. 110-7.

Mowbray, R. M. and Roger, T. F. (1963), *Psychology in Relation to Medicine*, Churchill Livingstone, Edinburgh and London.

Munn, N.L. (1966), *Psychology: The fundamentals of human adjustment*, Harrap, London.

Myers, I. B. (1962), *Manual of the Myers-Briggs Type Indicator*, Educational Testing Service, Princeton, New Jersey.

Oliveau, D. C., Agras, W. S., Leitenberg, H., Moore, R. C. and Wright, D. E. (1969), 'Systematic desensitization, therapeutically oriented instructions and selective positive re-inforcement', *Behaviour Research and Therapy*, 7, pp. 27–33.

Orne, M. T. and Wender, P. H. (1968), 'Anticipatory socialization for psychotherapy: method and rationale', *American Journal of Psychiatry*, 124, pp. 1202–12.

Ornstein, R. E. (1975), *The Psychology of Consciousness*, Jonathan Cape, London.

Osgood, C. E., Suci, G. J. and Tannenbaum, P. H. (1957), *The Measurement of Meaning*, University of Illinois Press, Urbana.

Overall, B. and Aronson, H. (1963), 'Expectations of psychotherapy in patients of lower socioeconomic class', *American Journal of Orthopsychiatry*, 33, pp. 421–30.

Pallis, D. J. and Stoffelmayr, B. E. (1973), 'Social attitudes and treatment orientation among psychiatrists', *British Journal of Medical Psychology*, 46, pp. 75–81.

Panayotopoulos, D. J. and Stoffelmayr, B. E. (1972), 'Training preferences, social attitudes and treatment orientation among psychiatrists', *Journal of Clinical Psychology*, 28, pp. 216–17.

Pearlin, L. I. and Kohn, M. L. (1966), 'Social class, occupation and parental values: a cross national study', in N. Warren and M. Jahoda (eds), *Attitudes: Selected Readings*, Penguin, Harmondworth.

Peck, D. F. (1973), 'Psychiatric nurse: an agent of behaviour change', *Nursing Times*, 69, p. 139.

Pinel, P. (1801), *Traité médico-philosophique sur l'aliénation mentale, ou la manie*, trans. D. D. Davis as *A Treatise on Insanity*, 1806; reprinted by Hafner, 1962.

Rachman, S. (1972), *The Effects of Psychotherapy*, Pergamon, Oxford.

Rapoport, R. N. (1960), *Community as Doctor*, Tavistock, London.

Ray, J. J. (1973), 'Conservatism, authoritarianism and related variables: a review and empirical study', in G. D. Wilson (ed.), *Psychology of Conservatism*, Academic Press, London.

Reichard, S., Livson, F. and Peterson, P. G. (1962), *Ageing and Personality: A Study of Eighty-seven Older Men*, Wiley, London, New York.

Revans, R. W. (1964), *Standards for Morale: Cause and Effect in Hospitals*, Nuffield Provincial Hospitals Trust, Oxford University Press.

Robach, H. B. (1971), 'The comparative influence of insight and non-insight psychotherapies on therapeutic outcome: a review of the experimental literature', *Psychotherapy: Theory, Research and Practice*, 8, pp. 23–5.

Robertson, A. and Kapur, R. L. (1972), 'Social change, emotional distress, and world view of students: an empirical study of the existentialist ethic and the spirit of suffering', *British Journal of Sociology*, 23, pp. 462–77.

Roe, A. (1951), 'A psychological study of eminent physical scientists', *Genetic Psychology Monographs*, 43, p. 121.

Rogers, C. R. (1957), 'The necessary and sufficient conditions of therapeutic personality change', *Journal of Consulting Psychology*, 21, pp. 95–103.

Rogers, C. R. (1961), *On Becoming a Person*, Constable, London.

Rokeach, M. (1960), *The Open and Closed Mind*, Basic Books, New York.

Rosenthal, D. and Frank, J. D. (1956), 'Psychotherapy and the placebo effect', *Psychological Bulletin*, 53, pp. 294–302.

Rotter, J. B. (1966), 'Generalized expectancies for internal versus external control of reinforcement', *Psychological Monographs*, 80, No. 1 (Whole No. 609).

Rowe, D. (1971), 'Poor prognosis in a case of depression as predicted by the repertory grid', *British Journal of Psychiatry*, 118, pp. 297–300.

Rowe, D. (1978), *The Experience of Depression*, Wiley, Chichester, New York, Brisbane, Toronto.

Ryan, D.V. and Neale, J. M. (1973), 'Test-taking sets and the performance of schizophrenics on laboratory tests', *Journal of Abnormal Psychology*, 82, pp. 207–11.

Rychlak, J. F. (1968), *A Philosophy of Science for Personality Theory*, Houghton Mifflin, Boston, Massachusetts.

Ryle, A. (1975), *Frames and Cages: The Repertory Grid Approach to Human Understanding*, Sussex University Press, Brighton.

Ryle, A. (1979), 'The focus in brief interpretive psychotherapy: dilemmas, traps and snags as target problems', *British Journal of Psychiatry*, 134, pp. 46–54.

Ryle, A. and Breen, D. (1971), 'The recognition of psychopathology on the repertory grid', *British Journal of Psychiatry*, 119, pp. 319–22.

Ryle, A. and Breen, D. (1972), 'Some differences in the personal constructs of neurotic and normal subjects', *British Journal of Psychiatry*, 120, pp. 483–9.

Ryle, A. and Lipshitz, S. (1976), 'An intensive case-study of a therapeutic group', *British Journal of Psychiatry*, 128, pp. 581–7.

Ryle, A. and Lunghi, M. E. (1969), 'The measurement of relevant change after psychotherapy: use of repertory grid testing', *British Journal of Psychiatry*, 115, pp. 1297–304.

Ryle, A. and Lunghi, M. E. (1972), 'Parental and sex role identification of students measured with a repertory grid technique', *British Journal of Social and Clinical Psychology*, 11, pp. 149–61.

Seaborn Jones, G. (1968), *Treatment or Torture*, Tavistock, London.

Shapiro, D. A. (1975), 'Some implications of psychotherapy research for clinical psychology', *British Journal of Medical Psychology*, 48, pp. 199-206.

Shapiro, D. A. (1976), 'The effects of therapeutic conditions: positive results revisited', *British Journal of Medical Psychology*, 49, pp. 315-23.

Sharaf, M. R., Schneider, P. and Kantor, D. (1968), 'Psychiatric interest and its correlates among medical students', *Psychiatry*, 31, pp. 150-60.

Silverman, G. (1977), 'Aspects of intensity of affective constructs in depressed patients', *British Journal of Psychiatry*, 130, pp. 174-6.

Skinner, B. F. (1953), *Science and Human Behaviour*, Macmillan, New York.

Slater, P. (1972), *Notes on INGRID 72*, M.R.C. Service for Analysing Repertory Grids, Biometric Unit, Institute of Psychiatry, London.

Slater, P. (ed.) (1976), *The Measurement of Intrapersonal Space by Grid Technique: Vol. I Explorations of Intrapersonal Space*, Wiley, London.

Slater, P. (1977), *The Measurement of Intrapersonal Space by Grid Technique; Vol. II Dimensions of Intrapersonal Space*, Wiley, London.

Slavson, S. R. (1964), *A Textbook in Analytic Group Psychotherapy*, International Universities Press, New York.

Sloane, R. B., Cristol, A. H., Pepernik, M. C. and Staples, F. R. (1970), 'Role preparation and expectation of improvement in psychotherapy', *Journal of Nervous and Mental Disease*, 150, pp. 18-26.

Smail, D. J. (1968), 'The place of conscious experience in clinical and medical psychology', *British Journal of Medical Psychology*, 41, pp. 169-76.

Smail, D. J. (1970), 'Neurotic symptoms, personality and personal constructs', *British Journal of Psychiatry*, 117, pp. 645-48.

Smail, D. J. (1972), 'A grid measure of empathy in a therapeutic group', *British Journal of Medical Psychology*, 45, pp. 165-69.

Smail, D. J. (1978), *Psychotherapy: A Personal Approach*, Dent, London.

Sperber, J. C. (1977), 'Personal constructs and child psychiatric diagnosis: A pilot study', *British Journal of Medical Psychology*, 50, pp. 65-72.

Sperlinger, D. J. (1971), 'A repertory grid and questionnaire study of individuals receiving treatment for depression from general practitioners', unpublished Ph.D. thesis, University of Birmingham.

Sperlinger, D. J. (1976), 'Aspects of stability in the repertory grid', *British Journal of Medical Psychology*, 49, pp. 341-47.

Stanton, A. H. and Swartz, M. (1954), *The Mental Hospital*, Basic Books, New York.

Strickland, B. R. (1978), 'Internal-external expectancies and health-related behaviours', *Journal of Consulting and Clinical Psychology*, 46, pp. 1192-211.

Strongman, K. T. (1974), *Decent Exposure: Living with Your Emotion,* Davie & Charles, London.

Sullivan, H. S. (1953), *The Interpersonal Theory of Psychiatry,* Norton, New York.

Szasz, T. S. (1967), *The Myth of Mental Illness, Foundations of a Theory of Personal Conduct,* Hoeber-Harper, New York.

Szasz, T. S. (1971), *Manufacture of Madness,* Routledge & Kegan Paul, London.

Teichman, M. (1970), 'Interrelationships among perceived family roles of neurotic and well adjusted students', unpublished manuscript.

Thouless, R. H. (1958), *General and Social Psychology,* University Tutorial Press, London.

Tollinton, H. J. (1973), 'Initial expectations and outcome', *British Journal of Medical Psychology,* 46, pp. 251-7.

Torrance, E. P. (1962), *Manual of the Minnesota Tests of Creative Thinking,* University of Minnesota, Bureau of Educational Research, Minneapolis.

Trauer, T. (1977), 'Attitudes of psychiatric patients to staff roles and treatment methods: a replication and extension', *British Journal of Medical Psychology,* 50, pp. 39-44.

Truax, C. B. and Carkhuff, R. R. (1967), *Towards Effective Counselling and Psychotherapy: Training and Practice,* Aldine Atherton, Chicago.

Truax, C. B. and Wargo, D. R. (1966), 'Psychotherapeutic encounters that change behaviour for better or for worse', *American Journal of Psychotherapy,* 20, pp. 499-520.

Tschudi, F. (1977), 'Loaded and honest questions: a construct theory view of symptoms and therapy', in D. Bannister (ed.), *New Perspectives in Personal Construct Theory,* Academic Press, London, New York, San Francisco.

Tutt, N. S. (1969), 'A study of psychiatric nurses' attitudes to treatment in a general hospital setting', dissertation for the degree of Master of Science (Clinical Psychology), Leeds University.

Tutt, N. S. (1970), 'Psychiatric nurses' attitudes to treatment in a general hospital', *Nursing Times,* 66, pp. 137-9.

Uhlenhuth, E. H. and Duncan D. B. (1968), 'Subjective change with medical student therapists: II Some determinants of change in psychoneurotic patients', *Archives of General Psychiatry,* 18, pp. 532-40.

Van Over, R. (ed.) (1971), *I Ching,* Mentor, New York.

Vernon, P. E. (1971), 'Effects of administration and scoring on divergent thinking tests', *British Journal of Educational Psychology,* 41, p. 3.

Walton, H. J. (1966), 'Differences between physically-minded and psychologically-minded medical practitioners', *British Journal of Psychiatry,* 112, pp. 1097-102.

Walton, H. J. (1969), 'Personality correlates of a career interest in psychiatry', *British Journal of Psychiatry,* 115, pp. 211-19.

Walton, H. J. and Hope, K. (1967), 'The effect of age and personality on doctor's clinical preferences', *British Journal of Social and Clinical Psychology,* 6, pp. 43-51.

Walton, H. J. and Last, J. M. (1969), 'Young doctors aiming to enter different specialities', *British Medical Journal*, 2, pp. 752–54.

Watson, J. P. (1970), 'A repertory grid method of studying groups', *British Journal of Psychiatry*, 117, pp. 309–18.

Watson, J. P. (1972), 'Possible measures of change during group psychotherapy', *British Journal of Medical Psychology*, 45, pp. 71–7.

Werner, H. (1947), *Comparative Psychology of Mental Development*, Follett, Chicago.

Whitehorne, J. C. and Betz, B. J. (1954), 'A study of psychotherapeutic relationships between physicians and schizophrenic patients', *American Journal of Psychiatry*, 111, pp. 321–31.

Whitehorne, J. C. and Betz, B. J. (1960), 'Further studies of the doctor as a crucial variable in the outcome of treatment with schizophrenic patients', *American Journal of Psychiatry*, 117, pp. 215–23.

Wijesinghe, O. B. A. (1978), 'The influence of personal adjustment strategies on the presentation and treatment of neurotic disorder', unpublished Ph.D. thesis, University of London.

Wijesinghe, O. B. A. and Wood, R. R. (1976), 'A repertory grid study of interpersonal perception within a married couples psychotherapy group', *British Journal of Medical Psychology*, 49, 3, pp. 287–93.

Wilson, G. D. (1973), *The Psychology of Conservatism*, Academic Press, London.

Wilson, G. D. and Nias, D. K. B. (1973), 'The need for a new approach to attitude measurement', in G. D. Wilson (ed.), *The Psychology of Conservatism*, Academic Press, London, New York.

Wilson, G. D. and Patterson, J. R. (1968), 'A new measure of conservatism', *British Journal of Social and Clinical Psychology*, 7, pp. 264–69.

Winer, B. J. (1971), *Statistical Principles in Experimental Design*. 2nd edition, McGraw-Hill, New York.

Wing, J. K. (1962), 'Institutionalization in mental hospitals', *British Journal of Social and Clinical Psychology*, 1, pp. 38–51.

Winter, D. A. (1979), 'Repertory grid technique in research on the psychological therapies', unpublished Ph.D. thesis, University of Durham.

Winter, D. A. and Trippett, C. J. (1977), 'Serial change in group psychotherapy', *British Journal of Medical Psychology*, 50, pp. 341–8.

Wolf, A. (1975), 'Psychoanalysis in groups', in G. M. Gazda (ed.), *Basic Approaches to Group Psychotherapy*, Thomas, Illinois.

Wolf, A. and Schwartz, E. K. (1962), *Psychoanalysis in Groups*, Grune and Stratton, New York.

Wolpe, J. (1954), 'Reciprocal inhibition as the main basis of psychotherapeutic effects', *American Medical Association Archives of Neurological Psychiatry*, 72, pp. 205–26.

Wolpe, J. (1958), *Psychotherapy by Reciprocal Inhibition*, Stanford University Press, Stanford.

210   *Bibliography*

Wood, R. R. (1977), 'Empathy and similarity of perception in a married couples' psychotherapy group: a repertory grid study', dissertation submitted for the British Psychological Society Diploma in Clinical Psychology, The British Psychological Society, Leicester.

Wootton, B. (1960), *Social Science and Social Pathology*, Allen & Unwin, London.

Wright, K. J. T. (1970), 'Exploring the uniqueness of common complaints', *British Journal of Medical Psychology*, 43, pp. 221-32.

Yalom, I. D. (1966), 'A study of group therapy dropouts', *Archives of General Psychiatry*, 11, pp. 393-413.

Yalom, I. D. (1971), *The Theory and Practice of Group Psychotherapy*, Basic Books, New York.

Zangwill, O. L. (1937), 'A study of the significance of attitude in recognition', *British Journal of Psychology*, 28, pp. 12-17.

Zigler, E. and Phillips, L. (1961), 'Psychiatric diagnosis and symptomatology', *Journal of Abnormal and Social Psychology*, 63, pp. 69-75.

Index

211